A PRACTICAL EDUCATION

A
PRACTICAL
EDUCATION

WHY LIBERAL ARTS MAJORS

MAKE GREAT EMPLOYEES

RANDALL STROSS

LC1023.S77 2017
Stross, Randall E., author.
A practical education : why
liberal arts majors make
great employees
Stanford, California :
Redwood Press, [2017]

REDWOOD PRESS
Stanford, California

Stanford University Press
Stanford, California

Printed in the United States of America on acid-free, archival-quality paper

Library of Congress Cataloging-in-Publication Data

Names: Stross, Randall E., author.
Title: A practical education : why liberal arts majors make great employees / Randall Stross.
Description: Stanford, California : Redwood Press, 2017. | Includes bibliographical references and index.
Identifiers: LCCN 2017022289| ISBN 9780804797481 (cloth : alk. paper) | ISBN 9781503603790 (electronic)
Subjects: LCSH: Education, Humanistic--United States. | College graduates--Employment--United States. | Employee selection--United States. | College majors--United States. | Stanford University--Alumni and alumnae--Employment.
Classification: LCC LC1023 .S77 2017 | DDC 370.11/20973--dc23
LC record available at https://lccn.loc.gov/2017022289

Typeset by Bruce Lundquist in 11.5/15 Baskerville

To
Emily, Hal, and Van

CONTENTS

1. The Major Decision — 1
2. The New Education — 18
3. Naturally Curious — 30
4. Proper Proportion — 41
5. A Foot in the Door — 53
6. Engineering Success — 64
7. The Different Perspective — 77
8. A General Understanding — 86
9. Underrepresented — 99
10. Normal — 111
11. Interesting Things Happen — 123
12. A Mania for Testing — 132
13. The Strength of Weak Ties — 147
14. The Shiny New Thing — 158
15. First Gen — 171
16. The Art of Living — 181
17. Bilingual — 194
18. A History of the Future — 205
19. Do-Over — 215
20. Liberal Education Is Vocational — 225

Acknowledgments   241

Notes   243

Index   281

A PRACTICAL EDUCATION

CHAPTER 1

THE MAJOR DECISION

STANFORD UNIVERSITY'S UNDERGRADUATES are a most fortunate group. Having been admitted to the most selective undergraduate school in the country and installed on an Edenic campus, they could not be any closer to Silicon Valley. Only a stone's throw or two beyond the edge of campus sit tech giants and tech adolescents and tech startups, which surveys anoint as the most desirable prospective employers in the world. Stanford undergraduates would seem perfectly positioned to approach their graduation without worry about what comes next.

The most sought-after students are the engineering majors, whose ranks have grown significantly in recent decades. But this is a book about the students who did *not* choose an engineering major, who instead chose majors for the joy of studying a subject that does not lead to a well-marked occupational destination. Their majors belong to the university's School of Humanities and Sciences, and many of these students face considerable uncertainty about their futures if they immediately seek professional positions without an advanced degree. For this book I have collected oral histories from their ranks, chronicles of the education, job searches, and initial work experiences of recent graduates. I've gathered enough of these histories to convince me and, I hope, convince others that graduates with these majors are well-equipped to land well and to thrive, if employers are willing to give them the chance.

I grant that the students who are profiled here, for the most part, come from privilege. Their parents, many of whom went to Stanford themselves, are financially comfortable. They sent their children to excellent primary and secondary schools and permitted their children, when they got to Stanford, to follow their own interests when choosing their majors. I understand that these students are not a random sampling of college students: these graduates are exceptionally smart and, let us not forget, are the champion go-getters of their age cohort. But they are not the only college students who are smart strivers; every college and university has such students. Whatever claims I make about the quick-learning capabilities of the students I followed at Stanford would apply to these other students, too, the ones who defy the ambient advice to major in business or an applied technical field, who instead major in a field that they genuinely enjoy studying and who excel in their classes.

I don't make a blanket claim that every student, at every college or university, who elects a liberal arts major will, ipso facto, make an outstanding employee upon graduation by dint of enrolling in the courses and earning passing grades. But those students who do choose for a major an academic field that is not tightly connected with a particular career and who do well in those courses, who demonstrate a sponge-like capacity to absorb new knowledge, whose academic record shows drive and diligence and a capacity for thinking hard and communicating well, should be seen by prospective employers as the multicapable candidates that they are.

If I am to persuade anyone of the practicality of the liberal arts, whether it be future employers, current college students, or the students' anxious parents, I need to be able to show actual liberal arts majors who are doing well in the workplace. This is why I have chosen to focus on Stanford only. Silicon Valley employers love Stanford graduates, even to the extent that they have been willing to take a chance on liberal arts majors from Stanford. For the most part, the graduates are not hired because of their choice of major but despite it. They were hired in many cases with the help of Stanford alumni connections. But what matters is that they managed to get in the door. Once they did, they were able to demonstrate the broadly useful strengths that characterize those who choose the liberal arts. Their employers then recognized their contributions, which were concrete and not related to the alumni networking, and gave them increased responsibilities, and that led to more achievements. These stories would have remained nothing but wishful hopes had the employers turned away majors that on their face had no relevance to the business. The Stanford tie is what sets the stories in motion, but what transpires once the job is secured speaks to the skills that liberal arts majors bring to their employers, skills that are sharpened in the course of majoring in the liberal arts wherever one earns a bachelor's degree.

This book also includes an abridged, episodic history of Stanford University, focusing on the tension between vocational and non-vocational directions that was present at its founding, and on the evolution of career counseling and post-graduation job placement. Immersion in this history will reveal how employers have rather arbitrarily changed their minds, again and again, about how and when they would like students to specialize in their undergraduate studies. One field becomes hot, and then it falls out of favor, replaced by another. The employers' message to undergraduate students is likely to continue to shift in the future, which suggests to me that the best preparation for an unknowable future is one that has been tested over time as universal preparation—that is, the liberal arts.

It is difficult, to be sure, to make this case in the face of considerable evidence that prospective employers of new graduates are far more keen to hire those with majors that are infused with quantitative skills or constitute an occupation-specific field, consigning far more liberal arts majors than engineering majors to first jobs that fit the labor economists' definition of "underemployed."[1] But not so visible is the way underemployment falls as the graduates spend time in the labor market. Also, lamentably, the casual observer or anxious parent cannot see that the initial earnings gap separating a baccalaureate degree with professional and preprofessional majors, the category that includes business degrees, from that composed of humanities and social sciences majors closes over time. By the peak earning ages, fifty-six to sixty, the humanities and social science majors earn $2,000 a year more, if those with advanced degrees in both categories are included.[2]

In assembling the oral histories of liberal arts majors to hearten others who will follow, I am recycling an idea that Stanford itself had more than thirty-five years ago. The shaky futures of liberal arts majors were visible in the 1970s, when visitors strolling across campus in the late evening might have come across the sight of students sleeping outside the campus's career center in tents or on uncovered beds.

In those years, as now, engineering majors had no difficulty in finding prospective employers who were eager to speak with them. But liberal arts majors then, as now, faced challenges. The number of companies that even deigned to meet with them was small; the number of students seeking an audience was large. So the university set up a reservation system, permitting students to sign up in advance for one of the precious few time slots by coming in person to the Career Planning and Placement Center.

On the day that sign-ups began, the more enterprising students arrived in the wee hours of the morning, long before the center opened, to be sure of snagging a slot. When those who arrived at 6 a.m. were too late to get one, students on later sign-up days began their vigils still earlier, at 4 a.m. and then even earlier, setting up tents or dragging their beds out of their dorm rooms.

This conspicuous tableau of liberal arts students desperate to gain access to the more desirable employers was an embarrassment to the university.[3] When a new university president, Donald Kennedy, was appointed in 1980, he faced sharp questions from a student reporter about the plight of liberal arts graduates who needed to be "prepared to go into the working world." Kennedy, a biologist by training who had spent nearly two decades teaching at Stanford and had recently completed a two-year stint in Washington, DC, as Commissioner of Food and Drugs, could have advocated that more students head for STEM fields—science, technology, engineering, and mathematics. But instead he defended the across-the-board utility of liberal education. Kennedy said he believed that students' interests were best served not by preparing them "for just one particular job or occupation" but rather by "making them exceptionally competent and capable people across the full range of activities."[4]

Kennedy took pains to show that he appreciated the need to strengthen, in particular, the humanities no less than had his predecessor, a historian. Speaking at a time when Stanford had become the third largest university recipient of federal funding for scientific research and development, he said, "We have to try in the 1980's to get the humanities where the sciences have gotten."[5]

Within his own domain, the campus, Kennedy had the power to bolster the humanities faculty. What he could not do, however, was change the way that corporate employers eschewed students who were humanities majors when they combed through lists of seniors seeking post-graduation employment. In 1979, the number of Stanford students who sought jobs had recently spiked. Five years earlier, the university's survey of seniors showed that only about one-quarter of the graduating class sought a job immediately after graduation. But the appeal of graduate school had diminished dramatically, and now more than half of the seniors were looking for work.[6]

"We hear scare stories about humanities graduates busing dishes in restaurants for lack of occupational alternatives," wrote sophomore Stan Young, in a column for the *Stanford Daily* titled "Pity the Fuzzy Study Major," which referred to the campus vernacular that speaks of students either as "techies" or as "fuzzies." Young was a history major, a choice that made his relatives "blanch." He was neither the first nor the last Stanford student with a major in the humanities to remark on the strangeness of being surrounded by those preparing "for technological occupations" and continually reminded of "the relative unmarketability of the transcript with which I will leave Stanford."[7]

Kennedy understood that liberal arts majors like Young felt anxiety about their future, and he did not promise that a highly desirable job awaited them as soon as they stepped beyond the campus. "One can't expect to walk into a prefixed kind of occupation," he told the student reporter. "It's going to take some experimenting and often that experimenting is going to be painful." All the university could do, he said, was provide the graduates with "the tools ultimately to cope."[8]

Saying that pain lay ahead for those who elected a major in the liberal arts was admirable in its frankness. But it would not serve well in attracting leery students into these fields. In an attempt to send more students down the less-traveled roads that led to indistinct futures, the university's School of Humanities and Sciences undertook a new initiative. The school, which was the center of liberal arts at the university, encompassing the humanities, the social sciences, and the natural sciences, undertook a survey of a large swath of recent graduates, inquiring into the details of their employment. The next year, it published a brochure, *The Major Decision*, that drew from the survey and featured profiles of selected students with liberal arts majors, including photos in some cases. It was a showcase of graduates who had found interesting work in places impossible to predict at the time of their graduation.

I was drawn to the students in the brochure who had elected the humanities, the majors that are seemingly most distant from the wish list of corporate recruiters. Students who were warily considering making the "major decision" in favor of the humanities could draw reassurance from the stories of actual graduates, and so, too, could their anxious parents.

In the introduction to *The Major Decision*, an administrator painted a sanguine picture for liberal arts majors, but it was the students themselves who best articulated the case for their majors.

Maryellie Moore, a history major who was the treasurer of Matson Navigation Company, spoke of the critical awareness that she had gained from studying history, which remained with her long after she forgot particular historical dates and events. Barbara Brown, a philosophy major, said she had never foreseen that she would become a manager for the San Francisco Municipal Railway, but

> I would almost be willing to go on a soapbox to sing the virtues of a good liberal education. At Stanford I learned how to think critically and in an organized fashion. It is only out in the "real world" that one can see the scarcity of that skill. Not a day goes by that I don't recognize the value of writing well, thinking logically, and developing work plans in an organized way. A person who gets those abilities out of college is incredibly marketable.[9]

The gallery of student profiles included an accountant, a writer, a doctor, a dentist, an attorney, and a student who had been a religious studies major who was now a programmer. Michael Crandell had graduated four years previously, and he was quoted in *The Major Decision* as saying, "I now have a job as a programmer only because I took one course in computer science at Stanford." He enthusiastically recommended a major in the humanities to others as "general preparation for work in some field that you may not even know of now, and that perhaps no one knows of now."[10]

The profile of Crandell was brief and did not explain how he had managed to get that job in programming on the basis of a single course. What subsequently happened to him and his nascent career in programming? Had he stayed in the field, or had his failure to take a full menu of computer science coursework proven to be an insurmountable barrier to advancement? Did the lack of specific preparation trump the amorphous advantage of "general preparation" provided by religious studies in the years that followed?

To find answers from the vantage point of the present, more than thirty-five years after Crandell graduated, I looked for his contact information and any public record of his professional experiences. He was not hard to find—and I immediately got the answer to one of my questions, whether he had stayed in the world of programming: he certainly had. Today, he is the cofounder and chief executive of a software company, RightScale, which offers management tools for cloud computing and has the backing of several prominent Silicon Valley venture capital firms. How had the religious studies major arrived at this destination, beginning with a single programming class while in college? I wrote Crandell to see if he would be willing to meet and supply a narrative of what had transpired after he graduated, and he obliged.

His story begins in 1974, in orientation week, when he was newly arrived on the Stanford campus and sitting with his parents listening to welcoming speeches and advice dispensed by the university's elders. Of all the inspirational wisdom and homilies that were offered that day, only one thing made an impression. One of the vice provosts predicted that computers would become an enormous presence in everyone's lives, and that students who did not take at least one course in computer science during their time at Stanford would be effectively illiterate, unprepared for the modern world. It was as if he had distilled career advice for the future into a single word—not "plastics,"[11] but software. It made an impression on Crandell, and he followed the advice.

Looking back, Crandell remembers enjoying the introduction to programming class. The students were taught SAIL programming—the *SAI* in SAIL came from the Stanford Artificial Intelligence lab where the language had recently been developed. The introductory class was large; the lectures were held in an auditorium. Outside of class, students typed their coding assignments on terminals connected to large machines in centralized computer labs. This was before the advent of personal computers, and though the machines were called minicomputers, they were "mini" only in that they were smaller than the mainframes that had preceded them. Near the end of the quarter, when class members rushed to complete assignments, the mere act of saving their work could stress the overloaded system, causing it to crash and lose the work. Still, it was technology that gave students the ability to run their code and see the results immediately, a capability that would draw many talented minds to the field of computer science.[12]

Two of Crandell's freshmen suite-mates were engineering students, and both had planned a linear future for themselves: study engineering, get a job, have a career, secure a stable life. No grand plan guided Crandell, however. A course on comparative religion that he took as a sophomore enthralled him. He was introduced to Taoism, Buddhism, Shintoism, and alternative views of Christianity. The course asked the big existential questions: Why are we here? What are we supposed to do with our time here? "It hit me like a train," he said.

After graduation, he began graduate studies at Harvard Divinity School, but he discovered that the program was not what he had thought it would be. He was following his intellectual curiosity; his classmates were preparing to head congregations, a prospect that did not interest him. He left and returned to his hometown, Santa Barbara, California.

When he looked for a job, Crandell's religious studies major did not match up neatly with available entry-level positions. But as a humanities major who had had abundant opportunities to hone his writing skills, he was hired to be the editor of *Center Magazine*, published monthly by a nonprofit organization, the Center for Democratic Institutions, for its forty-five thousand supporting members.

The center's staff used an outside firm to manage the subscriber lists and handle the printing of the address labels each month. The firm charged the center about $1 annually for each of the member-subscribers. As Crandell settled in to his new job, he saw that the outside firm did very little for the $50,000 it received each year. Were the center to purchase its own minicomputer, for a fraction of what it paid for a single year's service fees, and manage the labels itself, it would capture significant savings. The programming class that Crandell had taken as a student had not prepared him to write the program and handle the computer's administration by himself. But it had succeeded in stripping away the aura of mystery that enshrouded computers, and he could accurately gauge the size of the task were it brought in-house. As reluctant as the senior staff members were to embrace what seemed like a risky project, they were persuaded by Crandell's mantra: we can do this ourselves for much less. The center purchased the machine and realized the savings as promised.

During the day, Crandell worked as an editor; at night, he was the bass player in a rock band. But he fell in love with a woman who was a full-time graduate student and who had a young daughter, and he felt the need to increase his modest income. He decided to learn how to program at a professional level. His father introduced him to an acquaintance, Roger Marcus, an experienced programmer who offered to mentor him. Marcus was employed by CompuCorp, a manufacturer of pricey dedicated word processors, computers that only ran word processing software. They were expensive—CompuCorp's basic machine cost $10,000 and required the separate purchase of a $3,000 printer—but the ability to correct words at any time and save and retrieve documents led offices to replace electric typewriters with such machines. CompuCorp was located in Los Angeles, but Marcus was not offering a formal company-sponsored internship. The arrangement was wholly informal: Crandell would use a spare machine that Marcus had in the basement of his Santa Barbara home.

"We work in assembly language," Marcus told Crandell, who said, "Fine!" not having any idea what that meant. Assembly language is a "low-level language," meant to move bits in and out of particular storage places in a particular chip. Programming in assembly is demanding and exceedingly tedious. Today, most programming is done with a "high-level language," which insulates the programmer from having to know hardware details. But Crandell had no fear of assembly because "I didn't know what I didn't know."

Crandell spent about six months studying and coding in the evenings and on the weekends, mastering the Z-80 assembly language. The effort got him the entry-level job he had sought: he was hired by CompuCorp. It was at the company's lowest salary rung, but it was a significant raise for him. He remembers that when he interviewed for the job, he had heard someone in the room say, "Well, he's got one thing going for him. He doesn't have a degree in computer science." Crandell was not sure what that referred to—perhaps arrogance that the recruiters had observed among computer science majors—but he drily observed about his own religious studies major, "At least it's a plus!"

He landed at CompuCorp just as the IBM PC was arriving and rendering dedicated word-processors like CompuCorp's obsolete. CompuCorp, however, could not bring itself to make a less expensive version of its word processing software for the PC market and threaten its single-purpose machines. Crandell saw that those machines would soon disappear, whether CompuCorp acted or not. Crandell decided to leave the company and create word processing software for the IBM PC that would reproduce features in Compu-Corp's software. He was a one-person startup. He got a copy of Peter Norton's manual *All About the IBM PC*, taught himself the C language, and created his own software. He took the bold step of moving out of his office at home—a closet—into an actual office, a converted motel room that cost $250 a month.

The Crandell Development Corporation, as he called his tiny startup, eked out an existence, principally by selling the software to a distributor who paid Crandell $150 a copy and rebranded it for retail sale in Europe for $495 a copy. Crandell hired a programmer to help, then other employees. His little company eventually grew to ten employees before Microsoft introduced its Office suite, bundling the most popular software applications, including Word, into one low-priced package. When Office appeared, demand for high-priced word processing software such as Crandell's diminished.

Crandell next found an opportunity in developing LaserFAX, software that he licensed to forty other companies to give a PC the functionality of a fax machine. He sold his company to JetFax and became a vice president. Eventually the company would be renamed eFax and would merge with its major competitor, but Crandell left the merged company before it went on to multi-billion-dollar success as J2 Global ("I wrongly thought fax would die much sooner than it did," he says, looking back.) A short spell as a consultant was followed by stints as chief executive at two more startups.

After Amazon in 2006 launched AWS, Amazon Web Services, which offered computing cycles to anyone for minimal cost, paid for with the same credit card used to buy books at Amazon, Crandell joined with Thorsten von Eicken and Rafael Saavedra, both engineers, to found RightScale in 2007, which initially offered software tools to AWS customers to manage the computing resources that they rented from Amazon. As competing cloud services were introduced by Amazon's competitors, RightScale expanded its own offerings, giving its customers "cloud portfolio management" that handled many cloud providers simultaneously. These were highly technical services sold primarily to chief information officers of large companies.

Listening to the narrative of Crandell's professional career, one can hear a receptiveness to wondrous things that has ranged across topics, such as when he explored Saint Anselme's ontological proof of God's existence, the subject of his senior thesis at Stanford. Or when he discovered how he could use SAIL programming in the introduction to computer science class to create a rudimentary stick figure on the screen who, with the help of a randomizing function, would stagger along an unpredictable path like a drunken sailor. Later in life, he had not lost that ability to marvel: when Amazon offered to the public the ability to rent Amazon's own computer in-frastructure, at low prices that were unheard of in the industry, he called the moment "mind-blowing."

Crandell's career in the software industry shows the creative ef-florescence that is seen when an industry is young, still in the earliest stage of the life cycle, still welcoming to individuals who may lack particular credentials. Today, many parts of the software industry are now closed to the enterprising amateur. Would Crandell hire for a software engineering position someone like himself, essentially a self-taught programmer? He says the software world today is differ-ent from when he entered. Now a standard query is, where did you get your degree in computer science? But he says he still looks for the engineer who is a self-learner who will put in the hard work to continue learning.

And there are positions in his company for those without a tech-nical background. The day before we spoke, he had interviewed a candidate for a position as "customer success manager," who would work with customers on the one side and RightScale engineers on the other to resolve problems. This particular candidate's major was envi-ronmental studies, but he had the curiosity that Crandell prizes more than knowledge in a particular intellectual domain. "If he's willing to log the time and do the equivalent of reading Peter Norton at night, I'm all over that," Crandell said. "I think the people skills are actually harder to learn than the domain stuff on the technical side."

When Crandell is asked what advice he would offer to college students looking for a first job, he suggests that they concentrate their searches on smaller companies and startups. These work environ-ments are more open to contributions from the youngest members of the team.

The Major Decision included the testimonial of another religious studies major, Gary Fazzino, who had graduated in 1974 and was working at Hewlett-Packard as a government-relations manager. "My professors at Stanford forced me to learn how to think—the

most basic skill of all—through dialogue, reading, and long writing sessions," he said. This sounds generic, but Fazzino had a good
story to tell of his experiences, taking on new subjects about which
he knew nothing. He recalled writing a paper on Confucian thought
and receiving a distressingly poor grade. "After I picked myself off the
floor," he said, he listened to his professor's criticism that the paper
failed to acknowledge the different elements of Asian thought that
formed the context of Confucianism. Fazzino devoted the following
months to intense study of Chinese history. "As crazy as it may seem,
such an exercise has helped me both in political life and in my work,"
he wrote his alma mater. "My effectiveness is measured by my ability
to communicate the world of government to citizens and engineers.
I must try to understand the people I'm dealing with and the background they bring to an issue before I can hope to succeed."[13]

The phrase "as crazy as it may seem" anticipated a skeptical reception to his contention that his religious studies major had any
bearing on his current work as a manager at Hewlett-Packard.
"As crazy as it may seem" could have been affixed to every testimonial that Stanford collected for *The Major Decision*. All were attempts to convey that the students' experiences in the world of work
demonstrated that their liberal arts studies had proven to be utterly
practical.

In the years that have passed since *The Major Decision* was published, the labor market's preference for vocational majors has only
become more pronounced. The students' shift toward the vocational
reflects their reading of the labor market and the preferences of
future prospective employers. Attempting to sell the liberal arts to
undergraduates is premature without employers themselves moving
away from the vocational majors. Today, if asked, employers will
squirm away from admitting that their preferences have changed,
and they will affirm their fervent wish to hire college graduates who
have the "soft skills" that liberal education ideally bestows. Ninety-
two percent of executives surveyed by the *Wall Street Journal* in 2015

said that soft skills were equally or more important than technical skills, and 89 percent of these respondents said they had a difficult time finding candidates with those skills.[14] Corporate America's recruiting activities, hiring decisions, and compensation and promotion practices tell a different story, however.

This book seeks to persuade employers to take another look at their hiring practices by reminding them that there is no less need today than before for graduates who have demonstrated an omnivorous hunger for knowledge, who have honed communications skills, who can justifiably claim that their coursework helped them learn *how to think*. Rather than extolling the virtues of liberal education, as many other authors have already done and done well,[15] I have elected a different approach: spending time with Stanford graduates who received a liberal education recently, who did not go on to graduate studies, and who with only a bachelor's degree in hand found their first professional positions. The oral histories of their individual experiences are sufficiently detailed to show, rather than tell, the usefulness of their education.

The graduates' stories, which compose about half of the book, may provide some encouragement to current students who are contemplating majoring in the liberal arts but have not yet made "the major decision," and to their concerned parents as well. I make no claim that the stories constitute a statistically sound sample. Students who have not landed happily could not be expected to be willing to share their experiences. The group portrait is also unrepresentative on the employer side. By definition, the only employers who appear here are the enlightened ones—or the managers dwelling in nooks within less-enlightened organizations who welcomed the liberal arts majors whom I was following. But the stories serve an important purpose in showing to the skeptical what is possible.

I was purposely selective in assembling this gallery in one respect. I decided to focus on the students whose majors were as far from vocational as it is possible to get: those in the humanities. I also restricted my attention to students who had found work in positions that had no apparent connection to the major; no English majors who took positions in corporate communications or music majors who became music teachers. I wanted to show real-life examples of what advocates for the liberal arts claim, that the liberal arts, in the phrasing of Michael Crandell when he was a newly minted graduate himself, are "general preparation for work in some field that you may not even know of now."

Using the frame of a single campus, we can also follow the history of job searches by soon-to-graduate students and the advice dispensed to them, the changing attitudes of prospective employers, and the methods they used to winnow job applicants. By including the past as well as the present, we can see that at an earlier time, the appreciation of a liberal education was shared by employers as well as students.

I do not hide my sympathies here: I am an advocate for liberal education and I am happy whenever I hear of a liberal arts major who finds a congenial employer. I graduated from Macalester College, a small liberal arts college in St. Paul, Minnesota, but did not go through the harrowing job search that the graduates I follow here undertook. I double majored in history and East Asian languages and cultures, planning on going directly to a PhD program in modern Chinese history. I arrived at Stanford in 1976, having been accepted before graduation, so I never had to peer at the terrifying blankness of the day after graduation without a job. This book project gave me the chance to speak with students with much stronger constitutions than I had as an undergraduate, and to experience secondhand what I had not encountered myself. These students show that obtaining work immediately after graduating from college provides an informal form of graduate education.

My six years at Stanford overlapped a bit with Michael Crandell's years there, and we must have spent time during the wee hours in the same computer lab, though we did not know it then. In 1982, I completed my PhD in modern Chinese history and discovered there was no job waiting for me in the field. I took a position teaching U.S. history at the Colorado School of Mines, and a few years later I obtained a teaching position at San Jose State University in an unlikely place for a modern China historian: the college of business, where I have remained ever since, teaching courses on strategic management and business-and-society. I taught myself programming, and I've written books on technology companies (Microsoft; Google), on venture capital (Benchmark Capital; Y Combinator), and on inventors and entrepreneurs (Thomas Edison; Steve Jobs). For nine years, I wrote the "Digital Domain" column on technology businesses for the *New York Times*. How I learned on the job is a long separate story, which need not detain us, but I suppose it shows how my liberal education had bestowed "general preparation for work in some field that you may not even know of now."

CHAPTER 2

THE NEW EDUCATION

HARVARD WAS FOUNDED as "New College" in 1636, the first college in the North American colonies. Its longevity has seemed to be a defining strength: Harvard has been the preeminent institution of higher learning forever, the supplier of presidents and titans nonpareil, the possessor of an endowment of such unfathomable magnitude that it seems capable of making any administrator's wish come true. Harvard has always presented itself as an institution without peer.

Until now, that is.

Stanford has caused imperturbable Harvard to wonder aloud whether it has not only been matched, but perhaps even passed, by an arriviste. Stanford, the new New College, adopted a model different than Harvard's, providing the full menu of disciplines but treating engineering as *primus inter pares*. In 2014, Harvard all but officially disclosed that it was concerned that it had fallen behind Stanford when the *Harvard Crimson* published a long, at times anguished, feature story: "Seeing Red: Stanford v. Harvard."[1]

"I really have never encountered a place as exciting or as forward-looking as Stanford," said Harvard grad William Damon, Class of 1967, who in 2014 was a professor at Stanford's Graduate School of Education. David Spiegel, who graduated from Harvard Medical School in 1971 and became a professor at Stanford's School of Medicine, recalled in 2014, "When I joined the faculty at Stanford in 1975, the feeling was, 'it is a great place to be, but it sure ain't Harvard.'" He continued, "I don't feel that way anymore. Nobody does."[2]

Stanford's location, in the heart of Silicon Valley, drew the most attention from Cambridge. The *Crimson* article included a description of a visit to one Stanford class, and the choice was telling: introduction to programming, Programming Methodology CS 106A. "There is a huge number of students at Stanford now who concentrate in engineering, almost half," remarked Harvard's president, Drew Faust. "That's going to be a very different atmosphere from here."[3]

Stanford's celebration of the practical struck some observers at Harvard as vulgar, at least an abrogation of the values that the university should protect. "I have this romantic vision that a university is a really unique cultural institution whose purpose is to produce and conserve and disseminate knowledge," said Stephanie H. Kenen, a director of Harvard's Program in General Education. "It doesn't build roads."[4]

Harvard did not openly smirk at Stanford, the parvenu, but one detects an implied syllogism: Harvard is older than Stanford, and Harvard's much, much longer history confers a permanent superiority in what it does. Harvard English professor Derek Miller drew the ineluctable conclusion: "Stanford's still a startup."[5]

The practicality that Harvard observers saw in Stanford's institutional marrow today long preceded Silicon Valley—and was a direct contributor to the Valley's birth. It was the distinguishing characteristic that Leland and Jane Stanford, the university's cofounders, had in mind when they conceived of funding a new university. The occasion was a mournful one, however. The school was to be a permanent memorial to their only child, Leland Stanford Junior, who had just died of typhus fever at the age of fifteen while traveling with his parents in Europe.

Leland Stanford was the president of the Central Pacific Railroad—the company that supplied the western portion of the first transcontinental rail line—and a former governor of California, whose primary residence was in San Francisco but who owned a number of farms and other properties in northern California. San Francisco newspapers accorded the Stanford family extensive coverage, but it was the *Harvard Crimson* that two months after the death of the Stanfords' son was the first to hear of their plans. A small untitled item published in May 1884 said, "A writer from Paris says: 'I hear ex Governor Leland Stanford of California, who has been here for some time past and who is in very bad health, has decided to give several millions of dollars out of his immense fortune to the founding of a university for the sons of working men.'"[6]

When Stanford passed through New York City, the *New York Tribune* interviewed him, listening to his concern that universities did not provide graduates with the practical education needed to pursue a vocation:

> I have, in my business experience, found that too much of the current college training launches young men on the world void of such practical knowledge of any calling as will enable them to earn their living at once. Scores of educated youngsters have been sent to me as President of the Central Pacific Railroad, seeking employment, and I could not do anything with them, because they would not fit in anywhere. When business men wish to employ people, they have specific services in their mind and mere general brightness will not serve their purpose. I, therefore, intend as far as possible to seek practical educational results.[7]

The university he and his wife contemplated founding would ensure that its graduates "know some business or trade so thoroughly that the question of bread and butter shall not be a stumbling-block to them on their entrance to life."[8]

Leland Stanford's models were technical schools in the United States and in Europe. He said that while he was in New York he would seek suggestions from Cornell University, not for its liberal arts curriculum but for its agricultural and forestry programs. Even before leaving for Europe with his wife and son on the ill-fated trip, Stanford had already decided to devote five hundred acres of the horse farm he owned in Palo Alto to developing an arboretum with every known species of tree. Now he had decided that that this would be the appropriate site to build the university, where the graduates "would be fitted for action as well as for reflection."[9] A local newspaper imagined that the new university would impart knowledge in the hundreds of trades for which California most needed skilled labor, such as learning "how to grow grapes, make wine, cultivate all kinds of fruit trees, improve the breeds of domestic animals, till the soil to the best advantage and preserve it from rapid deterioration." These trades would be more remunerative than "any of the so-called learned professions"—and they would provide "more health and enjoyment" to boot.[10]

The practical, Leland Stanford felt, should not come after college but during it, dictating the college curriculum. He decried "the utter folly of attempting to convert the college-bred youth into the practical man of business affairs, without a larger amount of trouble than the manager of any enterprise can afford to bestow."[11]

Harvard had a classical curriculum at its core, and Leland Stanford was contemplating how to build a university that was, in essence, the un-Harvard. But long before Leland Stanford embarked upon his plans, others had viewed Harvard not as the exemplar of classical education but as a school that was overly concerned with applied learning. Thomas Jefferson was one of the most outspoken critics of Harvard for this reason.

In Jefferson's eyes, Harvard was the country's original vocational school. Harvard College turned out ministers; the medical school, doctors; the law school, lawyers. Jefferson did not want his new university, the University of Virginia, to be modeled after Harvard. In 1823, as his university prepared to accept its first students, he corresponded with George Ticknor, a Harvard professor of French and Spanish languages and literatures. "I am not fully informed of the practices at Harvard," Jefferson politely wrote Ticknor, "but there is

one feature from which we shall certainly vary altho' it has been cop-
ied I believe by nearly every college & academy in the [land?], that
is the holding the students all to one prescribed course of reading,"
restricting them to whatever is needed "to qualify them for their particular vocations to which they are destined." Jefferson wanted each
student at the University of Virginia to be allowed "uncontrolled
choice" in the lectures they would attend. Whatever the student
thought would improve his mind was fine with Jefferson. To him,
unfettered choice was the liberal education ideal.[12]

In contrast, others in the early nineteenth century moved higher
education in more applied directions. The U.S. Military Academy
at West Point, established in 1802, was an engineering school. So
too was the school that Stephen Van Rensselaer funded to establish
an institution for "the application of science."[13] Yale established the
Sheffield Scientific School in 1847, which for decades was operated
wholly separately from Yale College; its students lived separately
and took classes from only the school's faculty. (A historian writes,
"During the second half of the nineteenth century Yale College and
Sheffield Scientific School, separated by only a few streets, were two
separate countries on the same planet."[14]) Harvard added its own
scientific school, also in 1845, as did Dartmouth in 1852. Initially, at
least, these semiautonomous or wholly separate science-school affiliates accepted students who were less prepared than those accepted
by the classical colleges.[15]

Though higher education in the 1850s included degree programs,
here and there across the country, for education that we would cat-
egorize as professional or applied education—in agriculture, the
military, science, and engineering—one field was glaringly missing:
business. The only post-secondary business education was offered by
for-profit schools that sprang up, with short courses in bookkeeping,
arithmetic, business correspondence, and penmanship.[16]

This movement toward applied professional education, but excluding the field of business, would spread broadly with the passage

of the Morrill Act of 1862, providing federal land grants to the states for funding agricultural colleges and colleges devoted to the "mechanic arts," that is, engineering. With only a few exceptions, these would be public universities.

In early 1869, Charles W. Eliot, a Harvard-educated professor of chemistry at the recently founded Massachusetts Institute of Technology, wrote an influential article for the *Atlantic Monthly* titled "The New Education," critiquing in particular the experiments in nonclassical education that centered on the sciences and on living European languages rather than on Greek and Latin.[17] Eliot opened with the question that he imagined would be uppermost in the mind of his intended reader, a parent contemplating sending his son off to college:

> What can I do with my boy? I can afford, and am glad, to give him the best training to be had. I should be proud to have him turn out a preacher or a learned man; but I don't think he has the making of that in him. I want to give him a practical education; one that will prepare him, better than I was prepared, to follow my business or any other active calling. The classical schools and the colleges do not offer what I want. Where can I put him?[18]

Eliot did not recommend that parents send their sons to the new science-school affiliates. He said that these schools had recruited many good students, but also many who were "shirks and stragglers," those who were "incompetent to pursue the usual classical studies." Both the faculties of the new science schools and the students "necessarily felt themselves in an inferior position" to the main colleges, in resources and in reputation. "It is the story of the ugly duckling," said Eliot. He did not advocate that the science schools be integrated into the colleges, however. He said that combining the scientific and the classical on a single campus had already been tried in France and abandoned; in Germany, separation was maintained, to the benefit of both. He advocated keeping the main college, with its classical curriculum, separate from the places where that hypothetical parent sought "a practical education" for his son. Eliot recommended instead the freestanding polytechnic university, like Rensselaer or his own home institution, MIT. These universities were more than technical institutes; they conferred in addition to professional training an education that we would call liberal. Eliot wrote, "To make a good engineer, chemist, or architect, the only sure way is to make first, or at least simultaneously, an observant, reflecting, and sensible man, whose mind is not only well stored, but well trained also to see, compare, reason, and decide."[19]

Eliot's opinions about classical and applied education would affect Harvard directly. Within months of the appearance of the article, he was chosen in 1869 as Harvard's president and would go on to serve in the position for forty years, the longest tenure of any of the university's presidents, before or since.[20]

The inventors and industrialists who gained great wealth in the nineteenth century were not as concerned with defending Latin and Greek and keeping applied disciplines at a distance as was Eliot, a classically educated academic. In 1859, Peter Cooper, an inventor and industrialist, founded the Cooper Union for the Advancement of Science and Art in New York City, which provided free tuition and offered night classes so that a college education would be accessible to the working class. Following Peter Cooper's example was another wealthy patron of higher education who embraced practical subjects: Ezra Cornell, cofounder of the university in Ithaca, New York, which opened its doors in 1868, not so long before Leland Stanford prepared to visit the school in 1884. Cornell was an enthusiastic backer of education for agriculture and engineering and convinced the state legislature to designate the new university to be New York State's land-grant institution.[21] He also wanted to offer a free education to students who were willing to devote half of their time to manual labor, and he planned to build on campus a shoe factory and a chair factory for these students. But Andrew Dickson

White, the university's cofounder and its first president, talked Cornell out of the plan.[22]

Cornell University was one of several institutions that seemed to outside observers to be defining an entirely different kind of college education, a "Practical Education," as the *San Francisco Chronicle* headline labeled it, using the same phrase that Charles W. Eliot had used a few years earlier. Cornell, along with the Massachusetts Agricultural College and the University of Missouri, adopted a curriculum "in bold antagonism to old ideas," in which "theory is subordinated to practice, abstract speculation to utility, literacy and classical training to scientific, industrial and special instruction of a kind bearing upon the practical pursuits of life."[23]

Cornell University's first class was drawn largely from rural New York, described by one observer as "rough outside and inside." But students who tried to support themselves by working on the university's model farm earned less than was needed. Only one in ten members of that first class earned a degree.[24] Over time, "it became less of a school of training for poor boys and more of an ordinary college for the education of the sons of wealthy or well-to-do parents," said the *San Francisco Chronicle*.[25]

Shortly before Leland Stanford pondered how best to make his new university practical, the field of business had finally found a home within a university in 1881 when Joseph Wharton, whose fortune derived from the growth of the Bethlehem Steel Company and the American Nickel Company, made a substantial gift to the University of Pennsylvania for establishing what was initially called the Wharton School of Finance and Economy. And yet Stanford was more interested in the Cornell model, starting an entirely new university from scratch, rather than Wharton's, adding a new school to an existing institution.[26]

Stanford did not want to plunge into planning without learning what he could from the examples of established institutions. While on the East Coast, he visited not only Cornell but also Harvard,

Yale, MIT, and Johns Hopkins.[27] At Harvard, he and his wife, Jane, were received by Charles Eliot who, when he recalled the meeting many years later, said that the Stanfords told him that they were considering three possibilities as a memorial to their son: a museum, a technical school, or a university, and asked for his opinion on which would be most suitable. Eliot said a university, ideally a free university that would not charge tuition. This would require, he said, an endowment of at least $5 million (equivalent to about $120 million in 2017). Leland Stanford turned to his wife: "Well, Jane, we could manage that, couldn't we?"[28] The couple decided, in effect, to create all three: a university that would encompass a technical school and its own museum. The land, stocks, and bonds that they gave for the purpose would be worth not $5 million but $20 million.[29]

The one institution that made the deepest impression upon Stanford, the one that he said he wanted his university to emulate, was Cooper Union. Stanford wanted the polytechnic school, the school of design, the art galleries, and the museum of inventions that he intended to build to reach "the working classes."[30] At Leland Stanford's behest, a bill was introduced in January 1885 in the California legislature and subsequently passed, which provided for the creation of universities, using private funds placed in a state-protected trust, that would provide students with "a practical education, fitting them for the useful trades or arts."[31] In the summer, Stanford had Francis A. Walker, president of the Massachusetts Institute of Technology, come to California to spend several weeks conferring with him about plans for the university.[32]

When the Stanfords were ready later that year to unveil the detailed vision for the university, in the form of "The Founding Grant," spelling out their wishes to the university's trustees, they revealed that they were unable to pick one thing over another. They wanted it all: mechanical institutes—plural—and museums—plural—and galleries of art and laboratories and conservatories and "all things necessary for the study of agriculture in all its branches and for mechanical training." It was to include the liberal arts, too, everything needed for "the studies and exercises directed to the cultivation and enlargement of the mind." The conversations that the Stanfords had had with leading university educators had apparently led them away from the narrow conception of applied education that they had begun with. Now they wanted everything needed to "qualify its students for personal success and direct usefulness in life," and that meant supplying every existing form of knowledge, from the applied to the theoretical to the ethereal. The founders forbade "sectarian instruction" but did express their wish that the university would teach "the immortality of the soul, the existence of an all-wise and benevolent Creator, and that obedience to His laws is the highest duty of man."[33]

The Stanfords sounded economic and social themes in 1885 that are no less present in the early twenty-first century. The telegraph and railroad had made the world flat, or in the Stanfords' phrasing, had created "one great neighborhood in whose markets all producers meet in competition." Everyone's powers would be enhanced, the founders believed, by "labor-aiding machinery," whose development was so important, in their view, that "too much attention, therefore, cannot be given to technical and mechanical instruction."[34] The university founders' concern with fitting graduates "for some useful pursuit" impressed the *San Francisco Chronicle* as indicating a "liberal and catholic spirit;" the paper's reporter interpreted the absence of explicit admission restrictions as the expression of a welcome to students without "limit as to age, sex, color, race or nativity."[35]

Other elements of their vision reflected the founders' idiosyncratic concerns. They expected that a portion of the land of their Palo Alto farm would be rented out to parents of students and others, generating a "handsome income" for the university. But they directed the trustees to take care that "no objectionable people are allowed to reside upon the estate, and that no drinking saloons shall ever be opened upon any part of the premises."[36] (Leland Stanford believed that 25 percent of world production was "destroyed by the use of intoxicants."[37])

They also held on tightly to the idea that the university would maintain a farm for "instruction in Agriculture in all its branches." The university would have seven thousand acres to use, ample room for a fruit orchard and canning operations, for vineyards and viti-culture, giving students the means to work their way through college as well as receive both business and technical education. The Stanfords knew that work-study schemes had already been tried and abandoned at Cornell and Oberlin, but they were undeterred: they believed that theirs would be different and would somehow succeed where every other institution had failed.[38]

If others thought these plans unorthodox, Leland Stanford felt all the more vindicated in his determination to start a new university. If he had wanted to make a university like others, he would say later, he would have simply given his money to colleges already in existence.[39]

When the Founding Grant was unveiled in 1886 and the founders' vision was expressed most fully, at that moment before ground was broken and the grand dimensions were scaled down, before vision would be diminished by reluctant compromises or changes of heart, observers could be excited about whatever they wished to see in the Stanfords' philosophizing. Local boosters were palpably giddy at what they saw: here, at last, would be an education complex, preparatory school and university, that could train young people "in all the trades and practical arts," said the *San Francisco Chronicle*. Within the previous twenty years, France, Germany, and England all had founded excellent technical schools for the trades, moving well ahead of America. It was well past time for America to do the same, and Leland Stanford was credited for recognizing this.

The newspaper was so excited, in fact, that it urged Stanford to dispense with his plans to build a conventional campus: it urged him to follow the German model, spending $9 on faculty salaries for every $1 for facilities. In three months, a large temporary wooden building could be assembled and outfitted for the trades and be ready to open. "Doubtless many would say it was not fitting to start a great university in so modest a way," the paper said. "But the American public needs to have it brought home to it that teachers and not buildings are what make a great university."[40]

The editors in San Francisco possessed the boundless enthusiasm of local boosters, but they were patient boosters, looking out one hundred years. They predicted that before the end of the twentieth century, Stanford University would attract the greatest scholars of not merely the United States but the world, thriving when "Oxford and Cambridge, Paris, Bonn, and Berlin have exhausted their usefulness."[41] They tacitly presented a simple argument: old institutions, like living things, decline; new institutions possess the vitality of a newly born organism; therefore, Stanford University would possess that vitality. This neatly turned existing universities' own histories into liabilities and Stanford's lack of same into an asset. Stanford University was a blank slate and could be whatever its founders and trustees wanted it to be. Contemplating the possibilities, even if inchoate, was an exercise in heady fantasy. The actual institution that was created turned out not to be as different as its founders and boosters once hoped.

CHAPTER 3

NATURALLY CURIOUS

THE SMORGASBORD OF COURSE OFFERINGS that greets Stanford's freshmen today extends in all directions. The bountiful variety of majors—some sixty-four—is bewildering. Don't rush to decide on your major, the university says. Explore! The university even offers to freshmen and sophomores a two-unit course on choosing courses, called "Designing Your Stanford."

A foundational tenet of modern liberal education is that newly arrived college students do not have enough academic experience to immediately make a well-informed decision about what their area of specialization should be. But this tenet conflicts with many prospective employers' expectations that students will obtain a job-relevant summer internship before the senior year, and that, in turn, requires having a compelling story for the employer about one's preparation and experience by the middle of one's junior year. This leaves little time for the most intrepid students, whose academic explorations in their freshman and sophomore years covered more territory, to demonstrate their attachment to the occupational area or industry relevant to a given internship.

The lack of time is felt most keenly by the students who explore an initial academic interest, just as the university encourages them to do, but who then discover that they are not interested in, or actively dislike, the field and must set out for another destination. If the disillusionment comes during a study abroad or other off-campus experience during the junior year, there is scant time to reorient and acquire the expected experiences in a new field by graduation.

Meredith Hazy, née Colton, who arrived at Stanford in the fall of 2009, was unhurried about making a decision about the major. She loved reading and writing and enjoyed the English classes she took, so when it was time to declare a major in her sophomore year, English was the obvious choice. What she would do after graduation was a question that did not weigh heavily upon her. If she didn't find a path to interesting work, she figured she would go to law school.

The law-school option did not remain attractive, however. In the fall quarter of her junior year, she took advantage of Stanford's internship program in Washington, DC, where she interned at a community court. There she realized that, upon closer inspection, law was not so interesting after all.

In the spring of her junior year, she studied in Madrid, and after her return did an internship that summer at a nonprofit think tank in Menlo Park, the Kaiser Family Foundation, working on health policy. She had taken a class about nonprofits and philanthropy, and the internship seemed at the time to be a good way to see whether nonprofit work would turn out to be what she had yet to find, a field for which she had passion. Looking back from the present on that summer after her junior year, however, she sees what her classmates knew at the time: that is the summer when you are supposed to line up an internship with the one company or organization that you most wish will offer you a permanent position after graduation. "I was a little too naive to really realize that," Hazy says. "I was thinking, 'Hey, I'm interested in nonprofit stuff. I should do an internship related to that.'" She had been placed at Kaiser by an internship-matching service, and there was no possibility of being offered a permanent position there. She also noticed that summer that time passed slowly. Health policy turned out not to be an area she felt passionate about.

Good to know. But Hazy entered her senior year without any idea of what she was going to do after graduation. She stopped by the large career fair held in the fall, but had not realized that she should have attended with résumés in hand and dressed for success. She had gone expecting that the representatives in the booths would merely supply information, not do initial evaluations. "I was really clueless," she says.

Had Hazy been a senior in 1979, when the first career fair was held at Stanford,[1] her assumption that company representatives would do nothing more than dispense information would have been correct. The fair, which began as the "Job Faire," with the trailing -*e* that evoked a playful Renaissance Faire, had been organized as a response to the surge of students who in the mid-1970s sought post-graduate jobs instead of immediately going on to graduate school. About 55 percent of the Class of 1979 sought jobs after graduation, which was a doubling of the percentage of the Class of 1974 that sought jobs. But even though it was called the "Job Faire," a university coordinator emphasized that the representatives were "not peddling jobs"; instead, they were holding "an information session for students thinking about career opportunities to meet with employment organizations."[2]

That first generation of career fairs at Stanford that began in 1979 were organized expressly for the "undecided liberal arts student." The organizations who were represented were invited by the university, and few tech companies were included.[3] Later, Stanford career fairs would be filled predominantly by tech companies looking for tech majors. A separate career fair is now held annually for liberal arts students in the winter quarter, but it is small and dominated by nonprofit organizations and for-profit tutoring companies.

Hazy decided to apply for a year-long post-graduate fellowship, through Stanford's Haas Center for Public Service, that would support work at a nonprofit. This seemed to be the best available opportunity for her, and it would give her a year after graduation to investigate what would come next, time that she needed. She did not get the fellowship, however.

The disappointment was blunted somewhat by the Haas Center's invitation to apply to another public-service internship, similar to the other one but with a drawback: it would last only for the summer following graduation. She received word of acceptance in February. It was a fallback plan, in case she did not find a permanent position before graduation. Having that in hand did not eliminate the anxiety she felt about her future, but it at least kept the anxiety from climbing above the level it had reached already as she continued to look for permanent positions.

Hazy watched many fellow English majors finalize plans to start graduate studies; others knew by March that they would be teaching for Teach for America. Her roommate, who was a chemistry major, was, like Hazy, looking for a job during her senior year. Hazy thought, If she can't get a job, and she's a hard-science major, what am I going to be able to do?

Her roommate finally got a job, just before graduation, at a foundation, and Hazy ended up taking the summer internship. She landed at Pacific Foundation Services, which administered grants for small family foundations that did not have the staff to run grants programs on their own. Stanford's Haas Center paid her a stipend. Pacific Foundation Services tried to find funding to create a permanent position for Hazy but failed. All it could offer was a three-month extension, in which she would be paid an hourly wage, without benefits. Without a single job possibility in view, she entered a period of high anxiety that she describes as "the worst two months of my life."

She revisited her determination to find work in the world of nonprofits and foundations. This was her second stint in two summers, and the pace at work felt slow. She asked herself if she was excited to go to work every day, and the answer was no. Perhaps, she thought, she should look at tech companies. She did not have a particular role in mind, but having spent the past four years at Stanford, proximity made the tech industry seem accessible.

Hazy now asked herself, What tech companies did she think of as cool? The one that jumped ahead of all others was Twitter, which when she was not doing actual work, she was checking all day. She was no longer a student, nor was she sufficiently experienced to know how long the odds were that Twitter would find her work history of any interest. She saw that Twitter representatives would be on hand at a career fair to be held in a hotel in Walnut Creek, about ninety minutes away. This was not a job fair for college students or recent graduates. It was for experienced people. The position that Twitter had advertised was for "account management"—she could not say with certainty what that title even meant—and it called for five to six years of experience. She was rather desperate, though, and did not have other ideas. She figured she had little to lose, other than time, by showing up and seeing if the representative would speak with her. She investigated the term *account management* and learned that it was some kind of a sales role. She constructed a chain of logic that made it seem as if she was qualified: she could make the case that she communicated well; communication was a key component of sales; ergo, she could do sales.

When Hazy drove up to the fair, she expected to find the hotel filled with other tech companies, in addition to Twitter, that were recognizable names, and which would give her the opportunity to make her pitch many times. No such luck. She had not heard of any of the other companies and did not seek an audience with them.

Unlike the career fair on campus, where students milled about a plaza filled with booths, this fair was at a hotel that had no common area. Each company had rented its own room, and applicants formed a line outside the closed door, waiting for a recruiter to open the door and invite the next applicant in for an interview. Actually, Hazy did not see any lines in front of the rooms except in the case of Twitter's, and that one was long. She texted her fiancé, *I should leave. This is not for me. I don't know why I came. This was a bad idea.* Her fiancé, who had graduated from Stanford two years before her with a BS in engineering, urged her to stay and at least try to talk to the people from Twitter and see what they might say.

Hazy waited about an hour and then got her chance. When she entered the room, she faced two recruiters. She had prepared a spiel, explaining why Twitter should hire her for the account management role. This was greeted with patient smiles—and then a firm no. "I don't think you're a fit for this role," said one. Hazy remembers how her heart dropped and she thought, wistfully, "Getting the job would have been nice." Her reverie was interrupted, however. "I have this other role that I think would be a perfect fit for you," said a recruiter. It would be as an account associate—the meaning of the title was not clear and would require some investigation—but Hazy eagerly declared her great interest. She received an email message from the recruiter the next day, inviting her to come in to Twitter headquarters for on-site interviews.

There the soundness of Hazy's syllogism, with its assumption that good communication skills and good sales skills were indistinguishable, was tested. She was interviewed by three different people and was asked, at different times, to role play. Her interlocutor, for example, would invite Hazy to describe Twitter ads as if she were addressing an advertising prospect for Twitter. "What would you tell me about Twitter ads? How would you convince me to use Twitter ads?" It was a challenging assignment: all she knew about Twitter ads was what she saw as a Twitter user. She took up the challenge, "making it up on the go," she says. Picturing the exercise as a form of improvisational theater helped.

No one asked her about her coursework at Stanford. The closest any question came to inquiring about what she had studied was the one that asked her what her proudest accomplishment as an undergrad had been. She pointed to the senior paper she had written about food writer M. F. K. Fisher and remembered to cast it in biz-speak: "It was a great chance for me to work on a project from end to end."

She was also asked to prepare an analytical paper on "the digital ad space," a topic she knew nothing about. She looked through articles posted at Business Insider, *Forbes*, and other business news sites, gathering enough information to fulfill the assignment.

Twitter managers liked what they heard and read—and offered her the position. She had managed to leap from a soon-to-end internship at a nonprofit to a real job at a large tech company. It was enabled by a visit to a job fair that was for candidates who did not remotely resemble her, a newly minted, essentially inexperienced English major. We can safely assume that on that fateful day at the hotel, Hazy put very strong communication skills to good purpose.[4]

As an account associate, Hazy spent all day, every day, talking with businesses who had signed up to place advertisements on Twitter.[5] Some tried ad campaigns once or twice and then disappeared, clearly disappointed with the results. Hazy's job was to call such advertisers—six to nine a day—and have conversations with them about their business and how they might advertise more effectively on Twitter. It was a salaried position that happened to be in sales; there were no sales quotas to meet, no commission to earn.

Hazy joined a team at Twitter that had considerably more work experience than she. Two team members had worked at Google in a similar role. Another member was an attorney who had decided to change careers, and this position, as an account associate, would serve as a path into sales. Hazy was one of the few recent college grads that had been hired, and though a number of different types of majors were represented, including economics, journalism, and communications, she was the only English major in the immediate vicinity. What she soon saw, however, was that the major did not matter and she was not less prepared than teammates. The ability to learn quickly what you needed to know for the job was the only real prerequisite.

Twitter nominally provided four weeks of training, but the company was so eager to put the new hires to work that after two weeks of instruction Hazy was put on the phone with clients. Her charge was simple: help Twitter's registered advertisers, who had already signed up, use the service more effectively. The salary-based compensation and the absence of quotas made the work seem like it belonged to a helping profession. But after she had been at Twitter six months, the company introduced commission-based compensation and target sales quotas. Once a team member had spoken with an advertiser, the member was credited with whatever advertising revenue came in subsequently from that client. To prevent team members from cherry-picking the largest companies and speaking only with them, the members also now had to place a minimum of thirty calls weekly to different clients.

For Hazy, the quota came as a shock. When she had begun the job she had described it to herself in terms that made it feel familiar: "Hey, they want us to talk to advertisers; I can do that." She had never faced a quota before and initially did not feel comfortable. It turned out not to be onerous, but she was glad that she had joined Twitter in the earlier period and had had the chance to get comfortable in the position before the new regime was put into place.

After a year at Twitter, she became restless. She liked working on new internal processes and systems more than sales. She volunteered to take on ad hoc projects in addition to her regular responsibilities, relishing new challenges. She also looked around Twitter to see if she could step into new roles. Or, she wondered, would she be better off moving to an even younger Silicon Valley company? At Twitter, she saw senior managers who, like her, did not have the business degrees that would have been expected at older non-tech companies. She understood that those managers had been able to ascend at Twitter because the company had grown so fast. But now its growth had slowed. If she wanted to work at a company that was still growing exponentially, she would have to leave Twitter.

Hazy saw a job listing for "risk analyst" at Stripe, a fast-growing business-to-business software startup in San Francisco that made it easy for mobile app and web developers to accept credit card payments. A risk analyst was charged with identifying and predicting fraudulent purchases. She had seen the position advertised when she was applying at Twitter and recalled dismissing it, saying, "I don't know much about Stripe. And 'risk analyst' sounds boring—I don't even know what that means." But after working at Twitter and gaining work experience, she realized that "risk analyst" sounded like a position that would be anything but boring. As for Stripe, it had become more visible as it attracted venture capital from top Valley firms, raising about $200 million by the end of 2014; its valuation when it raised funds that year was more than $3 billion.[6]

Stripe's growth was rapid. In June 2009, Stripe consisted of just the two very young brothers who were its founders, Patrick and John Collison, who were only in their second year at MIT (Patrick) and first year at Harvard (John) when they cooked up the idea for the company during winter break. They had come out to Silicon Valley at the end of the school year to work on the company at Y Combinator, the Mountain View firm that funded large batches of startups twice a year, and had not returned to college.[7] In June 2015, the company had grown to about three hundred employees. That was the growth trajectory that Hazy was looking for. Twitter, with about ten times as many employees, looked stodgy and static in comparison.

Stripe's description of the ideal candidate for its risk analyst position fit a humanities major better than a statistics major:

Naturally curious: if something seems off, you want to figure out what's going on.

Decisive, yet open to learning: you will make many critical decisions every day, and you will be wrong some of the time.

Understanding and empathetic to the challenges of setting up a new business.

A strong believer in knowing and understanding the numbers behind a problem.

An excellent communicator and able to convey complex ideas succinctly.

Fluent in one or more non-English languages (not required, but a big plus as Stripe expands internationally).

Hazy had learned from her first job-hunt experience that meeting face to face with someone at the target firm was vastly preferable to submitting an application online. She did not know anyone at Stripe, but she had a Stanford friend who was a friend of someone at Stripe who had also gone to Stanford. Hazy got her friend to send an introductory email; she followed with an email to the Stripe person and got on the phone with her. At the same time, she contacted the Stripe recruiter to set an application in motion. She credits the friend-of-a-friend at Stripe for helping her résumé get noticed. She was invited in for a day of interviews.

Two years out of school, her academic experiences at Stanford were of even less interest to this prospective employer than they had been when she first spoke to Twitter as a newly minted graduate. When visiting Stripe, however, she could not talk up her day-to-day work at Twitter, holding the hands of clients, because the work of the risk analyst was so different, out of direct contact with clients and their hands. Fortunately for Hazy, the ad hoc projects that she had volunteered for at Twitter did involve analysis, such as one that required poring through phone records to see which calls for help came from customers with what kinds of attributes. She was also helped, we can safely assume, by her Stanford pedigree and the way the school's reputation for selectivity confers a competitive advantage to its job-seeking graduates over those who went to less selective schools. But her background consisted of more than just Stanford—it also included immersion in the humanities and in reading and crafting narratives. She had learned how to tell the story that she wanted to tell about herself, one that refused to accept a tacit presumption that an English major was unsuited for an analytical position.

Hazy was offered the job and accepted. She stepped into the company as the increase in its valuation became vertiginous. In July 2015, seven months after its last fundraising round, it raised more funds at a valuation that had jumped 40 percent;[8] the next year, it did more fundraising at a $9.2 billion valuation, more than triple what it had been two years previously.[9]

At Stripe, Hazy was placed on the team responsible for preventing fraud. No one expected her to know, upon her arrival, what she needed to know to perform her job, flagging suspicious customers or purchases. She received training, and she picked up on the job whatever the training did not include. In order to handle data analytics, she learned SQL, the programming language for working with databases, and used it every day.

When Hazy had more than a year of experience as a risk analyst at Stripe, she likened her daily work to preparing an English paper. In college, she read a novel, pulled out the themes, and then wrote a paper. At Stripe, she scrutinized quantitative data, pored over email from customers and anecdotes from team members about ambiguous situations and tricky calls, pulled out the themes, and then wrote a report, recommending actions that the company should take. "The method of analysis is surprisingly similar," she said, "it's just a different outcome."

Hazy also was grateful to have "soft skills" that she gained when she was at Twitter: the ability to build a good relationship with a manager, how to advocate for herself, how to get put on the projects that she wanted to join, how to balance her own interests with those of the company. She did not feel that these things came naturally to her; she had to learn them in the workplace and get better at them over time.

Hazy did not earn advanced degrees immediately following her graduation but she certainly continued her education. This was enabled by two enlightened employers who did not run away from "English major."

CHAPTER 4

PROPER PROPORTION

CONSTRUCTION of the new Leland Stanford Junior University formally began in May 1887 with the ceremonial installation of a cornerstone at the site on the birthday of Leland Stanford Junior. Leland Stanford, who had been elected the year before to the U.S. Senate, and his wife, Jane, were on hand, as were eighteen trustees who had come down by train from San Francisco to Menlo Park, the stop nearest to the campus-to-be. Carriages conveyed the guests to the empty location on the Stanford farm where building would begin. Local farmers and other curiosity seekers also showed up. The only built structure on the site was a wooden shed that had been thrown up to provide shelter from the sun for the trustees. Its canvas roof flapped in the breeze, as a short ceremony unfolded. A box of commemorative items was placed in a hollow, and Leland Stanford tamped the cornerstone into place.[1]

The site was a tabula rasa. The university could be, seemingly, whatever its creators wanted, beginning life as "one of the best endowed universities of the United States."[2] The plans for the physical plant were finalized, however, well before the curriculum was settled upon. The public was told to expect that the education would be "thorough, practical, useful."[3] But how the vision would be realized would be largely left to the university president.

The *San Francisco Chronicle*'s suggestion made the year before that the university start quickly with one large wooden building that could be assembled in a few months was ignored.[4] Leland Stanford had taken instead the advice of Frederick Law Olmsted and his nephew and associate John Charles to engage a Boston-based architectural firm that the Olmsteds recommended: Shepley, Rutan and Coolidge. The plan that they drafted did not express a significant break with the colleges of yore. At its heart was a quadrangle, with an arcade with arches that would run along the inner perimeter, bringing to the mind of a reporter who saw the plans "the cloisters of the old English colleges." Construction of engineering shops, a men's dorm, and a museum were immediately begun.[5]

Leland Stanford had many things on his mind besides the university: handling diverse business interests, serving as a U.S. Senator, contending with failing health. The opening of the university's doors to its first students approached, and Stanford had yet to complete the important task of finding the first president. This also held up the hiring of the faculty. Leland Stanford's first choice for the position was Andrew White, Cornell's president, who turned the offer down but recommended one of his students, David Starr Jordan, who was then the president of Indiana University.[6] Jordan had grown up on a farm in upstate New York, been a precocious member of Cornell's pioneer class—he had served as a botany instructor in his junior year—and had graduated with a master's degree. He was also the class poet.[7] In March 1891, Leland and Jane Stanford paid a visit to Jordan and offered him the position at an annual salary of $10,000, nearly three times what he made at Indiana, accompanied by the promise that he would have at his disposal for building the university "all the money he could use." Jordan accepted.[8]

Jordan's academic reputation rested primarily on his field work as an ichthyologist, and the news of his appointment was greeted by the Stanfords' hometown paper with cautious optimism, which saw in Jordan a practical-minded academic, a product of Cornell, the institution whose practical orientation was viewed as similar to what Stanford University's was supposed to be. "It is to be hoped for the sake of the success of this experiment in practical education," an editorial said, "that his hands will be left free, and that the theorists will not be allowed to have any controlling influences."[9]

Jordan's first hire was Orrin Leslie Elliott, a PhD student at Cornell, whom Jordan appointed as secretary, then registrar, of the university. Elliott was responsible for responding to the torrent of correspondence from prospective students who had heard about the "practical education" that the new university was to offer, teaching "things you could make your living at" without charging tuition.[10] Elliott also was responsible for granting admission to applicants. By September, one thousand applications had come in, far more than had been anticipated.[11] On opening day, October 1, 1891, 465 students were enrolled, about 350 of whom entered as freshmen but whose age was typically twenty or twenty-one and who were coming from work, not from school.[12]

They arrived to find a university that would provide a congenial home to engineering and science but not exclusively; it would also provide an equal place for the liberal arts. So instead of inaugurating a program teaching skills in the trades, or even adopting a polytechnic approach, Stanford University ended up with a plan that would not be all that different from older schools built around a quadrangle. Jordan set out "two great lines of work, the Liberal Arts and Sciences, on the one hand, and the Applied Sciences (Mechanic Arts, Engineering, etc.)" on the other, a plan for which he secured Leland Stanford's approval. What would be distinctive was placing the Applied Sciences on an equal plane with the Liberal Arts and Sciences. Jordan expressed his hope for "the two to be kept in close relation and, so far as may be, to be equally fostered."[13]

The $20 million that the Stanfords had entrusted to the university had attracted the country's attention. "No university ever received half the advertising in the American newspapers which we have had," Jordan would later write.[14] The founding gift also freed the new president from worry about financial limits. Jordan's plan was to start with a faculty of forty members, consisting of mostly senior professors who then could recruit junior talent as the university's hiring continued. But he discovered that academic stars, the professors that he most sought, were not interested in moving to a remote location in California. As a contemporary observer noted, "The pull of the great city is felt as strongly in university circles as elsewhere, and to Eastern professors, who thought they were making a great sacrifice in going to a frontier town like Chicago, residence on a California ranch was unthinkable."[15]

Jordan had been willing to come, but the proposition had been sweetened considerably by a salary that was multiples of what he had been paid in Indiana. The budget that Senator Stanford gave him to work with was nothing like the unbounded one he had been promised, however. Jordan could not offer a premium to others like the one he himself had received.[16]

When classes began, the university did not have the forty professors originally planned but only fifteen, the ceiling that Leland Stanford imposed on Jordan, saying that fifteen "ought to be sufficient to open with."[17] For the new university library, Stanford told Jordan that "I think a library such as a gentleman would have for his own use to cost about four or five thousand dollars would be sufficient."[18] Stanford also ordered Jordan to "defer" the plans for an agricultural department for the moment.[19]

Of the original fifteen faculty members, only seven were full professors; none were as old as Jordan, who was forty. This seemed to the *San Francisco Chronicle* a rather pathetic start for the institution for which money was to be no obstacle.[20] And though Jordan had expressed his wish that the applied arts and the liberal arts maintain a close relationship, that parity was not established at the beginning: of the first nine appointments that followed Leslie Elliott's as secretary and registrar, eight were in engineering, math, and science, and only one in the humanities, a "non-resident" professor of history.[21]

Jordan persuaded Leland Stanford of the need to fund the humanities by pointing out that the humanities would be the area in which Jordan expected Stanford's female students to concentrate. Leland Stanford conceived of the university as a "combination of Cornell and Johns Hopkins," Jordan would later say, created "to deal largely with the application of science and with advanced research in the various fields of knowledge." The qualifications for, and interest of, women in applied science or advanced research were assumed to be wanting. Neither the founders nor Jordan expected the number of women students to ever approach that of men.[22] But there would be some women, and when opening ceremonies were held on the first day of the school's very first semester, Leland Stanford revealed why he wanted women to receive a bachelor's degree: women would become mothers and the caregivers to infants. Noting that experts deemed the first five or seven years of a child's life as the most critical "to mold and direct the infantile mind," he said, "how important, therefore, is it to have mothers capable of rightly directing the young intelligence."[23]

Once the university opened, Leland Stanford praised Jordan for hiring young faculty members, whose youth made them "more open to new convictions than elderly men, and more liable to keep up with the progress of the times." But he continually hectored Jordan about appointing too many faculty members; it seemed to Stanford that the number "is rather large in proportion to the students."[24] He was irked even more when Jordan passed on to him complaints from the students that the gymnasium was uncomfortably cold in the winter. The senator, writing from Washington, DC, wrote Jordan that "I cannot believe that the boys are so effeminate" as to require steam heat.[25] This issue loomed large to the senator, too large to entrust his university president to manage it. The next day, Senator Stanford informed Jordan that he had independently telegraphed the university official who oversaw facilities to suspend work on heating the gymnasium until the senator had the chance to visit California to make a personal investigation of the alleged need.[26]

The senator's own health continued to decline. The next year, at the age of sixty-eight, he went to Switzerland to take in the restorative air of the mountains. But he walked with difficulty and could not get into a carriage without assistance. In one of his last interviews, in Paris, he rolled out the story he had been telling for years about how he had observed in the young men who approached him in his business life the impracticality of the traditional liberal education. In the multiple tellings, it had been burnished to a high shine:

> I have been impressed with the fact that of all the young men who come to me with letters of introduction from friends in the East the most helpless class are college men. They come from those I would like to oblige. They are generally prepossessing in appearance and of good stock, but when they seek employment and I ask them what they can do all they can say is "anything." They have no definite technical knowledge of anything. They have no specific aim, no definite purpose. It is to overcome that condition, to give an education which shall not have that result, which I hope will be the aim of this University. Its equipment and faculty I desire shall be second to none in the world. Its capacity to give a practical, not a theoretical, education ought to be accordingly for most [sic].[27]

When drafting the Founder's Grant, Leland Stanford had singled out agriculture as the field that would exemplify the practical education he had in mind, and by 1893 the university was working on plans that initially had been deferred to establish a department of agriculture.[28] But in June 1893, Leland Stanford died and the precariousness of the university's finances came into view. The $20 million gift, consisting mostly of real estate holdings, including the land upon which the university sat, was held in an endowment. Leland Stanford had borrowed $2 million to finance the opening of the university, a debt that he expected to be cleared when he received his share, $3 million, of undistributed earnings from the Southern

Pacific Railroad, into which the Central Pacific had merged. But the payment never came through.[29]

With Stanford's death, the Stanford estate was tied up in probate, and the income that the university depended upon for its operations was cut off. The university's ability to meet its payroll was thrown into doubt, and faculty salaries were reduced 10 percent. Students had to pay a new "registration fee" of $20 annually. Even so, the university stayed open only because Jane Stanford used the family allowance of $10,000 a month awarded to her by the court to meet the university's expenses. The crisis would not be eased for three years[30] nor fully resolved for six.[31]

David Starr Jordan had his own ideas about how to make a college education practical. One of his innovations was put in place when the university opened: teaching law to undergraduates, not as a replacement for post-graduate study but as a way to give students a start on such a course.[32] The other innovation that he sought, whose implementation he could never convince the trustees to support, was to make the university devoted exclusively to "technical and professional work" and to research. What he proposed was eliminating all introductory courses and instead requiring that all students complete two years of college at another institution before coming to Stanford.[33]

Jordan oversaw a faculty that held a range of mutually antagonistic opinions about professional specialization in undergraduate education. A debate played out in full public view in the form of thematically provocative commencement addresses given by Stanford faculty members. In 1895, when the first class to have spent all four years at Stanford graduated (they called themselves "the Pioneers"), John Maxson Stillman, a professor of chemistry, shared his thoughts on "specialization in education." The speech was a full-throated appeal for early and narrow specialization, commencing when the undergraduate student arrived on campus.

No student could master all that needed to be known, Stillman argued. The professions had become specialized: lawyers practiced only a particular branch of law; doctors specialized in a single sub-division of medicine; engineers did the same. So too should students. "Knowledge is indeed power—not, however, the superficial knowledge of a multitude of things, but the thorough knowledge of some useful thing," he said. Yes, graduate work provides for specialization, he granted, but it would be best if all students got its benefits. He argued, "It is better to make some sacrifice of general studies rather than to deprive the many of the benefits that arise from thus focusing their energies on some congenial subject." In his view, it was better to be narrowly trained, "out of touch per-haps with the common thought of the leaders of humanity" but able to do "useful work" in one's chosen field, rather than being "the highly cultured and accomplished college graduate with a smattering of twenty -ologies and -isms, but with not enough use-ful knowledge of anything to enable him to find a place in the world's work."[34]

The students that Stillman was addressing at that commencement ceremony did not see the world as he did. They had for the most part eschewed the majors that were most specialized, engineering and law, in favor of the humanities. Among the self-anointed Pioneers, 15 per-cent were English majors, 10 percent history, 13 percent foreign lan-guages; 3 percent drawing, and a smattering in philosophy. The social science majors consisted only of economics (6 percent) and psychol-ogy (less than 1 percent). Law accounted for 9 percent. In the sci-ences, physiology constituted 8 percent of majors. Stillman's home department, chemistry, drew 4 percent, less than the 6 percent that Latin attracted; physics, botany, zoology, hygiene, and entomology shared a few percentage points among them. Most students steered well clear of engineering, the area that was the most professionally specialized. Electrical engineering had 7 percent, civil engineering 5 percent, mechanical 4 percent, and mining 2 percent. The com-bined total for engineering, 20 percent, was less than half of those who had majored in the humanities.[35]

The Pioneer Class was not a uniformly distinguished one. In the view of one graduating senior who had served as the editor of the student paper, many of the students who had come to Stanford would not have been admitted elsewhere because of "their mental and moral disqualifications." Many had been expelled, or as this observer put it, "plucked by the score."[36] ("All who have failed and have been sent home are rich men's sons," said one student at the time.)[37] Nor was the quality of the teaching uniformly high. The senior recounted hearing of the instructor who spoke of "when the particle A has been drug along to here" or "Now, class, see what I have did." A course offered in corporate industry used Bible stories to illustrate points—Adam and Eve were held up as "the first co-operators in clothes-making." Most concerning to the former editor was the way that students despised those among them who showed interest in their classes. The most socially successful among students was the one who did not study and avoided class, the "quadrangle dawdler."[38]

One positive change that the senior had noticed since the university's opening four years earlier was the steady increase in the percentage of women in the student body. In the initial year, one out of every four students was a woman, but in the most recent year, the proportion had risen to one out of three. "The most logical assumption is that Stanford is better suited for ladies than other colleges since they do not show so rapid an increase in lady attendance," he surmised.[39]

Three years after Stillman's call for more specialization, when the graduating Class of 1898 assembled for its commencement ceremony, Walter Miller, a thirty-four-year-old professor of classical philology, took the stage and delivered an impassioned case for an education that was not specialized. He was not afraid to target in particular the keystone maxim of the university's late founder. "The world's call is for the man of learning who knows better than any one else how to do some one thing," Miller said, "but he cannot meet the requirements if he knows nothing but that one thing."

Far superior, he continued, is an education that allows the graduate to see one thing in relation to other things and to see all "in their proper proportion."[40]

Miller acknowledged that four years was not long enough to provide for grounding in the humanities and preparation for a profession. The solution was to discard the idea that the bachelor's degree was a terminal degree and instead think of graduate education as the final stage for all educated people, and not an elective stage only for some.[41]

Then, as now, Stanford's humanities faculty was placed on the defensive by the demand not to waste students' time with anything that was not immediately practical. Miller pushed back:

> Those who look upon knowledge only from the standpoint of "practical" utility are likely to see in the university only a bureau for the delivery of special information, a mere warehouse for literary, medical, or legal merchandise, instead of a temple of knowledge and truth. The enrichment of knowledge and power is not considered and therefore not desired. Too general is the conception in our land that nothing is practical, nothing is useful, even in matters of pure intellect, unless it can be translated into dollars and cents.

With an intuitive understanding of the power of the word *practical*, Miller wrested the word back: "In the truer sense of the word, anything is practical that makes a man or a community or a state or a nation stronger or better or wiser, anything that helps a man to live up to the best that is in him."[42]

At a superficial glance, Miller and the others on the humanities faculty seemed to be in the enviable position of drawing the most students. English, history, and foreign languages accounted for 22 percent of the graduating Class of 1898. The sciences had made gains and now were 19 percent, but engineering had lost a little ground, now totaling 15 percent. Education had been added and drew 5 percent; economics also drew 5 percent; law had edged up to 10 percent from 9 percent. Another new major was "bionomics," experimental biology that the Stanford registrar explained was synonymous with "Evolution," which had 2 percent.[43]

What the university's tallies for the individual majors did not show, however, was the split among men and women. In 1907, the professional fields were almost exclusively male. Engineering majors consisted of forty-four men and no women; law had thirty men and one woman. In the humanities, women predominated: Latin majors consisted of eighteen women and one man, English had identical numbers, and German had sixteen women and four men.[44]

The pattern suggests that men were specializing early and electing vocational paths, while women were receiving the broad liberal education that was expected to be put to use not in the paid workplace but in the way that Leland and Jane Stanford had envisaged, at home in the care of infants and young children. When John C. Branner, a professor of geology, addressed the Class of 1898, the same group of seniors as had Miller, he praised the senior women: "Members of the Faculty know that the women in the class are smarter than the men." But he did not give the women valedictory encouragement to go forth and make their mark on the world. He only told them and the men to "get married as soon as you can afford to do so."[45]

The women of Stanford were much on the mind of Jane Stanford as well. One year later, when she formally transferred more than $10 million worth of real estate, stocks, and bonds to the university, she requested from the trustees, and received, a change in the university bylaws that placed a limit of five hundred on the number of women who could be enrolled simultaneously at the university. At the time, there were 480 women among the 1,100 students.[46] "I have watched with interest the large growth in the attendance of female students," Jane Stanford told the trustees, "and if this growth continues in the future at the same rate, the number of women students will, before very long, greatly exceed the number of men, and thereby have it regarded by the public as a University for females instead of males. This was not my husband's wish, nor is it mine, nor would it have been my son's."[47] She died in 1905 at the age of seventy-six, but the cap of five hundred was not lifted until 1933.[48]

By limiting the number of women who would be enrolled, the university would take in more male students whose interest in studying was marginal or nonexistent, and the longer it would take for the wider world to perceive a university that produced well-educated graduates. In the 1907–08 academic year, almost one out of every five male students, but only 2.5 percent of the women, were thrown out of the university for "delinquent scholarship."[49]

Having an artificially higher percentage of men also meant the university would have more demand for engineering and law, the professional tracks, and less for the humanities. It was only when the limit was removed—that is, only when the directive of Jane Stanford was nullified and women could be admitted without imposition of a cap—that the undergraduate curriculum could outgrow the effects of earlier stunting. Without the rebalancing of the gender ratio before World War II, professional narrowing would have been much more pronounced, decades before the present tendencies in that direction manifested. It is the flourishing of liberal education that would follow in the mid-twentieth century, and the broad embrace of that education by prospective employers of new graduates, that shows us an encouraging example of liberal education being recognized by all parties as practical.

CHAPTER 5

A FOOT IN THE DOOR

WHEN LELAND STANFORD VIEWED the typical college student of his time as "void of such practical knowledge of any calling as will enable them to earn their living at once," he could have been referring to a history major like Stephen Hayes, who graduated from Stanford in 2010. At that point, the subject that Hayes knew best was the history of South Africa. Yet the education embodied in his history major is demonstrably practical, if understood not primarily for subject matter but as marking a process of honing how to learn, how to analyze the unfamiliar, how to write well, how to speak persuasively.

Hayes grew up in Arlington, Virginia, without television and video games. His parents were liberal arts majors who got law degrees and who wanted their three children to spend their free time with things other than screens. Hayes became a voracious reader who developed a special love of history, beginning with a Civil War phase, then a World War II phase. When he arrived at Stanford in the fall of 2005, he walked into an introductory freshman seminar on the politics of contemporary South Africa and became fascinated with that country's history. He spent one quarter in his junior year studying in Cape Town, and when he returned to campus, he took a passel of courses in African history and spent long hours in the stacks of the university's libraries. One of his seminar papers, on the Natives Land Act of 1913 that stripped black South Africans of land ownership, was selected for inclusion in the history department's student journal, *Herodotus*.[1]

Outside of his classes, Hayes enjoyed working for Stanford as a tour guide, especially when leading tours for prospective students and their parents. He was one of about thirty guides, chosen from about two hundred students who apply each year.[2] The guides stock up on Stanford trivia to dispense ("We have 8,100 acres of land here; to put it in perspective, we can fit twenty-six Disneylands right here on campus"). They also field substantive questions about the university, from general education requirements to university policies governing underage drinking. At the start of every tour he thought to himself, "Game time!" He also worked as a tutor in the university's Program in Writing and Rhetoric, helping students improve their oral communication skills. His summers during college were occupied with internships in Washington, DC: in the first, he worked in Senator Dianne Feinstein's office, doing research on carbon cap-and-trade legislation; in the next, he worked in the Washington office of California utility PG&E; and in the third, he was a White House intern in the first year of Barack Obama's administration.

By the fall quarter of his senior year, about one-third of his Stanford friends already knew what they would be doing after graduation. These were the students who had done an internship the previous summer that converted into a job offer. Hayes was not paying a great deal of attention. He had taken Introduction to American Law, which he had much enjoyed, and he thought he would go to law school eventually, viewing a law degree as useful in a number of careers, including government or business. But he was not anxious about what he would do immediately following graduation. He was occupied with classes, continuing to take almost twenty units each quarter as he had since he had arrived, well more than the fifteen units in a normal load. One day, as he was crossing campus, he came upon the fall career fair and had a conversation with a person representing the consulting firm Monitor, who took pains to say that the company welcomed a humanities major. But Hayes was not excited about working in a job where he would live inside spreadsheets all day, so he did not pursue consulting possibilities.

The next quarter, Hayes applied to Teach for America, which ran a campus recruiting operation no less sophisticated than those of the consulting firms and investment banks. There were deadlines and interviews and winnowing. Its national acceptance rate was 15 percent,[3] which gave those who were selected a feeling of belonging to an elite. The consulting firms and investment banks wanted to be affiliated with TFA. One of Hayes's friends, who had done an internship at Bain after his junior year, applied to both Bain and TFA, and Bain offered him a job with a start date that was deferred two years so he could first be a TFA volunteer. About 10 percent of the senior class at Stanford applied for TFA when Hayes did.[4]

Hayes was accepted into TFA, which would start in the fall. He still planned to eventually go to law school. At the end of his winter quarter in his senior year, he had enough credits to graduate, so he spent the spring quarter at "Camp Stanford," the students' name for the quarter in which, for payment of a nominal sum, a student remains officially a student and can live on campus but does not take courses and does not pay tuition. Hayes used the quarter to study for the LSAT.

Hayes received a high LSAT score, but when he looks back at his time at Stanford, he has a regret: that he had done whatever would optimize his chances of getting into a top law school and avoided anything that would hurt those chances. In retrospect, he wishes he had done more academic exploring. He regrets in particular not taking the introductory course in computer science, CS 106A, to avoid a risk of hurting his GPA.

Hayes got off to a good start at TFA. He was sent to a crash course in Los Angeles to learn some rudiments of teaching and was assigned to a kindergarten class at a charter school. "I was bright-eyed and full of optimism about the experience I was about to embark on," he recalls. His assignment for the school year would be teaching seventh-grade English and social studies at a charter school in San Jose, where the reading level of the typical seventh-grader was at the fourth-grade level. He taught three two-hour classes each day. The first two classes went well, but not the third, which was in a stiflingly hot classroom, without air conditioning, the perfect incubator for what the teaching world calls "behavior management" problems. When he turned to the school principal for assistance, he not only failed to get help, he found himself marked for transfer or dismissal. He decided he would end his TFA stint after one year and began applying to law schools for the class that he would enter one year later.

Hayes needed an interim job for the intervening year, and he sent out applications to a variety of companies, small and large. He was living in Mountain View in an apartment; his roommate, a Stanford friend who had been his roommate in their freshman year, was working at Google and put in a good word for him there. When Hayes was invited for an interview, he discovered that his prospective employer was not much interested in the courses that he had taken at Stanford. What he was asked about most was his recent job experience at TFA. But he was able to talk about the relevance of his academic experience at Stanford in general terms, highlighting the training that gave him the ability to present ideas effectively, whether orally or in writing. The one time in the interview when he got to talk about specifics was when the interviewer asked, "What are you passionate about? What do you enjoy doing when you're not within the walls of this office?" Here Hayes talked about his interest in South Africa, his studying abroad there, and his seminar paper that had been published in the history department's journal.

Google gave him a job as a contractor in the People Operations group, its human relations department. Hayes's contract position was to last six months; no promises were made that he and his fellow contractors would be offered permanent positions. The only permanent Google employee in his team was the manager to whom the contractors reported. But contractors nonetheless got to enjoy some of the amenities of working at Google. Hayes felt dizzy at the change, going from the decommissioned motel in San Jose that had housed the charter school at which he had taught to Google's gleaming campus, with its cafeterias, gym, laundry pickup service, and other luxuries.

Hayes was fortunate that the team to which he had been assigned happened to be tackling an interesting project. Google had come to the realization that its use of brain teasers to screen applicants had not been an effective evaluation tool, and it had generated a good deal of negative publicity and ill feelings among talented prospects, to boot. *Fuck that! I don't want to tell you how many ping pong balls fit in a bus.* The company was also rethinking the way it had always filtered recent college graduates, asking only how selective was their school and what was their GPA. "There are a ton of false negatives," Hayes says, "and they realized that there are exceptional candidates who just might have a slightly more unconventional background." His team was charged with developing new questions for Google's interviewers, which ideally would reveal an applicant's ability to excel at her or his job, says Hayes, "regardless of whether or not they went to Stanford or regardless of whether or not they had a 4.0 GPA during college."

The team came up with questions that were similar to those used by consulting firms, such as this:

> Say you want to start a small business in a new town. You have a choice between starting a lawn mowing company, opening a frozen yogurt shop, or a beauty parlor. Walk me through the considerations and the questions that you would ask in order to land at the right outcome and explain your reasoning to me.

Hayes most enjoyed crafting interview questions, but he and his team also carried out interviews with real job candidates, putting the new questions to a test in the field. He recalls one applicant in particular, "a total rock-star candidate," who had applied for a sales role at Google, but who had never gone to college. Under the old hiring procedures, Google would never have given him serious consideration. But the candidate had done exceptionally well in his sales career, and he was offered a job, which greatly pleased Hayes.

Before Hayes had gotten the contractor job at Google, he had had a conversation about job possibilities with another Stanford friend who was working at a year-old startup named Inkling, which made software for publishing interactive textbooks for the iPad and was based in San Francisco. He did some research and was sufficiently intrigued that he sent in an application. He never heard back, and when the Google job materialized, Inkling dropped from his mind. But a few months later, Inkling got in touch and invited him in for an interview. Hayes was feeling a bit restless—the daily routine at Google had begun to feel easy, and he itched for work that was more challenging—so he went in for the interview and got an offer to be an editorial assistant. He accepted, telling himself it would be just for a year if he got into one of the law schools that he most wanted to go to.

Inkling had about thirty employees when Hayes joined in 2011. Before the iPad, textbook publishers created digital versions of textbooks by converting static print pages into static PDF pages. The iPad offered a way to display pages that dynamically resized themselves, depending on the size of the screen, and contained interactive features, such as clickable links and animations. First, though, the PDF pages had to be rewritten. A publisher would give Inkling responsibility for creating a dynamic version of a digital textbook, Inkling would send it off to a subcontractor in India, and then editorial assistants like Hayes would have to compare the new version with the original one and identify the discrepancies, which were plentiful, that needed to be fixed.

To Hayes, Inkling was engaged in an exciting mission, creating textbooks for digital media that would engage students more than printed books did. He also remembered his unhappiness when as a student he had been forced to purchase entire textbooks every quarter in which only a few chapters were assigned. Inkling offered students the option of purchasing only the individual chapters that they needed. The proofreading that filled his work day was not as exhilarating as the grand mission, but he was pleased to have gained entry into a company whose product he believed in.

Producing each title involved organizing many files and making entries in Excel spreadsheets, coordinating work spread out among many people, inside and outside of Inkling. The finished product was beautiful, and every time a title was released to Inkling's online bookstore, champagne would be uncorked for the occasion. But the workflow was too messy; it was hard to be sure that the several dozen people involved in production were always looking at the same working version of a given page. The company decided to build software for its own use to handle the management of the content. Six months after starting, Hayes found himself promoted to a newly created Content Operations Team, which initially consisted of just two people: a manager and his assistant, who was Hayes. At that point, he had been accepted into law schools, including his first choice, Stanford, but he relished the prospect of new responsibilities and challenges. He got permission from Stanford to put off starting for a year.

Hayes had no background in project management, nor did he have any experience in defining quality standards for service, but he learned on the job. He also picked up enough knowledge of HTML and CSS, used in building web pages, to be able to fix some things without having to assign them to the front-end designers. Startups are perpetually overstretched and are averse to imposing rigid rules about positions and titles. Employees do whatever needs doing, and if they don't know how, they get someone else to teach them or figure it out on their own. Hayes's education continued.

The software that Hayes's team built worked well, and Inkling was able to develop templates for entire series of trade-book titles, such as Frommer's travel guides or Wiley's Dummies series, that sped up production. Inkling had published only about thirty titles at the time Hayes joined the company; at the end of the following year, its library had grown to four hundred. Inkling's publisher partners took an interest in the software that Inkling was using for itself. The partners had to manage content that was being worked on simultaneously not by dozens of people, but by hundreds. Inkling decided to add a new line of business, licensing its internal content-management software to large publishers in the form of software-as-a-service.

Another year passed, and Hayes asked Stanford Law School to defer his start one more year. As Inkling grew, so did his responsibilities. The software licensing business became so successful that Inkling dropped book publishing entirely to focus on its software-as-a-service business. But when year three rolled around, Hayes could defer law school no longer. He let his supervisor know he would be leaving in the fall to return to Stanford.

When he had begun at Inkling, Hayes had hoped to acquire some interesting business experience before he went to law school, and his hope had been fulfilled in full measure. Joining this startup, which grew greatly during his three years there, had given him a position with real responsibilities, a seat in the room where important decisions were made, an opportunity to learn new domains of knowledge. Having had this remarkable experience at Inkling, he wondered how well he would adjust when he returned to the quieter and less exciting life as a student.

When Inkling's CEO heard of Hayes's plans to leave for law school, he sat Hayes down and presented him with an offer that demonstrated in a most persuasive way that Hayes's services were valued. Hayes decided to let go of his original career plan and told Stanford Law School that he would not be coming. In doing so, he officially jettisoned the predictable career path that many of his Stanford peers had chosen. He elected instead to follow opportunity wherever it revealed itself.

Hayes had started at Inkling proofing textbooks, a job he now calls a "foot in the door" job. It required an unrelenting focus on the smallest of details, which he says he was not particularly adept at. But once in the door, he was able to find roles within the company to help build the operational systems necessary for scaling up, work that he did enjoy. As the mission of the company shifted over time, however, it was less engaging to him. When he started, he had thought Inkling would usher in the future of digital textbooks. As the company matured, it moved beyond textbooks to become a software service for large corporations that needed Inkling's software to manage online training material, such as for sales teams, which was not so inspiring a mission.

In 2015, Hayes felt it was time to leave Inkling for another reason: he was in a romantic relationship with another employee who had been in a separate department, but after a reorganization, the two found themselves in the same one. Both he and his girlfriend decided to leave at the same time. Their work had required that they travel extensively, and with their accumulated United Airlines miles they were able to purchase two round-the-world tickets and embark on a four-month trip: New Zealand, Australia, Southeast Asia, South Africa, Europe, South America.[5]

Upon their return, Hayes had two networks of friends to help him find a new job: Stanford friends, and others whom he had gotten to know in the course of working at Inkling. He had coffee or lunch with them, and the friends, in turn, put him in touch with others and with a recruiter. He faced a choice: Did he want to return to a company that sold to consumers, as he had in the first two years at Inkling, or did he want to work for a business that sold to other businesses, B2B, which was where he had ended up when Inkling made that shift? Preferring a company whose product would be visible to everyone, he met with a Stanford friend who worked at Lyft, and then with another Stanford graduate, a mutual friend of the two, who had been one of the first employees hired at the company.

Lyft viewed Hayes's work experience in operations at Inkling as highly relevant. Would he have been invited in for interviews on the strength of that experience alone, without having Stanford friends at the company? There is no way to run an experiment to determine with certainty. But even with the Stanford connection and the work experience, he still had to do well in the interview process in order to receive an offer. He was asked to prepare a kind of case study, addressing the question of how he would go about launching a new market for Lyft in Las Vegas, which the company had just begun serving. He was invited to do consultative interviews, before his presentation, with relevant teams within the company—compliance; government relations; operations; marketing; partnerships—and then give an hour-long presentation to all with whom he had spoken. This exercise entailed quickly acquiring essential information about unfamiliar topics, distilling, rearranging, and adding his own original insights, then presenting the result. It was not dissimilar from the process of preparing a history paper; it did not throw Hayes, the history major.

Hayes got the job, joining Lyft's operations strategy team, which works on expanding the company's scope of business, converting expansion experiments into actual operations. His first assignment was to work on Lyft's partnership with Hertz, which worked with Lyft drivers who did not own a car or whose car Lyft deemed unsuitable. This was followed by assignment to the Lyft team working with General Motors, a new partner, as the two companies prepared to open the partnership's first rental location in Chicago. Hayes worked in the group that was filling in operational details, such as how to get the new vehicles to the rental hub and how to structure the rental agreement to provide the most incentive to drivers to use the vehicle for Lyft and not for its competitors.

Lyft was growing. By March 2016, the company had about eight hundred employees, and Hayes spent about one hour of each work day interviewing prospective new hires. For the most part, the hires have come from predominately elite schools. They come with a wide array of majors, not because Lyft seeks broad representation of majors but because the major simply does not matter: these are candidates who have work experience that is relevant to the roles Lyft seeks to fill, and just as it was Hayes's work experience that mattered when he was hired at Lyft, so too work experience is the primary consideration for the new hires. Hayes uses phrasing that is heard so often among hiring managers today: "We're looking for people who can really hit the ground running." The most junior candidates that he interviews at Lyft have at least two or three years of work experience since graduation. He reflects,

> It makes me have a very real appreciation for the companies like Inkling that took a bet on me early on and were patient, giving me the time to get the hang of things and develop professionally because that's kind of a luxury that we're not really extending right now at Lyft.

Sixty years ago, when large corporations hired new graduates in large annual batches, the green new employees were trained and then had the opportunity to move up while staying with the original employer. Today, movement from one employer to another is expected by all parties—and many of the most visible startups in Silicon Valley, like Lyft, stand aside and let other companies do the training, waiting for young employees to gain experience elsewhere before hiring them. Stephen Hayes was not ready to "hit the ground running" when he left Teach for America and sought a position in the private sector. Fortunately for him, he would end up in a startup that appreciated his ability to learn new things quickly. But he has not been able to pay the favor forward when hiring at his current employer.

CHAPTER 6

ENGINEERING SUCCESS

HERBERT HOOVER was a member of Stanford's Pioneer Class of 1895. Determined to be a mining engineer, he chose the major that got him as close as he could get: geology. Nonetheless, I think of his education and interests as resembling those of humanities majors of our own time in important respects. The subject matter of Hoover's coursework at Stanford was not particularly useful to his early professional work. But his classes helped sharpen his ability to learn new things quickly, and a mining engineer he indeed became. Then mine manager and globe-trotting mining consultant and ultimately a successful investor in the mining sector. When Hoover was elected in 1928 as the president of the United States, he attained a lofty perch—arguably the loftiest of all—in a domain with no direct link to his undergraduate major.[1]

Hoover's ability to learn new things quickly was more evident at the beginning of his professional life than in the latter. Or at least we can say that he did not learn quickly enough when, as president, he faced economic cataclysm. When we look back at his administration, we cannot help but also see in the same frame the market crash of 1929, the high-tariffs protectionism, and the start of the Great Depression. Hoover was the president who signed off on high tariffs, who was infamously intransigent in his defense of a balanced federal budget, even as unemployment rose to unprecedented levels, and who attempted to keep wages from falling by browbeating employers. His economic policies cannot be attributed, however, to the economics he learned at Stanford: he did not take economics.[2]

Hoover's poor handling of the economic disaster that doomed his presidency obscures the engineer-administrator's strengths that had shone earlier: in his much-praised administration of flood relief following the Great Mississippi Flood of 1927 and, before that, in refugee relief in Europe during World War I. He did know how to get many sorts of things done, even if dealing with the Great Depression was not one of them.

Before the refugee relief, and before Hoover had become a wealthy investor in the mining industry, he had been an impecunious college student. We know quite a bit about his college experience because his worldly success, which followed rapidly, brought two biographies when he was still middle-aged and biographical materials were still fresh.[3] One of the two was by Will Irwin, a journalist who was a near-contemporary, having been a freshman at Stanford when Hoover was a senior. Both biographers collected anecdotes from Hoover's classmates and gathered documentary materials that captured details about Stanford University's earliest years, about engineering, the liberal arts, divisions of economic class within the student body, and the post-graduation job searches of graduates, details that would not have been preserved otherwise.

Herbert Hoover was orphaned at a young age—his father died of typhoid fever when he was six and his mother of pneumonia when he was eight[4]—and was raised by relatives. Moving from Iowa to Oregon at the age of eleven, he went for three years to a small all-grades school, the Friends Pacific Academy, that was headed by his uncle, a doctor and missionary who also raised Hoover's older brother, Theodore, as well as four other orphans and four children from his own marriage. But when the same uncle left the school to found a real estate development company in Salem, Hoover became a full-time factotum there, the "office boy." He learned to type, added the rudiments of accounting to the bookkeeping he had already learned, and took some math classes at the Capital Business College.[5]

At their uncle's urging to attend a Quaker college, Theodore Hoover returned to Iowa to attend William Penn College, and Herbert was encouraged to follow a similar path. In spring 1891, when he was sixteen, relatives arranged for a scholarship at another Quaker college, Earlham, in Indiana. Herbert wanted to become a mining engineer, however, and Earlham did not offer engineering courses.[6] Another possibility appeared just then: Herbert saw an advertisement for Stanford University, the soon-to-open school with free tuition whose founders emphasized a *practical* education, encompassing science and engineering.[7] The university was just then holding admissions examinations for its first class. Stanford mathematics professor Joseph Swain was to visit Portland, Oregon, to conduct examinations for applicants in the region, and Herbert Hoover arranged to get to Portland to take the exams.

Hoover did not pass. But the university's administration was not confident of the school's ability to attract sufficient numbers of applicants to produce a full-size inaugural class, so second (and third and fourth) chances were offered to some applicants who appeared to have unrealized academic potential, and Hoover was deemed one of them. Swain told him he had failed math and English but he was admitted to the university conditionally as a "special." If he moved to Palo Alto a few weeks before the start of school and hired tutors, Swain said, he should be adequately prepared to pass the two exams when he retook them just before the new school year began in September.[8]

Having just turned seventeen, Hoover headed to Stanford as its very first dormitory was being completed—Hoover and his roommate would be the first students assigned to a room. His preparations for retaking the entrance exams were only partially successful; he passed math but again failed English. The university permitted him to enroll in classes, with the proviso that he would still have to pass the English exam at some point before he graduated.[9] The professor of English was adamant that every graduate, without exception, be able to express thoughts well in written form. For Hoover, meeting this requirement would prove to be an almost insuperable difficulty.

Hoover had a small inheritance managed by a court-appointed guardian that he could use toward his living expenses at Stanford.[10] But it was not close to being sufficient to cover the expenses, so he worked part-time in various jobs during the school years, as well in the intervening summers (even so, the inheritance was entirely spent before graduation). His first job was as a temporary assistant clerk in the registrar's office, staffing a desk on registration day.

Some of the students who registered came from backgrounds of limited means, like Hoover, to whom the absence of tuition was a primary attraction of the school, and who came closest to realizing Leland Stanford's ideal students, the ones who would not have been able to go to college without free tuition. These students, also like Hoover, had considerable work experience before arriving. Most of these students were older than Hoover and were well into their twenties.

Other students, however, had no reason to worry about finances. These included those who had come from the East Coast and who, responding to a Stanford survey, said that the California climate was the principal reason they had chosen the school. "To kill two birds with one stone—California and college," said one. Another: "I wanted a liberal university education. I was disgusted with fossil teachers in a school run by politics. I wanted to see and know Western life. I wanted to be a stranger in a strange land. Stanford filled the bill. I came."[11]

Even before classes had begun, local observers had noticed the presence of the wealthy among the young new arrivals—conspicuous consumption being a hallmark. "A jolly party of students, sons of rich Eastern men, have arrived here in a Pullman car," reported a local newspaper. "They have come to take courses at the Leland Stanford Jr. University. While they are waiting for the university to open, which will be on the 1st prox., they will travel about the State in their car and have a very merry time."[12]

On registration day, students were to present themselves at a registration desk so that details of their birth, guardianship, and academic plans could be officially recorded.[13] When these well-dressed gentlemen, with their fathers in tow, looked down to see a very young clerk, Herbert Hoover, dressed in a cheap suit, they were perplexed. Where was the adult in charge? But Hoover would not be ignored. "I'm here to register you, and I'm going to do it," one biographer has him saying. "Name, please?"[14]

Leland Stanford did not want students like Hoover to feel that their status on campus was anything less than that of students who came from wealthy families. Stanford thought that a university blind to class should not accept donations from grateful parents, at least donations that were not earmarked for a special purpose. In 1892, the father of Edmund Doyle, a classmate of Hoover's, sent Stanford President David Starr Jordan a check for $150 as a donation in the place of tuition. When Jordan told Stanford about the contribution, Stanford said it could not be accepted as a proxy for tuition; it had to be directed to the library or a department from which the students would directly benefit. He wrote Jordan, "Our idea is, if you remember, that while the Institution is to be open to all without regard to their fortunes, nothing must occur that might humiliate students of small means."[15]

When Herbert Hoover turned to choosing classes for himself, the starting point for a student who wished to major in mining engineering, what the university would eventually name "Geology and Mining," was geology. But in the very first semester, fall 1891, not all of the newly appointed professors had arrived, and John C. Branner, the first and only professor of geology, was not yet in place. Hoover began his college career with classes in algebra, geometry, trigonometry, woodworking, and drawing, all of which were required of mechanical engineering students.

In the spring, Branner was installed and offered geology, which Hoover took in place of drawing. Branner also hired Hoover as a part-time assistant, whom he would later praise for his ability to figure out how to get things done on his own. In a reminiscence, Branner supplied a story that illustrated this talent. Before coming to Stanford, he would ask a new student assistant to get his office's loose copies of German periodicals and U.S. Geological Survey reports bound. The assistant invariably needed his hand held every step.

"Where?"

"Send them to a binder in the city," Branner would answer.

"How?"

"By express."

"How shall I pack them?"

Branner's exasperation mounted with each question. But when he told Hoover to get the periodicals bound, the volumes appeared on the office shelves without any ado and a bill for binding and shipping lay on Branner's desk.[16]

Hoover had picked up other jobs, in addition. Even before classes began, he wrote a friend that he had "considerable buisness [*sic*] worked up & 300000000000 schemes for making more."[17] For a year he was the campus agent for San Francisco newspapers and delivered the papers before breakfast. Later, he was the agent for a San Jose laundry service, picking up dirty laundry on Mondays and delivering parcels with clean clothes on Saturdays.[18] He tried out for the school baseball team, but his time as a player was short; he was better suited to overseeing the team's finances and schedule, so he became the team manager instead.

Jackson Reynolds, a law major who was in the class behind Hoover's and who also worked throughout the school year to provide funds for room and board, went on to become a bank president. He looked back with gratitude for having had to work while at Stanford:

> The greatest benefit to me was derived from the necessity for my concentrated employment of every spare moment in my college day. I had only about half the time of other students for attention to

my studies and I therefore had to accomplish about twice as much in the same space of time. That training has been of more benefit to me than any other single phase of my college life and it taught me that a great deal can be accomplished in the odd moments which most of us waste.[19]

In the summer following Herbert Hoover's freshman year, Branner arranged a paid job for him doing survey work in the field for the Arkansas Geological Survey. It was a position that today would be called a paid internship, giving him professional experience at the same time he received modest compensation. In the summer after his junior year, he carried out survey work for the U.S. Geological Survey in the California Sierra.[20] He returned to campus five weeks after the fall semester began because of the demands of the assignment.[21]

Today, Stanford students who do internships in the summer after their junior year, and who like the work, hope to receive at its end an offer of a permanent position that begins after graduation. Having the offer in hand removes the need to look during the senior year for post-graduate work and contend with the anxiety that accompanies the search. In Hoover's case, he returned to campus for his senior year feeling optimistic about a permanent position with the U.S. Geological Survey. He wrote to a friend in November,

Learnd much and am better morally, physically & financially than 6 months ago. . . . Pleased the cheif some and am in consequence sceduled to return to the U S Geol Survey June 1st 1895. The position to be perminent in all probability. Salary—if perminent—$1200.00 a year to start.[22]

Before Hoover would be able to accept a "perminent" job, he would have to graduate, and that would require that he take care of the English exam that he still had not passed, despite retaking the exam twice a year since he had arrived. It was a cloud hanging over his senior year in an otherwise sunny sky—he had been elected as treasurer of the student body,[23] a prestigious position—but he could take some consolation in observing that about one third of the members of the early classes at Stanford also had failed the English exam and had been admitted conditionally. Engineering students featured prominently among this group.[24]

It was a professor of English, Melville Anderson, who guided university policy in this matter, defending the requirement that every graduate should be able to write an essay that, in the words of Will Irwin, was "correctly spelled, grammatically and rhetorically accurate."[25] Had Leland Stanford lived until Hoover's senior year, however, it is unlikely that he would have supported the requirement. Stanford had once admonished David Starr Jordan for spending his valuable time writing, "if someone else can do it just as well."[26]

Hoover never did pass the English exam. As commencement neared, his paleontology professor offered to help him meet the requirement by working with Hoover to polish a paper that Hoover had earlier submitted for his class. The professor then took it to the English department to plead for a special dispensation, arguing that it served as evidence of basic competence in writing.[27] It was accepted.

Was the exemption evidence of less than full commitment to requiring all students to show competence in writing clear, error-free English? Of a university willing to give favorable treatment to engineers that was not extended to others? If it was the latter case, it should also be noted that engineers composed a small minority of the student body in the early years.[28]

After graduation, Hoover returned to field work for the U.S. Geological Survey. But funding for a permanent position did not materialize, so when his short-term position ended in October, he was out of work. Needing cash, he accepted an opening in an underground mine performing brute labor, pushing an ore cart. The job required getting up at 4:45 a.m. The pay was modest, but it brought the opportunity to gain an acquaintance with a working mine. He felt fortunate to have snagged the job amid many unemployed laborers and despite the fact that "everybody here [is] prejudiced against college men."[29]

It was work that was, at best, merely endured. After two months in the job, Hoover's spirits were low. "If my college education can't get me any thing better than pushing an ore-car for a living, I'd better quit mining," a biographer has him saying to an acquaintance who was an experienced mining engineer. The acquaintance urged him to seek a position with a consulting mining engineer named Louis Janin, whose office was in San Francisco and to whom Hoover had been introduced briefly by Waldemar Lindgren, the U.S. Geological Survey geologist who had supervised Hoover's field work in the Sierra. Hoover acted on the suggestion.[30]

When Hoover called on Janin, he said that he sought a "tryout in his office in any capacity." Janin asked him to join him for lunch at Janin's club (Hoover would later recall that Janin "spent enough on that lunch to keep me for a week") and explained that he had all the assistants he needed. The only job that he had was as a copyist. Hoover said he knew how to type and would like the job.[31]

Hoover calculated that any position, even as a copyist, would enable him to be "near the throne," in position to claim a job of more responsibility and higher pay.[32] Janin asked Hoover for letters of reference, which Hoover had to arrange. In the meantime, Hoover started work in the office's most lowly position. For $30 a month, which was even less than the $2.50 that he had made daily as a common laborer in the mine, Hoover handled correspondence and looked for other ways to make himself useful.[33]

Preparing the letters of recommendation for Hoover did not pose a difficulty for his former professors. When the first student cohorts passed through Stanford, the close relationship of the faculty and students was like that found at a small college, what Hoover would later describe as "a small community of intimate association."[34] Another graduate, a member of the Class of 1896, recalled the closeness in the same way, also speaking of the "intimate" contacts that students had with professors—and with the university president as well. This student would later say, "I knew Dr. Jordan well, and he did more to shape my life than any other man I have ever known."[35] Hoover also knew Jordan well, and, more important, Jordan knew Hoover well, and wrote a glowing reference letter for him, as did Branner.

When Janin received the letters, he raised Hoover's salary and asked him to prepare a technical report on a mine that was at the center of a civil suit for which Janin had been hired as a consultant. The mine was in the Sierra, where Hoover had done field work, and he was able to write the report, sketch maps, and prepare exhibits for the courtroom quickly. Janin was impressed, and his firm's client went on to win the case.[36] Hoover was then dispatched on assignments to Colorado, New Mexico, Nevada, and California. In March 1896, he supplied the Stanford newspaper with the update that he had been promoted to "membership" in the San Francisco firm he had been working in for several months. This was in recognition of "his recent services in experting some mining properties."[37]

While he was in New Mexico, the U.S. Geological Survey notified him that funding had finally come through for the permanent position that he had sought after graduation. Should he take it? If it were only a matter of selecting the position with the highest salary at this early point in his career, there was nothing to ponder. The U.S.G.S. position offered an annual salary of $1,200; he presently was earning $2,000 at Janin's firm. But Hoover was concerned with a less obvious question: Should he continue on the path of mining engineering or should he switch to one in geology? He wrote Branner seeking career advice. His geology professor and mentor urged him to stay with Janin, where he could be promoted rapidly. The fact that he had already been given responsibilities showed Branner that "you are quite up to the work and that your continued promotion [is] assured." Were he to join the U.S. Geological Survey, however, his position would be insecure, as continued funding was uncertain.

"You can never know when it will end," Branner wrote. "So I suggest that you stay where you are, and Dr. Jordan thinks as I do about it."[38]

The consultancy that Hoover worked for was in no way a large organization with the abundant promotion opportunities that Branner imagined. But Hoover did not stay at the consultancy for long. In early 1897, Bewick, Moreing and Company, a British mining company that had operations around the world, asked Louis Janin to recommend an expert mining engineer who would be sent to West Australia to introduce American mining technology to their gold mines in the region. Bewick, Moreing asked, with a wink, that the candidate have at least seventy-five years' professional experience— such would be needed "to handle their problems down there," Janin explained to Hoover.[39] The annual salary would be about $5,000, which seemed unfathomably large to Hoover, who was only twenty-two. Janin offered to recommend him for the job, if he wanted it. Hoover accepted it, and began growing a mustache and beard to try to appear older and more experienced than he was.

In the new post, the young American replaced incumbent staff managers, closed inefficient mines, replaced two-man drilling teams with single-man assignments over the miners' protests, and earned promotions and raises quickly.[40] In late 1898, he accepted an offer from Bewick, Moreing to take up a post in north China. More success followed, and he was made a partner. By 1901, only six years after he had graduated, David Starr Jordan was proudly pointing to Hoover's annual salary—$33,000—and speaking of him as "the highest salaried man of his years in the world."[41]

When Jackson Reynolds, the law major from the Class of 1896, looked back on his Stanford education, he made the case for a broad liberal education, "training the mind as one trains the body, and then the mind can do any kind of work it later finds to do."[42] Hoover, however, expressed a different opinion when he offered advice about a mining engineer's education. He was willing to grant a place for "the groundwork of education in the humanities," but that should be

completed before college began. He advocated that technical education, undiluted by humanities (and though he did not say, presumably
free of English-proficiency exams), should extend at least four years.[43]

The technical education would be most practical if it centered
on theory. Colleges should not attempt "so-called practical instruction," which in Hoover's mind was nothing more than "play-house."
Speaking as a manager who oversaw thirty mines that employed
"about 9,000 white men," he said that he and his staff did not have
"the time nor the inclination to knock out of the heads of these men
mis-impressions which they have gained by so-called practical training in the technical school."[44]

The practical training should come once the degree was earned,
after which new graduates should spend two years working in different roles within the industry, in a self-directed apprenticeship. Regrettably, Hoover said, he had found "in throwing our mines open to
young men fresh from technical institutions, that not one out of ten
have been content to go through this period of apprenticeship."[45]

At the time that Hoover graduated, he did not realize the degree to which American mining engineers would soon be in great
demand. But the field was promising enough to have attracted his
older brother, Theodore, who had left William Penn College without
graduating, worked for several years, and then enrolled at Stanford
in 1898 after Herbert had graduated, joining the Class of 1901 and
graduating with a degree in geology. After working for various mining companies around the world, he returned to Stanford to head
the newly formed Department of Mining and Metallurgy.[46]

In the nine years after Herbert Hoover graduated in 1895,
American mining engineers became the era's masters of the universe. By then, British mining companies, which controlled about
75 percent of the world's gold output, had turned over management
of the mines to American engineers, who were employed by the
hundreds.[47] A Stanford student who majored in a field of engineering would be received well.

Herbert Hoover's education and professional career began in one era, when engineering was not accorded special status, and extended into another, when it was. To get his footing, Hoover endured a mindless first job, pushing ore carts, that did not utilize his college education, and his second job, at Janin's firm, paid even less initially but was instrumental in launching his career because he saw how he could make himself useful. In these general terms, everything he endured and did would be familiar to a newly graduated liberal arts major of today who is given the chance to be a versatile contributor. The story of Hoover's early work experiences can inspire today's students, steeped in the liberal arts, who seek, just as he did, nothing more than a tryout.

CHAPTER 7

THE DIFFERENT PERSPECTIVE

JENNIFER OCKELMANN, a member of Stanford's Class of 2011, a history major and psychology minor, did not keep a careful account of how many job applications she completed. "It might have been depressing," she recalls thinking at the time about keeping a tally. But she would be asked by friends for a definite figure, and so she did some calculations and estimated that the total, at a minimum, was three hundred.

The first 299 were unsuccessful.

Ockelmann's problem, from a career counselor's perspective, was that she loved history. She got A's in every history class she took at Stanford. Her paper about the 1920s, subtitled "Flappers and the Struggle Between Modernity and Modesty,"[1] was selected for inclusion in the history department's journal, *Herodotus*. If she had made plans to go directly to graduate school, she could have proceeded smoothly, without prompting onlookers to raise their eyebrows with puzzlement and concern about her choice of major. But during her senior year at Stanford, she decided to do something else: she would look for a job.

What friends and family wanted to know was, *What are you going to do with your history degree?* Until she lined up that first job, she would not have an answer.

Among those concerned about her future was her father, who had majored in economics at Stanford, worked at Arthur

Andersen, then gone on to Harvard Business School. He did not press her to follow the same path as he, but he made clear that he would like her to choose a major that offered some job prospects that he could see.

The unrelenting what-are-you-going-to-do? question forced Ockelmann to make some vague gestures in the direction of teaching, maybe, or law school, eventually, gestures that her fellow history majors had quickly learned to offer. Her roommate, who happened to be an art history major, said wryly that this was the one major even less useful than history. The two of them watched enviously as their friends, the computer science majors, the economics majors, the biology majors, spoke of the clearly marked paths that led to their futures. In contrast, Ockelmann and her roommate had no idea what was ahead.

At the beginning of her senior year, Ockelmann went to the large fall career fair. Hundreds of companies sent recruiters to the event, but Ockelmann could not find any that even pretended to be interested in history majors or in the all-purpose abilities honed by study in the humanities: thinking critically, analyzing deeply, writing clearly. At the career fair, the only humanities field that she heard employers mention that was of possible interest to them was English, the most obvious match for staff editor and similar positions.

The campus's Career Development Center was no help to Ockelmann. She had gone to its offices when she was a sophomore, looking for an internship for the following summer. A staff member had told her that the internships handled by the center were only for juniors. This was followed by the question that Ockelmann did not need the university to pay a full-time staff member to pose to her: *Do you know anyone who might be able to get you a job?*

No, she did not have family connections to industries in which she was potentially interested. She did not return to the career center the next year, and she did not again look for an internship. She spent the summer after her junior year doing what she had enjoyed doing the previous summer: she worked as a counselor at Stanford's Education Program for Gifted Youth, work experience that, by its nature, did not lead to a permanent post-graduate position.

In the middle of her senior year, she began searching for a future job in earnest, visiting the online Stanford Job Board, where hiring managers expressly sought Stanford students and alumni. She also increasingly spent time at Indeed.com, the job-postings website that aggregates millions of posts from many sources. Looking back on the senior-year search, she laughs, "I applied to pretty much anything that seemed like it might take me." The one filter she applied was geographic: she was looking for a job in the Bay Area.

She also visited the websites of companies that she was interested in, looking for the email address of an actual person to whom she could send her résumé, rather than filling in a form, pressing send, and never knowing who would receive it. "Now that I'm on the other side," she says, "I know where those things go: no one sees those."

The listings she found at Indeed.com turned out to be more helpful than the companies' websites. She got some telephone interviews, the initial screening. She was invited to in-person interviews in two cases, but it was her psychology minor that her interlocutors wanted her to talk about. No one asked her about her history courses or appeared to notice her GPA, which was on the transcript. The lack of interest in her grades and her major suggested that prospective employers regarded admission to Stanford as a proxy for general intelligence and drive—qualities that presumably were present on the first day that the students had arrived on the Stanford campus. What humanities majors like Ockelmann had subsequently learned in their major field from the distinguished Stanford faculty was greeted with a shrug.

When Ockelmann was engaged in first- or second-round interviews, what drew attention was an absence on her transcript: computer science courses. In her freshman year, she had taken the introductory computer science course, Programming Methodology

CS 106A, and it had been tough going. It was a large class, 250 students, about half of whom would end up being computer science majors. A separate, highly accelerated version of the course siphoned off the most serious computer science students, but even so, Ockelmann, who had never taken a programming class before, struggled with the course material.

The course had fulfilled for Ockelmann the one-course distribution requirement in engineering, and she had not taken additional programming courses after that. As she spoke in her senior year with startups about job possibilities, she now regretted that she had not taken additional computer science courses. These prospective employers looked over her transcript and remarked, "Oh, we'd love it if you had some programming experience, too." They would not have put her to work as a full-time coder, but if she had completed coursework that went beyond the intro computer science class, she would have fulfilled their ideal of the graduate who, as she puts it, "could do anything."

Spring sped by, and Ockelmann found herself in the position she had worked so hard to avoid: greeting graduation without a job in hand. After commencement ceremonies, friends who had jobs lined up prepared to move their things into newly leased apartments. Others headed to medical school or master's programs. Ockelmann, however, had to pack up her stuff, get in her parent's car, and move back into her childhood bedroom at her parents' house in Redondo Beach, in southern California.

"It was very scary," she says. "And it was really embarrassing, too. Almost a stronger emotion than fear." The only consolation was that she was not the only one among her classmates who moved back home. Her roommate, the art history major, had done the same (her job search came to an end when she was accepted into a PhD program in art history). Others in her graduating class shared the same plight.

At home, she redoubled her searching at Indeed.com. She searched for keyword phrases: "marketing associate," "account manager," "editor," or "PR assistant." Each application she submitted required preparation of a new, customized cover letter.

In the first months after graduation, she and her classmates stayed in close touch, tracking who had landed where. Only one's closest friends, however, heard dispatches of disappointing news, of spirits drooping as the job search continued. Ockelmann did not post on Facebook what was actually going on, which was a growing feeling of despair. She feared that with every week that passed, her résumé would preserve this blighted stretch of unemployment as part of a permanent record.

In August, Ockelmann allowed herself to become hopeful again. Rocket Lawyer, a forty-five-person startup in San Francisco, seemed impressed with what they'd learned from a phone interview with her and invited her for an in-person interview for an associate marketing position. This had been preceded by several phone conversations with the woman who would be her boss, should she be offered the position. The invitation was not accompanied by an offer to pay for her airfare and travel expenses, but she knew that startups did not cover those expenses for entry-level job candidates, at least for the non-engineering positions she was looking at. She leapt at the invitation, and all went well in her interview. "You'll be a great fit here," she was told. Only one thing remained: the CEO insisted on meeting every new hire, and he could not interview her that trip. "Would you be able to come back?" she was asked. Of course!

Paying for her expenses, back she would come for The Interview. It lasted six minutes. The chief executive asked about her previous experience that related to the position. That experience did not exist, a fact that Ockelmann had not hidden in her résumé. Had he not looked at it? She attempted to convey her willingness to learn on the job, but received no signals that could be interpreted as encouraging.

When she walked out of the room, her principal contact, the one with whom she had felt an easy rapport, did not seem aware that the

CEO had not been impressed by her résumé. "We're so excited," she told Ockelmann. "I'll let you know as soon as I can."

The email came the next day: the company had decided it would not fill that role "at the present time."

This was crushing. How could she ever get started if experience were required even for entry-level positions? In late August, she sent off a message to her closest friend:

> i am so. sick. of looking for jobs. there's nothing out there. i think i've been doing really, really well at not getting despondent, but this recent round of failures is getting to me personally . . . if only there were even jobs to apply for, but there really aren't.

The next month, she was invited to interview at another company and she became hopeful again, but this came to nothing. She wrote to her friend:

> i have just reached a new low: applying for an administrative assistant position. its at a marketing firm, so the hope would obviously be to move up quickly, but still. i just spent two hours searching for jobs and only four to apply to. im THISCLOSE to becoming a "discouraged worker." im also going to sign up for a temp agency down here i think, just to have something to do/possibly save up money to move.

She gathered herself and returned to the listings at Indeed.com. She got a positive response when she applied for a position at another San Francisco–based startup, Huddler, which handles online discussion forums for websites with niche audiences, such as the one for Head-Fi.org, for aficionados of expensive headphones. The position was "account coordinator," a title of ambiguous responsibilities, but she had noticed it had come up in other searches and was invariably housed within the marketing group.

Huddler did a phone screening and then invited her in for an interview. Once again, she flew to San Francisco at her own expense and was interviewed by seven of the company's forty-odd employees. She got what seemed like a welcoming reception, but after returning home, weeks went by without word.

When Ockelmann received an invitation to return—once again, the presumptive last step would be an interview with the CEO— she could not help but remember her unhappy encounter with the CEO of the last company at which she had reached this stage. This interview would proceed differently, however, because Ockelmann and Huddler's CEO, Dan Gill, shared a significant experience: Stanford. Gill had graduated only seven years earlier, majoring in biological sciences. When Ockelmann walked into his office, the two quickly exchanged information about undergraduate identities, telling the other about their freshman dorm assignments and joking about the associated stereotypes.

No secret handshake was exchanged, no job offer was assured on the basis of the shared alumni tie. And the tie did not lead automatically to a wink and a pass. A hiring manager at another company had grilled her mercilessly about the one quarter at Stanford in which she had taken slightly less than a full load. The manager told her, "I went to Stanford; I know how it works." Nor, before that moment in the CEO's office at Huddler, had the Stanford connection spared Ockelmann the need to win the approval, one by one, of the employees she had met with earlier. Still, the convivial sharing of Stanford memories did mean that her professional inexperience was not disqualifying. She was offered the position and began work in December 2011, six months after graduating.

Ockelmann was employee #45 at Huddler. The company grew to about sixty-five employees, experienced layoffs and other departures, and then had more layoffs after it was acquired by Wikia, a much larger company that also hosted forums. Only about fifteen of the original Huddler employees remained, but Ockelmann was one of them. She says she was not nervous about losing her job because she was managing all two hundred of Huddler's accounts.

In Ockelmann's view, it is not what is learned in college but rather personality attributes that account for the best fit for entry-level positions at her company. Her work as an account manager does not demand a business degree, nor would a major in economics be helpful. It requires a personality that handles the needs of clients well: detail-oriented, well-organized, courteous and friendly. The ability to remain even-keeled and not lose one's temper is also helpful, she adds. A sales position requires a different kind of person: gregarious, brimming with energy and enthusiasm. "It doesn't really matter what you did before," she says, "if the company is willing to teach you what to do now—which is what they did for me."

Ockelmann is not a hiring manager, but she has interviewed many job candidates at Huddler. "I definitely think I bring a different perspective than some people, who didn't experience what I did," she says about her fierce advocacy for applicants who don't have experience and are currently unemployed. Instead of using an interview to walk through the applicant's previous work experience, or the lack of such, she tries "to get people's personalities and figure out if they seem competent and if they seem smart and capable and passionate." She tells the CEO that she was given the chance to prove her competence without experience and she wants to give others the same opportunity.

When asked if she regrets her choice of history as a major, she says that were she given the chance to go back to her freshman year and choose a different major, she would not. She allows that it would have been helpful to her if she had taken a few more computer science classes and economics classes, not for what she would have learned but for making a better impression on prospective hiring managers. "It's all about appearances in the job hunt when you have no skills," she says. "It's just about what they can see and what kind of conclusions they can draw, based on an incomplete evidence set."

The language that Ockelmann uses to describe herself and her fellow history majors as graduates "who have no skills" is the derisive phrasing used for the humanities by academic disciplines centered on technical or quantitative fields. It sets up a false dichotomy: technical domains of knowledge, like computer science, supposedly impart "skills"; humanities disciplines leave graduates without "skills." Ockelmann's own work record belies such talk. As an undergraduate, when beginning work on her paper on flappers in the 1920s that would be published, she did not have deep knowledge of Clara Bow, the movie star, or of early advertising campaigns for the newly invented disposable sanitary pad for women, or of any of the other topics taken up in her paper. No matter: she learned what she needed to know. So too as a newly baptized account coordinator, fresh out of college, she knew nothing about account coordination. No matter: she learned what she needed to know. Adeptness at learning is arguably the most valuable single skill one can possess.

CHAPTER 8

A GENERAL UNDERSTANDING

ON A FRIDAY MORNING in spring 1894, Stanford students, faculty, administrators, Jane Stanford, trustees, and sundry guests gathered in the gym for speeches and prayers to pay homage to Leland Stanford, who had died the previous year. The morning's principal speaker, Horace Davis, a businessman and member of the university's board of trustees from its inception, described Leland Stanford's genius as "a practical one" that found expression in actions, like founding the university, rather than in words.[1]

Much of the public still thought of colleges as places that were inherently unsuited for a practical education, a prejudice, in Davis's mind, that was received from an earlier time when colleges taught only Greek, Latin, and mathematics. The prejudice remained alive and well, however. Davis said that he had recently heard Andrew Carnegie argue that a college education would actually inflict an "injury to a boy meaning to enter the practical walks of life." Davis, a Harvard graduate himself, was familiar with the oft-told story of the Harvard graduate seen collecting fares on a streetcar. The way Davis went about constructing a defense of college, however, reveals his own lack of conviction that a college education outside of science or engineering would be useful in a career. He was all too quick to grant that college "is of no use in some varieties of what we call business." Investors in the stock market, for example, required an "instinct" for buying low and selling high, and the university could not instill such an instinct.

What the university could do well, according to Davis, was provide a specialized technical education. For an illustration of "the power of technical training," he invited his listeners to consider the backgrounds of the men who had risen during "the war"—the Civil War—to the positions of highest responsibility on both sides. Grant, Sherman, Lee, Sheridan, and Thomas—all were graduates of West Point, which showed that "technical training won in the end." Additional evidence of that statement's truth could be found, he said, by looking at the accomplishments of a school such as the Massachusetts Institute of Technology.

Davis was oblivious to how he chose as models of a practical form of higher education institutions that were not like Stanford University: an engineering-centered military academy and a polytechnic science-and-engineering university that made no claim to offering a liberal education. When Davis got around to praising Leland and Jane Stanford for including in the founding charter the "museums, galleries of art, and the studies and exercises directed to the cultivation and enlargement of the mind," he devoted his most flowery phrasing to extoll poetry, art, and religion, "the bloom and aroma of our existence." But he did not attempt to make the case that studying them would be of professional benefit; they were only for the end of the day, after work was complete. "Cultivate the useful for your daily bread," he said, "but cherish the beautiful for the solace of your leisure hours."[2]

The university allowed students to choose the beautiful as their principal area of study, not just the useful. Upon admission, every student had to declare his or her major field of study. They could choose any field represented by a faculty member—a limitation, to be sure, with only fifteen faculty members initially. They could change their major later, as Herbert Hoover had done when John C. Branner, the first geologist, arrived. But the requirement that a student declare a major at entry, however provisionally, was one means by which the university sought to force students to think about what they would eventually do with the education they received. In the words of Jane Stanford, requiring students to declare a "particular calling" served to protect the university "from the cost of instructing and from the baneful influence of a class, bound to infest the Institution as the country grows older, who wish to acquire a University degree or fashionable educational veneer for the mere ornamentation of idle and purposeless lives."[3]

The education that was most unambiguously practical provided entry into one of the three largest professions in the late nineteenth century: engineering, law, and medicine. Engineering was the first of the three to become institutionalized. Long after the United States Military Academy at West Point (1802) and Rensselaer School (1824) moved the professional education of engineers in the United States into classrooms and laboratories, law and medicine continued to rely upon an apprentice model, studying under a mentor. By the time these professions standardized and institutionalized training, the idea that college students should have a liberal education as undergraduates before tackling professional training was well accepted in the United States, and the professional education was placed at the graduate level, at least in most places. (Stanford would briefly be one exception.) Engineering is the sole well-paid professional track in U.S. higher education that stands apart for universally using undergraduate education for the training.

Taking even a minor step of lengthening the undergraduate training of engineers to five years instead of four in order to include more liberal education, a proposal that engineering educators have floated from time to time, has failed to be adopted because it requires all accredited engineering schools to act in concert. Were a single school to attempt to lengthen the course unilaterally, students would flee for programs that stick with a four-year course that is light on non-engineering requirements. Guido H. Marx, an engineering professor at Stanford, observed in 1907 that "the callow, flippant 'kiddishness,' often seen in youths who come to college solely at the desire of their parents or because it is 'the thing,' has been noticeably

absent among our engineers." But Marx saw that this same seriousness did "make the men impatient with those things of which they
cannot see the immediate practical bearing, resulting in a tendency
toward unwillingness to broaden their courses of study."[4]

The second profession whose training Stanford University offered at the undergraduate level when the university opened was law,
and this was most certainly not standard practice in U.S. higher education. Stanford offered law as just another major for undergraduates and required for the AB degree no more than the four years
required for that of the others.[5] The Stanford experiment allowed
the university's alumni magazine to boast that its law graduates left
not only with knowledge of the law and "the gift of gab" but also
with a broad liberal education from courses in history, English, and
other courses outside of law, "a full supplementary education."[6]

How "full" that "supplementary education" could be, compacted
as it was into the four years that were also supplying a complete legal
education, was questionable. But from the perspective of students, it
was an arrangement that was most welcome. Law quickly became
the most popular major on campus.

When students graduated, they needed recommendations from
the law department for securing placement in law firms. "Only the
proven good men" received the department's official blessing. The
department viewed its withholding a blanket recommendation of
every graduate as helpful in building its reputation.

Competitive rankings among colleges and universities were
closely followed in the early twentieth century, many decades before *U.S. News & World Report*'s rankings ruled. In 1905, a Stanford
author took pride in a survey of unspecified "authorities" that regarded Stanford's law program as third best nationally and another
that, more conservatively, ranked it as the best among those located
west of the Mississippi and the eighth best nationally.[7] The recent
loss of two of Stanford's law professors, who had been lured by
much higher salaries to the University of Chicago, was not deeply

mourned: in the eyes of the Stanford booster, the raid spoke to the strength of his school's reputation.

The law department's placement of professional training at the undergraduate level attracted plentiful students, but the law faculty recognized that liberal education had to be squeezed to an unacceptable degree. In 1906, it stopped offering a Bachelor of Arts in law, which effectively moved professional training to the graduate level. A newly offered Juris Doctor was only for those who had already earned a bachelor's degree.

For Stanford undergraduates who planned to go into law, the university introduced an "A.B. in Pre-Legal Course." Before, when students could major in law, fully three fourths of the units required for the bachelor's degree were specified by the law department. But with the shift to a pre-law major, the required coursework was much reduced. In the freshman and sophomore years, students were to take only non-law courses; in their junior year, they took a single course in law, Contracts. And only in their senior year was their schedule packed with courses in the subject.[8]

The law faculty also saw that undergraduate campus life undermined the seriousness expected of students pursuing professional studies. Charles Henry Huberich, the head of the law department, wanted his department, which by 1908 would have the most students of any department on campus, to move from the Quad, where it shared offices with other departments, to a building of its own, to be built some distance apart, "somewhat removed from the distractions of undergraduate life."[9]

Whether Stanford graduates majored in law, when the major was offered, or in another field, those who went on to law school constituted a large and highly visible bloc of alumni. A Stanford alumnus who lived in Portland complained in 1909 that "we are getting too many Stanford lawyers." He lamented that few alums were "engaged in mercantile lines," which was a shame, he thought, as "business here is the best ever."[10]

Stanford did not have a department of business to match the department of law. Its absence was typical for private universities at the time—the only business school was the Wharton School at the University of Pennsylvania—but its absence at Stanford may nonetheless seem surprising at a university dedicated to providing a "practical education." In Stanford's early years, the only business coursework was shorthand courses taught by George Clark, who worked in the university president's office. Clark, who had graduated from the University of Minnesota in 1891, had come to Stanford to work on a master's degree in Latin. Once the university administration learned that Clark happened to be an expert in shorthand, he was offered a full-time position as stenographer. Five years later, he was appointed secretary to President Jordan, and later was named as university secretary and academic secretary.[11]

In 1892, Leland Stanford expressed his wish that his university offer instruction in shorthand, typewriting, bookkeeping, and telegraphy. Acting on this, George Clark offered a beginning course in shorthand in spring 1893 and hoped to offer an advanced course that would follow.[12] But he had difficulty attracting students to the course and never got to the point of teaching an advanced course. After two years of struggle to sign up students for beginning shorthand,[13] he abandoned the effort for a while.

The Stanford faculty did not stand up to support him (and Leland Stanford). From the faculty's perspective, "shorthand was unacademic and out of place as part of the requirement for a university degree," said Clark.[14] Shorthand, typewriting, and bookkeeping were subjects offered by the for-profit business colleges, whose use of the noun *college* made them seem closer relatives to nonprofit colleges and universities than the latter felt warranted. But such colleges offered many courses that actually did overlap with those of Stanford's engineering school. For example, Heald Business College ran advertisements directed at Stanford students in 1900 that explained it had been established in San Francisco almost forty years previously and was composed of the following departments: Book-keeping and Business Practice; Shorthand and Typewriting; Pen-manship; Modern Languages; English Branches; Telegraphy; Civil, Mining and Electrical Engineering; Surveying; and Assaying. Its of-ferings were "practical in every detail," phrasing that Leland Stan-ford would have been pleased to apply to the education offered by his own university.[15]

Stanford University did not move quickly to add business to its offerings, but its faculty did notice the gradual spread of busi-ness schools among private colleges and universities elsewhere. The University of Chicago in 1898 became the second private research university to add a school of business. In 1900, Dartmouth College added the first graduate school of business, adopting a "3+2" pro-gram: three years of undergraduate study in the liberal arts, followed by two years of graduate study in business.[16]

Seeing the subject of business become legitimized, George Clark patiently waited for a propitious moment to reintroduce the busi-ness subjects that he had tried to offer at the time of Stanford Uni-versity's founding. After a hiatus of almost twenty years, he secured in 1912 the support of the Department of Education to return to the classroom and offer a new course in stenography. Clark, still the academic secretary, did not have a formal faculty appointment—his added title was "instructor in commercial subjects."[17] But he be-lieved fervently in the importance of equipping college students with shorthand skills. He had at his fingertips anecdotes that supported his mission. The head of the Civil Service Commission in Washing-ton had asked President Jordan to send twenty-five or more Stanford graduates who were competent stenographers, eschewing the gradu-ates of business colleges who "were lacking in general education and so incapable of rising to positions of responsibility and executive du-ties as occasion required," or so at least the story went in Clark's tell-ing. And President Jordan, while on a train in Arizona, had chanced into a conversation with an executive of an English mining firm who hoped to hire a Stanford graduate who had majored in mining but who was also trained as a stenographer and bookkeeper, so the college graduate could write his letters, keep his accounts, and be entrusted with the details of the executive's professional work. The executive did not have a budget to hire two assistants: he needed one assistant who could handle all of the tasks. When Jordan returned to campus and made inquiries about who might be likely candidates among alumni, he failed to find a single person who had the necessary qualifications. "There were graduates in Mining," Clark said, "but they were not stenographers; there were stenographers, but they were not assayers."[18]

The story that topped all the rest came from Clark's visit in 1908 to Wharton, where he asked the dean why the school did not include shorthand and bookkeeping in its curriculum. The answer he received was that the subjects were not sufficiently academic for university students. But Clark then paid a visit to Peirce School,[19] where he found a dozen Wharton graduates "taking there at an additional outlay of time and money, which they could ill afford, these same nonacademic and elementary subjects, because they realized the need of a practical key to unlock the door of business opportunity." Clark argued that universities should have no compunction about offering the courses its graduates would need to find jobs, however practical in nature the courses were.[20]

Clark took heart in the "marked change" he could see in the way that commercial subjects were viewed by academics. More public high schools taught shorthand and bookkeeping, and though these had not yet been included in any curriculum in a university's school of business, he was pleased to see that more colleges and universities "have found it necessary, or at least fashionable, to establish schools or departments of commerce." He believed that with the passage of time, shorthand and bookkeeping would become "as essential a part of the commerce course as the shop practice—forge, machine, pattern-making, etc.—is now of the training of engineers."[21]

Forty-five students were enrolled in Clark's new course in the education department, many of whom were expected to find positions after graduation in high schools, teaching shorthand and stenography, but some of whom were, Clark hoped, headed for a career in business. Addressing Stanford students who had chosen economics as their major, Clark argued that adding training in stenography would be a mark of distinction, training that is "something distinctly in advance of what any other university offers."[22]

The shorthand course, reborn with Clark's great hopefulness, apparently did not last long. Clark himself died six years later, at the age of fifty-three,[23] and no one replaced him as an energetic advocate for shorthand. But shorthand and typing classes did not go away entirely. They popped up in the 1920s in the economics department, but then were shut down in 1926 when budget cuts pinched departments.[24] Ten years later, when students asked for courses in typing, shorthand, and cooking, the faculty committee that fielded the suggestions was surprised to learn that a professor in the psychology department was offering a course in shorthand.[25] The courses disappeared again, and then, one month after the attack on Pearl Harbor, typewriting and shorthand were reintroduced to campus, offered as part of "the national defense education program."[26]

The lack of shorthand training in Stanford graduates that had so troubled Clark in the early twentieth century did not seem to bother the business people who were his contemporaries. In fall 1907, the *Stanford Alumnus* published an essay by Harris Weinstock titled "A Business Man's View of College Training." Weinstock was the co-owner of the Weinstock-Lubin Company, a department store in Sacramento, and a trustee of the University of California who had given the commencement address at Stanford earlier that year. His "business man's view" of college was highly favorable and depended not at all on the presence or absence of shorthand courses, or even of a business school. Weinstock was impressed with "the American college-bred man of to-day," especially the one who had been trained in the sciences, where he had been taught "how to think and how to do things." His appreciation of the humanities in particular was not visible—in passing, he told the story he had heard that "a large portion of Paris cabmen are unsuccessful students in theology" and were bad cabmen at that. But he did credit college with instilling the kind of all-purpose agility in learning new things that the humanities confers, and which gave a college graduate who entered the workforce the ability to "learn in five years what it may take the man with an untrained mind about twenty years to acquire."[27]

Stanford University would ultimately disagree with Harris Weinstock's contention that an unspecialized training in learning how to learn was all that "the college man seeking commercial employment" needed to acquire while a student. But the university never fully embraced the training in stenography and typewriting advocated by George Clark. Instead, it followed the lead of Dartmouth, Northwestern, and Harvard and established in 1925 a graduate school of business. By declining to offer a business degree for undergraduates as the Wharton School at the University of Pennsylvania did, Stanford confirmed the model that undergraduates—engineering majors excepted—should receive a liberal education, postponing professional training until later.

Stanford students who majored in economics had long pressed the Stanford administration to establish a school of business. In 1917, Clem J. Randau, a freshman who was majoring in economics, wrote an opinion piece that argued that economics majors, who were "Stanford's embryonic business men" and composed the second largest department, were as entitled to have the chance to do "practical graduate work" as was "the coming civil engineer." Stanford did not force its graduates to go to the East Coast to get a law degree. Why, Randau wanted to know, did it do so when it came to a business degree? In his view, the university's failure to provide the opportunity to obtain a business degree was nothing less than discrimination.[28]

When Stanford finally established the Graduate School of Business, it announced that its two-year curriculum would include a half year of observation or employment "in some actual business concern." But as the school prepared to accept the first batch of students, the faculty did not view economics majors, those "embryonic business men," as the school's most desirable applicants. The school sought instead students who as undergraduates had taken courses in lab sciences, history, literature, social sciences, and mathematics, essentially anything and everything that avoided "too much preliminary specialization." Statistics and elementary accounting were two exceptions, but even these were recommended only "if that can be done without sacrificing general educational aims."[29]

Ten years after the Graduate School of Business opened, it was filled with the very students that it had hoped not to attract. Economics majors composed two-fifths of its student body, engineers another fifth. Only the remaining two-fifths were from a broad range of fields, including those in the humanities, where they were more likely to have addressed what J. Hugh Jackson, the founding dean of the school, defined as an "imperative": that applicants to the school possess "a thorough groundwork in English composition."[30]

In a 1935 talk presented to Stanford students, Jackson made clear that he was not pleased with the way that economics majors predominated. He said he wished to see more students who majored in what he called "the social sciences," which was his way of referring to history, philosophy, political science, and psychology. In the question-and-answer period that followed, he was asked, "Why is not economics as good a major as social sciences in preparation for this School?" Jackson, whose own academic specialty was accounting, responded with several reasons: that business in the future would have to work more closely with government; that psychology and engineering were no less important to business than was economics; that the broader the undergraduate curriculum, the more the student would gain a "general understanding of business."[31]

Even if all the Graduate School of Business's students had majored in history, philosophy, or English, the school still would not have had a significant impact in shaping the composition of the ranks of business executives, because the program remained tiny even ten years after its founding. In the 1934–35 academic year, the school conferred MBAs upon only 36 students (three of whom were women). After the end of World War II, a spike in enrollment peaked in 1948, when 287 students earned MBAs. But enrollment was soon capped at a lower level, with only 179 getting the degree both in 1955 and in 1960. (The number of women remained infinitesimal: 1 percent of the 1960 class were women.) Even when the school expanded to a larger size—394 MBAs in 2013–14—it still did not produce great numbers (though women had made gains, then composing 35 percent of the class).[32]

Along the way, the business school decided to give interested undergraduate students a glancing acquaintance with business subjects, in the form of a four-week summer program, open to students from any college or university who were not business majors. The inaugural session ran in 2004 as the Summer Institute for Undergraduates;[33] in 2006, it was rebranded as the Summer Institute for General Management, acknowledging it was open to recent graduates in addition to rising juniors and seniors. Its first batch had 56 students.[34] By 2016, it had 125 in a batch. The participants did not receive credit or even a suggestion that they would have an advantage over others were they to later apply to Stanford's MBA program. But they were promised "a strong foundation in business and management fundamentals" and "the tools you need to distinguish yourself and get hired."[35] All in four weeks.[36]

In its marketing, the school preyed on the anxieties of students. "Companies are hiring young professionals who can make an immediate impact in the workplace," the school's website warned.[37] An investment of four weeks and $11,125—the posted price in 2017 for its tuition, room, and meals—was offered as the way to acquire that ability.

Surprisingly, the school also marketed the program directly to the parents of prospects, as if the students needed to be taken firmly in hand and pulled in the direction of practicality. In 2006, readers of the business school's alumni magazine were invited to "imagine your son learning how to write a business plan. Imagine your daughter learning how to manage a distributed global team." The institute promised to "prepare your son or daughter for a career in business," if the child's major was not business and the child was either an undergraduate or—in a breathtaking expansion of paternalism—even a graduate student.[38]

Stanford's School of Humanities and Sciences made funds available to cover the Summer Institute for General Management's costs for any current student who was majoring in the humanities and needed financial aid to attend. An administrator said in 2013 that the funding was meant to encourage students "who feel like otherwise they might need to major in something that does have more of a business focus."[39] Even with that enticement, however, the institute's appeal to humanities majors remained limited. In the 2016 session, more students represented engineering majors (30 percent) than the humanities (28 percent).[40]

The school offered no data that showed that attendees actually did "make an immediate impact in the workplace" in a fashion that their peers who had not attended could not. But the mere fact that such a program in the business school existed asymmetrically—the School of Humanities and Sciences did not offer a four-week humanities institute for non-humanities majors, to help participants make a different kind of immediate impact in the workplace—speaks to the reputational ascent of business and a concomitant decline of the humanities.

CHAPTER 9

UNDERREPRESENTED

JESSICA MOORE'S parents met at Stanford, when her mother was an undergraduate, majoring in chemical engineering, and her father was a graduate student in computer science. After marriage, they began a family that become large: Moore and her twin were the oldest and three siblings would follow. The parents settled not far from Stanford, in East Palo Alto, and Moore went to elementary and middle school in nearby Menlo Park. Hers was a religious family whose life was organized around a church in East Palo Alto.

When she was thirteen, the family moved to a suburb of Denver when her father, who worked for Visa, was transferred there. The family kept in close touch with their church's pastor in East Palo Alto, returning every year for a church conference. When Moore was admitted to Stanford, she was overjoyed; it meant she could return to the place that still felt like home.

When Moore stepped onto Stanford's campus in fall 2008, she was a minority in two senses: she was African-American, a member of a group that constituted about 10 percent of Stanford's undergraduates,[1] and she was interested in history, which within her family placed her into a minority composed of just her. Not only were both of her parents engineers, so were two aunts, one of whom had a PhD in chemical engineering. Moore could not help but feel the press of family expectations that she too should head into engineering.

She also was a minority in a third sense: she was going to college when most of her same-age friends at church were not. Many of them had children of their own, were unmarried, and had, in Moore's words, "made very different choices and had different options." Moore recalled that when she had rejoined the church community when she moved back to start her freshman year at Stanford, a woman at her church had told her, "You're just so young to go to college!" Moore had tried to explain that eighteen was not young but the standard age, but she stopped herself, struck by how different her world was from the parishioner's.

In her freshman year, Moore did not immediately begin on an engineering track. She held her family at bay and took several history classes; she was drawn particularly to African-American history and to women's history. The twin interests were combined in a single enthralling seminar, on African-American women from 1865 to 1955, which was taught by Alyson Hobbs.

Moore's mother, who grew up in Washington, DC, was fearful that her daughter would major in history and lack the skills needed to become employable. She periodically told and retold the story of a time when she was in college and traveling between Washington and the Bay Area, when she hopped into a cab at the airport and exchanged small talk with the driver, an African-American man. When he learned that she was a Stanford student, he said that he had graduated from Stanford himself: he had been a history major. Moore's mother did not want her daughter to end up driving a cab for a living. The story had the desired effect: Moore was scared to pursue her love of history.

In her sophomore year, Moore decided that public policy, an interdisciplinary major offered at Stanford, would be a good major for her, serving as a middle ground between her interest in the humanities and her family's desire that she major in a technical subject. She signed up for a sociology class and then filled up the remainder of her schedule with math, computer science, and economics.

Moore looks back upon that quarter as a disaster. The preceding freshman year, filled with the intensive reading and writing assigned in her history classes, was poor preparation for this slew of classes that were quantitative in nature. She had to drop her math class, and she finished the computer science class only by opting to take it as pass/fail. The experience brought an end to the plan to major in public policy.

Having recently struggled in her accelerated calculus class, Moore felt relief in returning to history, a field in which her strengths shone. She was named a Mellon Mays Fellow, a fellowship funded by the Mellon Foundation for minority students who are considering a PhD in certain fields, mostly in the humanities. One fellow used the $5,000 research grant that came with the fellowship to pay for archeological field work in Australia. Moore's research did not require travel, however; the newspapers she would use for her thesis were available online, so she used the grant to purchase a new computer, printer, and software.

Moore's thesis was on press coverage of sexual violence in the United States between 1920 and 1945, and it compared differing coverage of rape in newspapers aimed at white readers and at black readers. Her thesis advisor, Estelle Freedman, cited Moore's thesis in her own book,[2] and a short version of the thesis was chosen for publication in *Herodotus*.[3]

Moore did not give serious consideration to doctoral programs in history,[4] however, because she had also applied to, and been accepted into, a business-oriented mentoring program for black, Latino, and Native students that was provided by a nonprofit, Management Leadership for Tomorrow (MLT).[5] Beginning in her junior year, Moore worked with a career coach who supervised monthly assignments for the participants. One assignment asked them to prepare a brief "elevator" pitch about themselves; another was to reach out to an MLT alumnus and ask for feedback on the current state of the student's résumé. The preparation was aimed to enable the participants to land an internship in the summer following their junior year that, in turn, would lead at the end to a job offer for after graduation.

The MLT program provided its student participants with deep access to the program's corporate sponsors, who were eager to increase the number of underrepresented minorities in their executive ranks. To companies such as Google, Deloitte, and Citi, MLT provided not merely minority students from elite institutions but students that had passed another layer of screening before being selected by MLT. The program's application requirements were considerable—a transcript; SAT or ACT scores; lists of extracurricular activities with "description of impact" for each; honors and awards; essays on "career goals" and "leadership potential"; and at least one letter of recommendation. This saved the corporate sponsors from doing the culling themselves. Moore estimates that in her year there were about 120 students in her year's MLT cohort nationwide, and one in ten were from Stanford.

At the same time Moore was receiving résumé-polishing advice from her MLT mentor, in her junior year, she was dispensing résumé-polishing advice as a student employee of Stanford's Career Development Center. But she did not have a clearly formed picture of what kind of work she wanted to do herself. She knew only what fields she did not want to enter: consulting and finance. She applied for a summer internship at Google and looked around for other possibilities at the campus career fairs, including the one for liberal arts majors, but nothing caught her interest.

Moore's friends who were humanities majors shared their own dispiriting accounts of their job searches at the career fairs. "If you're not engineering-focused," Moore says, "it's not even worth going." To her, the different parts of the Stanford campus reflected the disparity in opportunities for engineering majors and for everyone else: in the tech quad, the generous donations of the large tech companies or their founders are highly visible. The difference in "feel," she says, is another example of the different worlds defined by "the techie/fuzzie divide."

Moore placed herself, unapologetically, among the fuzzies. But Google did not care what her major was. She had applied to the company's internship program, BOLD (Build Opportunities for Leadership & Development), which was expressly for underrepresented groups in the technology industry: black, Latino, Native, students with disabilities, and veterans. All majors were welcomed. Other than asking that the applicants have an interest in the Internet and Google's technology business, the only other preferred qualifications were "interpersonal and organizational skills, with the ability to navigate an ambiguous environment" and "analytical skills and an interest in tackling business problems."[6]

Moore was accepted, despite the blemishes on her transcript left in her sophomore year when she was, as she puts it, "trying to find my way." She felt especially fortunate to have been accepted, as she watched a good Stanford friend who was also a history major and who, like Moore, was a Mellon Mays fellow, fail to find a position after sending out dozens of applications. Perhaps the difference that accounted for Moore's getting the offer from Google was her being selected for the Management Leadership for Tomorrow program. That alone, however, may not have been sufficient. Moore also was the beneficiary of a recommendation made by a highly placed person within Google, a recommendation that came from Moore's personal network.

Moore was well-connected in the Valley not from help from the Career Development Center or from family connections or even from Stanford roommates or friends. Her connections came from her part-time work—as a babysitter. When she came to Stanford, she had first worked at the checkout desk of one of Stanford's libraries. It did not require her full attention every minute, but attending to patrons made uninterrupted study impossible for any extended period of time. In her sophomore year, she got her own car and could take up babysitting, work she had done in Colorado while in high school. The Stanford campus was surrounded by affluent households; the pay was much better than the jobs on campus; she enjoyed playing with the children; and after they were put to bed, she continued to be paid for time that she could use however she wanted, including studying.

Babysitting led to conversations with her employers, who became a network of unofficial career counselors with extensive work experience. Without her asking, they took it upon themselves to work with her on her still-vague career plans. One woman in particular, a senior executive at a large semiconductor company, pressed her, "What do you want to do?" a question for which Moore did not have a satisfying answer. Acting as a friend, not as Moore's employer, she urged Moore to pay more attention to the search for an internship after her junior year, a critically important thing. When Moore told her that she was applying to Google's BOLD internship program, her friend contacted a close friend of hers who worked at Google to put in a good word on Moore's behalf.

When Moore learned that she had landed the Google internship, she was able to soothe her mother, who was worried about Moore's professional future. Her father stood back and trusted Moore to make her own decisions, but her mother could not resist the temptation to take a more active role in Moore's planning than Moore wanted. When Moore got the internship, she imagined her mother thinking, "She might be OK after all, especially if this turns into a full-time job." Moore herself did not dare expect a job offer at the end of the internship. But she figured that it would help her find future work because the imprimatur of Google would always be on her résumé.

For her internship, Moore was placed on the Diversity Team in Google's People Operations. She created modules used in the company's internal training program that explained Google's programs for veterans, for women, for racial and ethnic minorities, and for people with disabilities. She and her team also invited outside support groups to campus, and she did event planning. At the end of the summer, Google offered her a full-time position in People Ops for after graduation.

Google knew that Moore had neither a business degree nor work experience in a corporate setting, other than her brief stint as an intern. The company nonetheless greeted Moore and her fellow liberal arts majors with a welcome that recognized the students' ability to learn new subjects quickly. Google paired that welcome with an extensive rotational training program for twenty of the new hires in People Ops that would take twenty-seven months to complete.

Moore was one of four Stanford graduates among the twenty in the training program. None of the others, whose majors were political science and drama, psychology, and communications, had business or technical majors either. In her building at Google Moore noticed many familiar faces from Stanford, people who were not official Google employees, Googlers, but were TVCs—temps, vendors, and contractors, identifiable by their identification badges. (This was Stephen Hayes's status when he worked at Google before moving to Inkling.) The contractors referred to the system derisively as a "churn and burn" model: they were given the chance to work as hard as they could for six months or a year, vying to be one of the lucky few who were "converted" into permanent Google employees. Most would be discarded, however, and fresh bodies would be brought in to start another year's cycle.

Moore noticed another cluster of Stanford students in Google's marketing group, some of whom were in a rotational training program similar to Moore's. The marketing program had forty participants in each cohort and started new cohorts twice a year. Another training program, the first at Google, was begun in 2002 by Marissa Mayer[7] to train newly minted college graduates for product management roles throughout Google. The Google training programs lacked the scale of the management training programs that industrial giants like General Electric ran in the heyday of training.[8] Competition for one of the limited slots in Google's programs was keen. But those who were admitted were given learning opportunities in the field that far exceeded what a business school's classrooms could offer, and the participants were paid a regular salary to boot.

The training that Moore received was put into place by Laszlo Bock, the head of People Ops, who left GE Capital to join the company in 2006.[9] Bock appreciated the contributions that liberal arts majors could make: he himself majored in international relations at Pomona College, graduating without, he would say later, "any sense of what I wanted to do." When he spoke to college students, he recommended the liberal arts: "There is no better preparation for living your life," he told students at a talk in 2014 at Ursinus College. "It gives you the insight and ability to make connections."[10]

Bock implemented a host of changes at Google that made the company receptive to applications from any major, at least for positions that were outside of software engineering and account for about one out of every two positions at Google. Bock collected data that showed college GPAs were not a good predictor of an applicant's future performance at Google, nor were SAT or ACT scores. Bock said this was partly because an academic environment is artificial in the way that professors are looking for a particular answer and students become good at figuring out what the professor wants to see. At Google, he sought people who would be able to solve problems "where there is no obvious answer."[11]

On another occasion, when Bock said that Google seeks people who "have the ability to process on the fly" and "the ability to pull together disparate bits of information,"[12] he was describing the abilities that history majors use when speaking of the practice of history. Bock ruefully described how, when he completed his MBA at Yale and failed to receive a single callback from the employers he first approached, he gained an appreciation of the need to be able to "tell your story well," which was one of "the most important skills you will have in your entire life."[13] Moore, the history major who had written an honors thesis, was well-practiced at crafting narratives.

Had Bock personally looked over Moore's application, with the transcript that Moore feared looked "spotty," he probably would not have been greatly concerned about her grades in her sophomore year. Bock espoused the importance of "intellectual humility," a prerequisite for learning. In a 2014 interview, he said that the careers of many graduates of elite business schools fail to rise beyond a certain point because those graduates "rarely experience failure, and so they don't learn how to learn from that failure."[14]

The training program for new hires in People Ops that Bock had set up consisted of three nine-month rotations: a generalist role, in which Moore was embedded in the team that supported David Drummond, the company's chief legal officer; a specialist role, in which she was assigned to the benefits team and learned much about health and wellness; and an analyst role, working on projects related to finding engineering talent from untapped sources—this was the role she occupied when I spoke with her.

As a junior analyst in training, Moore became comfortable with spreadsheets and learned the basics of SQL, the programming language used for searching the databases that Google maintained to track prospective candidates and the performance of current employees. She was surprised that she became comfortable working with large data sets. The newly acquired quantitative skills were joined with the writing skills that had been sharpened by taking writing-intensive history classes. "Ultimately, you need to make your data tell a story, one that drives business decisions," she said. She could see that many engineers lacked the knack for constructing a story. "The language piece isn't always there immediately," she said of her colleagues who were engineers. "They're a different breed, I kid you not," but, she added, "they run things!"

One difference separating the engineers from herself, Moore said, is that the engineers are persistent, heedless of how they come across to others, which isn't necessarily a bad thing. "I think my EQ [Emotional Quotient] is much higher and I don't want to offend somebody," she said, but the engineers don't care about anything but getting an answer. She recalled attending one particular TGIF meeting at Google where the engineers had pressed Google cofounder Larry Page so hard that she was uncomfortable even on the sidelines, merely witnessing the exchange. The TGIFs are held late in the afternoon on Fridays on the Mountain View campus, when refreshments are served and senior executives make a few announcements and field questions from employees. On this one occasion, Page had spoken of the importance to the company of a "Mobile First" strategy. An engineer—Moore, the daughter of two engineers, recognized an engineer when she saw one—asked Page, "What do you mean by 'Mobile First'?" Page offered a rambling answer. The engineer was not satisfied: "I don't understand what you mean by that." Page answered again and the engineer renewed his request for a clear explanation. Moore wanted to say to the questioner, "Oh, my God, please be quiet! He *is* the CEO!"

Sitting where she did, in the midst of the analytics group in People Ops, Moore got the chance to work on bias-related issues in human resources management. One project she worked on examined Google's hiring of African-American software engineers, dating back to the company's founding in 1998. She could see that Google's preference for graduates of the most selective colleges and universities presented an obstacle to hiring more engineers who were underrepresented minorities; the pool of prospective candidates from a short list of schools was small.

Google was reexamining that preference. People Ops launched an internal education program called "Unconscious Bias" that brought attention to the subconscious form of bias that influences decisions made in a fraction of a second. Moore offered an example from her own experience:

> You fly Southwest, you get to choose your own seat, and you're walking down the aisle, you're looking at people and making split-

second decisions as to whether or not you sit by them. For me, I'm, "Eh, I don't want to sit by a huge burly guy." So I'm kind of looking for a woman who I can sit by and feel more comfortable with for this flight. So I think both consciously and unconsciously, there are decisions being made based on where people go to school and where they've worked for before, like if they've worked at an Apple or a Yahoo—they're drinking the Kool-Aid, they probably know what to do.

An internal Google study done a few years previously concluded, in Moore's words, that "the top CS student at one of the second-tier schools is just as qualified as, and may be more qualified than, the fiftieth-ranked CS student at Stanford or Caltech or MIT." She said that more people at Google had come around to accept the notion that the company should be looking more actively for "the big fish in a small pond."

Google was enlarging the net for bringing in candidates, developing a more sophisticated way of reviewing the résumés of candidates than simply looking for the name of one of a handful of selective colleges or universities or the name of a large tech employer. When *Forbes* magazine ran an article about venture capital funding in the Midwest, members of the People Ops's analytics team wondered about the software engineers in those startups in the Midwest: "Is there talent there that we should be aware of?" The answer of course was yes.

At the time I spoke with Jessica Moore, the People Ops group and the Finance group were about to move from the main campus in Mountain View to a new satellite campus in Sunnyvale, about three miles away. The facility was beautiful, and included a swimming pool, which the main campus lacked. "If you get kicked off the island," she said, laughing, "they try to make it nice."

The best thing that Google provided Jessica Moore, however, was not a gleaming new office campus or anything else that was tangible or visible or quantified. Rather, it was giving this history major the on-the-job training that enabled her to contribute to a company founded by engineers, run by engineers, and filled with engineers. For all of Google's fondness for PhDs, the ultimate in terminal degrees, the company showed a laudable dedication to the idea that a liberal education is suitable for many positions, if the company is willing to supply education in the workplace.

CHAPTER 10

NORMAL

LEWIS TERMAN, a psychology professor who joined the Stanford faculty in 1910, played an outsized role in the development of intelligence tests and in the spread of testing to workplaces. He became Stanford's first nationally renowned scholar. He coined the phrase "intelligence quotient" and shaped the early years of industrial psychology, promoting a reductionist model of human potential centered on IQ that, while still enormously influential, thankfully has failed to remain the preeminent means of assessing an individual's potential.

When Terman bothered to take a look at the humanities, which was not often, he stared uncomprehendingly. In his view, the humanities were subjects that provided no practical use. Yet in a most roundabout way, Terman's research would greatly help future Stanford graduates who majored in the humanities find professional positions. Prospective employers would need assurance that a degree from a given institution could be interpreted as a proxy for a certain level of knowledge and mental dexterity, at least enough to warrant investment of time and attention in investigating a particular individual's fitness for a position. Terman was instrumental in putting into place at Stanford the academic tests for admission, which he designed, that raised the level of academic preparation of all students who entered the university. When the tests were required of all admitted students, all enjoyed the presumption of clearing a high bar, regardless of choice of major.

Nothing in Terman's early years augured a career in academia. He grew up on a farm in Johnson County, Indiana, the twelfth of fourteen children.[1] He attended a one-room schoolhouse, with about thirty children scattered across grades one through eight. The school year ran for six months, from October through March, to accommodate the labor needs of the surrounding farms. Its resident teacher was invariably a man whose own formal education had ended in the eighth grade.[2]

The school had no library and offered no supplementary readings. Terman occupied his school day committing to memory entire textbooks. "The school day was long," he drily remarked in an autobiographical sketch written when he was fifty-three, "and the time had to be put in somehow."[3]

When he turned eleven, he was put to work on the farm full-time each year, from April to September, working with a team of draft animals, plow, and wagon. Many work days lasted from 5 a.m. to 7 or 8 p.m. "Any mental development that may have occurred during this part of the year must have been due to maturation rather than to intellectual stimulation," he wrote in the sketch.[4]

No high school was within reach of his home, so once Terman completed eighth grade at the age of twelve, his options dwindled. He stayed at the school one more winter. The following winter, he embarked upon what he later would jokingly call "post-graduate work" at another one-room elementary school at which one of his brothers, who had attended college, taught.

The only path open to Terman that led off the farm to a college education led first to a teaching position at a rural school, which provided an income, modest though it was, that could help finance college. When Terman was fifteen, his parents sent him to Central Normal College in Danville, Indiana, a private school that, despite the "College" in its name, would best be thought of as a residential high school at a time when high schools were rare in less populated regions. Schools like Central Normal College "took raw country boys fresh from the grammar school and in a few ten-week terms made them into teachers," he wrote.[5]

Terman also took several correspondence courses, in German and in the history of education, and earned three degrees from Central Normal, which Terman said "lavished" degrees upon its students: a BS in what was called the "scientific course," a BPd in pedagogy, and then an AB in the "classical course." These gave him the qualifications to secure his first permanent position, as the principal and full-time teacher of a tiny township high school of about forty students in his home county. He taught every course in the four-year curriculum. He was twenty-one years old.[6]

While he was teaching, he married a teacher whom he had met at Danville, and in 1900 they had their first child, Frederick. Terman had succeeded in getting out from behind the plow. But he still had an unfulfilled ambition, to become a professor at a teachers college or regular college, specializing in either psychology or pedagogy. To attain that, he would need a bachelor's degree from what Terman called a "standard university," and, he dreamed, maybe he would be able to collect a master's degree.

Terman resigned from his teaching position, borrowed money, and moved his family to Bloomington to study psychology at Indiana University. When the registrar at Indiana University had finished evaluating the courses on his Central Normal College transcript, Terman was granted two years of credit and entered with junior standing. In the two years in Bloomington he was omnivorous, devouring as much education as he could—every psychology course offered; a year of neurology; generous helpings of philosophy and education; German; French; sociology; economics. At the end, he had both a new AB and an AM. Influenced by the teachings of his psychology professors, William Lowe Bryan,[7] John A. Bergstrom, and Ernest H. Lindley, Terman had acquired a new ambition, to become a psychology professor himself. The place to become properly trained would be at Clark University, in Worcester, Massachusetts, under Stanley

Hall, the pioneer psychologist who had been the first to earn a PhD in psychology in America and who had been the first president of the American Psychological Association. Terman's favorite teachers—Bryan, Bergstrom, and Lindley—all had obtained their PhDs under Hall at Clark.[8] Terman, who now had a daughter as well as a son and was already deeply in debt, did not have the financial means to pursue a doctorate, so he began looking for positions at teachers colleges and principalships.

The first offer he got was for a position back at Central Normal College. But the salary was too low for him to pay off his debt and save for further training, so he turned it down. Then the unexpected happened: a fellowship offer from Clark University. It would not cover all costs, and would require more borrowing from his family, but it made studying for a PhD a realistic option. With the support of his wife, he decided to accept.[9]

At Clark, Terman found unimagined freedom to study whatever he wanted; informal, close relationships between the few students—only fifty or so—and the faculty, whose members had the freedom to lecture whenever and on whatever topic they wished; and the heady pleasure of Stanley Hall's weekly seminar on Monday evenings. At the seminar, two students would present a report on their research and then Hall would lead group critiques. At the end of each discussion, Hall would provide an insightful summary of the discussion that was so exhilarating to witness that when Terman left for home, he was "dazed and intoxicated" and "lay awake for hours rehearsing the drama and formulating the clever things I should have said and did not."[10]

Hall had recruited for Clark's faculty younger men who approached psychology with an interest in precise measurement, using, for example, instruments to measure a subject's reaction times to stimuli. They sought to move psychology away from its roots in philosophy and shore up its identity as a branch of science. Terman, however, was not interested in using the "brass instruments" of the new psychology laboratories. He found himself drawn to an area that was on the margin of the discipline: "mental testing." Terman dreaded telling Hall; he felt such gratitude to Hall for making it possible for him to come to Clark that Terman felt "it cost me a heavy soul-struggle" to choose mental testing as the area for his thesis. When he met with Hall, Terman recalled, "he expressed very emphatically his disapproval of mental tests, but, finding that my mind was made up, he finally gave me his blessing and some advice on the danger of being misled by the quasi-exactness of quantitative methods."[11]

For his doctoral dissertation, Terman devised tests that he hoped would reveal the constituent components of what was then referred to as "general intelligence." He recruited fourteen students with whom he spent more than three months, thirty-six hours a week, testing and interviewing them. "My subjects were specially selected as among the brightest or most stupid that could be found in the public schools within easy distance of Clark University," he wrote.[12] At the end of his write-up, his closing observation was that his study "has strengthened my impression of the relatively greater importance of *endowment* over *training*, as a determinant of an individual's intellectual rank among his fellows."[13] He would title his thesis "Genius and Stupidity." (Terman and his fellow psychologists, enthusiastic eugenicists almost to a person, relied upon a taxonomy of intelligence whose categories included not just the "stupid," but also the "feeble-minded" and "morons.")

When he was awarded his PhD in 1905, he did not immediately join a college faculty. Suffering from tuberculosis and eager to move to a sunny climate, he accepted a position as a high school principal in San Bernardino, in southern California. After a year back on the front line of education, he was invited in 1906 to join the faculty of Los Angeles State Normal School (which would later become UCLA) as a professor of child study and pedagogy.[14]

In 1909 Terman wrote a piece for *Scribner's Magazine* about external pressures to make the high school curriculum better suited to the needs of the employers of students. Rather than decrying the encroachment of "commercialism," Terman said that commercialism was not a bad thing at all. He defended high school students who disliked "intellectual" courses, who could not see why they had to study academic subjects that seemed useless to their futures.

Writing in the education journal *The School Review*, Terman, who then was thirty-two, mocked adults who panicked when they heard that students were increasingly demanding from their teachers answers to questions like "What good will Latin do me?" and "How will Greek History help me earn a living?" To Terman, who believed that any subject that could not provide "fruit in action" should be dropped, it was the students with whom he sympathized, not the teachers who fumbled for answers and an adult society that wrung its hands worrying about "the so-called progressive degradation of ideals in the young."[15]

To Terman, Germany provided a cautionary lesson. There, thousands of graduates of the classical *Gymnasien*, which "for the most part ignore the problems of real life," were idle or underemployed, misfits who were drifting into the ranks of German socialists. In the United States, Terman wrote, "our more practical sense has brought it about that few of our secondary schools dish out the formal studies to all indiscriminately." Still, he urged high schools to do more to provide an education appropriate for "a busy practical life." He thought the future would bring schools that universally offered apprenticeships, modeled after "the best industrial schools now conducted for Indians and negroes."[16]

The next year, E. P. Cubberley, the head of Stanford's Department of Education, sought a psychologist for his department—in particular, a psychologist who had been trained by the great Stanley Hall. He recruited from Indiana John A. Bergstrom, Terman's former teacher, but soon after arriving to campus, Bergstrom died from a brain tumor.[17] Cubberley then offered the position to Edmund B. Huey, another Clark PhD and a friend of Terman. Huey was more interested in clinical psychology than teaching, and when he declined the offer from Stanford, he recommended Terman for the position.[18] Terman accepted the offer to come as an assistant professor of educational psychology.[19]

When describing the job offer in his autobiography, written many years later, Terman listed the serendipitous events that led to his landing at Stanford, "the university that I would have chosen before any other in all the world."[20] Stanford was included in the itinerary of Edwin E. Slosson, a science journalist who undertook a comparative report in 1909 and 1910 of the country's top fourteen universities, living on each campus for week-long visits, visiting classes, and speaking with as many students and faculty members as he could. Slosson, who held a PhD in chemistry from the University of Chicago, wrote up detailed impressions of each and comparative observations that were first published in *The Independent* and then gathered in a book, *Great American Universities*. In choosing the fourteen, Slosson used a list assembled by the Carnegie Foundation for the Advancement of Teaching that ranked schools by their annual expenditures on instructional staff. Columbia was first and Stanford was eleventh on the list.[21]

When judging the quality of Stanford's student body, Slosson said the university sought the best students but was not as strict about imposing particular requirements on applicants as the other universities. He contrasted this approach with Princeton's, which he said effectively excluded applicants who had not studied Latin, or who lacked $150 in cash above what would be needed for living expenses, or who failed to answer correctly a certain proportion of questions in subject-matter tests, or who, as Slosson decorously phrased it, "do not belong to a particular race or sex." Stanford's admissions criteria were much looser, seeking only to exclude those of "mediocre ability" or those who were not "serious-minded"—or those who drank "intoxicating liquor." Slosson described the Stanford administration's attitude this way: "The university has no use for the boy who comes to enjoy a congenial club life, nor for the girl who strolls up to the campus at 12 dressed in her prettiest to take drawing."[22]

Stanford's registrar did not actually know enough about student applicants to determine whether they possessed the seriousness that was desired, so the university went ahead and admitted many and then unceremoniously suspended them if their grades were poor. It was a system that Stanford students called "the flunking-out system," and Slosson compared it to the weeding done at West Point. In the 1907–08 academic year, 28 percent of Stanford's fraternity members were suspended for failing grades (while only 3.2 percent of sorority members were).[23]

For the most part, Slosson was not impressed with Stanford students. He had heard stories that the success of Stanford in intercollegiate athletics had brought misfortune to the campus by attracting "a class of young men more interested in athletics and other amusements than in work, not at all the Stanford type of students." Clashes with the administration, enforcers of temperance, had followed; students threatened to strike; and the university had to quell the uprising with mass suspensions.[24]

Slosson had heard plenty of grumbling among faculty members about the decline in the numbers of students who were at Stanford principally for educational purposes. He also had heard complaints about President David Starr Jordan, in particular Jordan's prohibiting faculty members from supplementing their income with outside paid work. Jordan's policy was instituted in order to ensure that teaching was not neglected. But Slosson sided with the faculty. "It is hard enough to get first-class men in engineering even when they are allowed to carry on professional work," he said, "and this [outside consulting] is in most schools regarded as rather an advantage, because it keeps them efficient and up to date."[25]

It is amusing to look back on this moment, in 1910, when Slosson's report appeared just as Lewis Terman arrived to assume an assistant professorship. No one then could have known that after

World War I Terman would effect a dramatic improvement in the academic quality of Stanford's student body by introducing subject-matter tests in the application process at Stanford.[26] Terman would also became wealthy from royalties for developing intelligence tests that would be widely sold and regarded as the standard tests of intelligence. In the words of one of his biographers, Lewis Terman would live "to see America become test-conscious."[27]

In his 1910 report, Edwin Slosson was sympathetic to the Stanford faculty's complaints about outside work, but his sympathy did not prevent him from aiming his strongest criticism at the faculty's lack of achievements in scholarship. He listed the advantages that the members of the Stanford faculty enjoyed over professors at peer institutions: the salaries of Stanford professors were higher than all other places, other than at Columbia and at Harvard; they "were not overburdened by the number of students"; university policy prevented them from being distracted by outside consulting; the library and laboratories were well-equipped; they did not have to "make grandstand plays" for the benefit of a state legislature that controlled finances; they lived "in a quiet country place, having easy access to a large city, but untroubled by its noise, distractions, and obligations." Slosson recalled that William James had declared that "the advantages of the place for steady mental work are unparalleled." But Slosson could not see evidence that Stanford's scholarly achievements reflected the superior conditions for research.[28]

If any one single newly hired assistant professor would turn out to be an exemplar of scholarly achievement, fulfilling the scholarly expectations that Slosson and others outside of Stanford had of the school's privileged faculty members, it would be Lewis Terman. Arriving at Stanford, he took none of its Elysian research conditions for granted and quickly went to work on a number of monographs and a textbook that came out within three years. Three of these addressed school hygiene, a subject that was much on the minds of educators then and particularly so for Terman, suffering from tuberculosis that he must have contracted from a student when he was teaching.[29] The other area he worked in was the measurement of intelligence that, along with the psychology of genius, he had addressed in his doctoral dissertation and that would occupy him for his entire career. (He would later observe the unchanging nature of his professional research interests over the decades and ruefully quote Samuel Johnson's remark when he had reached the age of fifty-seven: "It is a sad reflection, but a true one, that I knew almost as much at eighteen as I do now.")[30]

The attention of all "mental testers" among American psychologists at that moment was trained on the work of the French psychologist Alfred Binet and his assistant Theodore Simon. The two had developed tests for evaluating the intelligence of children that were published first in 1905 and then, in revised form, in 1908. The Binet-Simon Scale was immediately translated into English and spurred many American psychologists to use the tests on child subjects to see if the scale, which defined "normal" intelligence for various ages, proved valid.[31]

When Terman arrived at Stanford, he immediately began testing children with the Binet-Simon Scale. With the help of graduate assistants, he tested four hundred in the first year, another three hundred the second year. He tinkered with the content of the Binet-Simon tests, adding new components such as vocabulary tests and having subjects recall backward the digits of a long number. He adjusted scoring norms so that the battery of tests would yield a bell-curve distribution of scores for each age. In 1916, he published *The Measurement of Intelligence*, his version of what had begun as the Binet-Simon tests and what he called the Stanford Revision Extension of the Binet-Simon Intelligence Scale, a wordy concoction that became known more simply as "Stanford-Binet."[32] It was based on testing 1,700 "normal" children, 200 "defective and superior" children, 150 adolescent delinquents, 30 businessmen, and 150 homeless men.[33] Whether it was out of a feeling of gratitude to his new em-

ployer or an inclination to be self-effacing, or both, Terman's decision
to use "Stanford" in the name of the new test rather than his own
surname was unusual; the last names of psychologists who were the
principal investigators were attached to dozens of psychological tests
that were proliferating just then. Terman would again place Stanford
in the limelight when he later named the Stanford Achievement Tests
that he developed. The wide circulation of these tests, it would turn
out, greatly enhanced the university's public stature.

Psychologists had experimented with intelligence tests for at
least twenty years before Binet developed his scale, but Terman
credited Binet, who died in 1911, with making three important ad-
vances: Binet used age standards when measuring intelligence; he
tested more complex mental processes; and he abandoned older
"faculty psychology" and focused on "general intelligence."[34] "Faculty psychology" attempted to measure particular aspects of intelligence, such as memory, attention, and sense discrimination, and
this is where Binet himself had begun his research. But after years of
frustration, he had abandoned the attempt and simply tested what
Terman approvingly said was the "combined functional capacity
without any pretense of measuring the exact contribution of each to
the total product."[35]

Terman took Binet's "age-grade" method and devised a point
system in which the intelligence score for a given subject was compared with the median score of "normal" subjects of the same age.
If it was identical, it produced an "intelligence quotient" of 100, referring to 100 percent of the age-related norm. Terman recognized
that removing age from the label affixed to an individual child's intelligence gave it an aura of immutability. Age did not matter, he
said. An individual's IQ does not change. "Children of superior intelligence do not deteriorate as they get older," he said, "and dull
children do not develop average intelligence."[36]

Fourteen years after *The Measurement of Intelligence* was published,
Terman would look back on the moment with some incredulity

about what followed its publication. He said he knew at the time that his revision of Binet's tests was superior to others that were also then available, "but I did not foresee the vogue it was to have and imagined that it would probably be displaced by something much better within a few years."[37] No less astonishing, he felt, was the way that "mental tests" would gain acceptance as quickly as they did.

In a short while, we will return to Terman's story, in Chapter 12, to watch how intelligence tests would be reconfigured for testing in the military and then in the workplace. The Scholastic Aptitude Test would also emerge from the stream of work that Terman undertook. The notion of protean mental ability, which the SAT carries on, is one that is crucially important to humanities majors on the job-search trail.

CHAPTER 11

INTERESTING THINGS HAPPEN

FRESHMAN SEMINARS IN THE HUMANITIES could never exist in a world wholly given over to vocational tracks. Not only do they address an *impractical* subject, they are inefficient, providing a mere handful of students with a tour of one corner of a field, one that engages the professor's own interest. But when taught well, students will find themselves so infected by the professor's enthusiasm, so engaged with the subject, so eager to learn more without heed of vocational considerations, that the students take another course in the department. And another and another, following intellectual curiosity. At the heart of a liberal education is the student's pursuit of interest wherever it might lead, Thomas Jefferson's "uncontrolled choice," and the freshman seminar in the humanities gets students started as soon as they arrive.

Andrew Phillips caught the contagious enthusiasm of a classics professor in his first quarter at Stanford in fall 2006. The very first class he stepped into on the first day happened to be Odysseus of Many Turnings. The seminar was limited to just twelve students, who would trace Odysseus through three millennia, reading not only *The Odyssey* but also Sophocles' *Ajax* and *Philoctetes*, Shakespeare's *Troilus and Cressida*, and Derek Walcott's *Omeros*, among other assignments. Phillips was enthralled by the professor, Richard Martin, and by the readings and class discussions.

Phillips then signed up for a course on ancient athletics, and then one on archaic Greek art. These were followed by courses on the Stoics and Epicureans; on appropriations of Greek art; on ancient urbanism and, separately, on urban sustainability in the ancient world; on Mayan mythology. He had taken two years of Latin in high school, at Georgetown Preparatory School, and he took two more years at Stanford. And he also started Greek. "Before I knew it, I had a good number of credits for a major," he recalls. "At that point, I'd just enjoyed it so much, it seemed like an easy choice."

When Phillips made the decision, he planned on becoming an attorney, and his father, who was an attorney who practiced in Washington, DC, encouraged him to pursue classics. Handling a great volume of reading and condensing it into smaller bits would be good preparation for a law career, his father said. For three summers, Phillips worked as an intern at a law firm.[1]

Outside of class, a good portion of Phillips's time was occupied with football: he was an offensive lineman who was a starter at Stanford for three years. His line protected quarterback Andrew Luck, a player who shattered many school records and was twice the runner-up in the Heisman Trophy balloting. (Phillips told me that in his senior year his team "went" to the 2011 Orange Bowl; he modestly left out the outcome of that game, a decisive 40-12 win for Stanford over Virginia Tech.)

Before Phillips's final season with the team, however, just as training camp was to begin, he and his family encountered tragedy. His father was killed and his younger brother, then thirteen, was injured in a small-plane accident in Alaska.[2] In the wake of his father's death, Phillips found himself reexamining his plan to become an attorney, a plan that now seemed to him to have been based mostly on unquestioningly following the path that his father and other family members had taken into law. In the fall of his senior year he went to several career fairs that were directed at athletes, but nothing caught his interest.

After the Orange Bowl, he decided he would aim for the National Football League, and for the next four months, he trained full time. He was not chosen in the draft, however. He could have continued to train, hoping to be picked up by a team as a free agent, but his prospects were cloudy. Even were he picked up, he would most likely have faced an itinerant career, playing for one team for six months, getting cut and moving to a new city for another short stint. "I don't think I was up for that," he says. "I was emotionally at a point where I was ready to move on from football."

If professional football was out, however, and so was law, what would he do with a classics major? He had a brother at the University of Virginia, also a football player, who had watched some of his teammates go through a master's program at Virginia's McIntire School of Commerce that was marketed to liberal arts, science, and engineering majors who sought to remediate the absence of business courses in their undergraduate education. Instead of asking these students to invest two years of study in a conventional MBA program, McIntire offered these students a shorter alternative: a one-year program that would lead to an MS in commerce.

Enrolling in the program, Andrew Phillips relocated near his mother and brothers for a year, family members supplying comfort to one another. When he arrived on campus, he was pleased to be among students who were like him, who had not majored in business and who were utterly lacking in business experience. Of the various paths the participants had taken to get to Virginia, though, his was not typical: he was one of only three classics majors among the hundred or so in his class.

While Phillips was taking classes on Virginia's campus,[3] the school videotaped students who were willing to offer testimonials about their experiences for use on the school's website. Phillips was among those who volunteered:

> I was an ancient history and classics major. I found out after coming here and being involved in strategy classes, accounting, finance, brand management, project management, what I learned did matter. As useless as I thought my ancient history degree would be

coming into a business context, there were people who studied architecture, art history, biomechanical engineering and thought the
same thing about their disciplines. But you put us all in a room and
interesting things happen. I'll bring up a context from something
I learned in classics, somebody else will bring up something they
learned in architecture. Whatever it is, all those backgrounds matter, all those backgrounds end up having a voice in the conversations we have.[4]

The McIntire School's alumni network was most closely tied to
the worlds of finance and consulting, and students in the MS program could contact alumni and secure interviews at investment
banks and consulting firms on the East Coast. Phillips paid a visit to
the Washington office of a consulting firm early in the fall semester,
not long after he had started the program. One of the interviews
involved thinking out loud about a hypothetical fast-food chain that
was weighing a drive-in model versus drive-through, and he experienced paralyzing anxiety during the exercise. That was the end of
his investigation of consulting.

After conversations with alumni from whom he sought career
advice, Phillips decided to shift his search away from the consult-
ing-and-finance firms that most of his classmates were pursuing
and instead look to technology companies in the Bay Area, where
many Stanford friends worked. During football season he flew out to
the Bay Area on two weekends that coincided with Stanford home
games to reconnect with old friends and to work the Stanford network, meeting with individuals for coffee to talk about possible job
openings. Invitations for formal interviews followed.

Phillips was twenty-four when he was looking for his first professional job. As the interviews proceeded, one obstacle that he encountered was being seen as older than the other candidates who were
being considered for entry-level positions. The master's degree he
would complete the next year made him appear "overqualified" for

the positions he was seeking. He was older than others because he had completed Stanford in the fall quarter of his fifth year, having spent his first year in college as a red-shirt member of the football team, practicing but not playing, preserving until his second year the start of his four years of playing eligibility. Then he had finished the fifth year with training, followed by the start of graduate school.

Phillips was told by interviewers "our worry is that you're too expensive for this entry-level job, but you're too inexperienced to take a higher role." Whenever he heard this, he rushed to remove the concern: "Wait, wait! I know I'm inexperienced! That's why I'm getting this degree! That's why I'm supplementing my education! Because I had no experience!"

When Phillips explored junior positions in venture capital firms, he ran into another obstacle that was wholly unrelated to his education or work experience: his size. "You're 6-feet-4, 300 pounds; you're not going to get hired in a culture of techies." Two people delivered this message to him, separately, about what was running through the minds of his interviewers. The bluntness of it took him aback. It was not disguised with something like "You don't have the skill set; we're looking for somebody with more quantitative skills." It was this: we do not hire people who look like you.

Forming a startup with others was another possibility, but Phillips understood that he was far too green to be a cofounder. What he wanted was a place in an established startup, one that had already secured venture capital, was growing at a healthy rate, and would provide him with an opportunity to gain some experience in a real business. A former teammate was working at Wildfire Interactive, a software marketing startup that enabled client companies to set up contests (which involve some element of skill) or sweepstakes (which do not), and other campaigns on the client's Facebook fan page. Electronic Arts, for example, set up a contest on the eve of the release of an iteration of its futuristic horror video game Dead Space. With Wildfire's software, Electronic Arts invited visitors to come to its Facebook page to submit a creative "kill" sequence, either with photos or a video. Finalists were selected; visitors to the page were invited to cast votes for their favorite. By harnessing the self-propelling effects of online social networks, the contest created a sensational response.[5]

Wildfire fit Phillips's template of a fast-growing startup. Three years earlier, it had been one of five just-hatched startups to win a $225,000 grant in a competition organized by Facebook for software startups that used the Facebook platform.[6] Facebook followed with an equity investment of $100,000, and as Wildfire grew, expanding from 7 employees to 120 within eighteen months, it raised a total of $4.1 million from venture capitalists and angel investors. When Phillips applied, the company was sufficiently well-established that its client list included Pepsi, AT&T, and Unilever.[7] It was growing in revenue and headcount by 10 percent each month.

Phillips was interested in Wildfire, but why would Wildfire be interested in the inexperienced Phillips with his classics major and just-begun MBA-lite master's degree program?[8] He discovered that Wildfire's sales organization was receptive to hiring newly minted college graduates as trainees in its sales organization without restrictions related to major. Wildfire was too small, the remuneration too uncertain, for experienced salespeople in well-compensated positions elsewhere to be willing to join. Necessity forced Wildfire to hire graduates coming out of college, lining up sales prospects and acquiring experience that would permit them to be promoted to the position of account executive, the salesperson who met with prospective clients.

The Wildfire manager who hired Phillips, Daniel Davis, looked for three attributes that he deemed most important for salespeople: a strong work ethic, above-average intelligence, and a knack for staying organized.[9] To be sure, salespeople had to be articulate, but all serious candidates for sales positions were articulate; it was not a distinguishing characteristic.

Davis was not looking to hire graduates from Stanford and the Ivies; he was looking to hire the hardest-working smart people he could, and two of his finds were graduates of Arizona State and Chico State. When Andrew Phillips applied, his Stanford pedigree did not establish that he was a hard worker, but his holding a starting position on a college football team that played at the most elite level, with the outsized demands on his time that that entailed, and at the same time seeking out challenging classes in the Department of Classics, did suggest that his appetite for work matched what Wildfire was looking for. When Phillips went in for his interview, he was asked why a classics major would want to work in tech. The question came across as originating in the interlocutor's curiosity, not skepticism. Phillips told his story, of his original intention to become a lawyer, his love of studying languages and of adding Italian to his Greek and Latin, of loving his first Stanford class and the small seminars that followed and enjoying the conversations he had with his classics professors. He recounted how he realized that he should supplement the classics with an analytical component, which the UVA program would give him. Wildfire offered him a position as a sales associate. It was January 2012, and the company agreed to postpone his start until after he had finished his master's program. He returned to Virginia no longer burdened by worry about finding a starting position: he was set.

His program ended; he got married; he and his wife headed west, going to Napa for their honeymoon before Phillips was to report for his first day of work at Wildfire. A friend had given the couple a special winery tour as a wedding present, and the day of the tour, just as Phillips was savoring the scene, vineyards on all sides, he received a text message from a friend at UVA: Wildfire had just been acquired by Google for $350 million.[10] He gulped, thinking, "I don't have a job now." His wife, a nurse, had gotten a position at Stanford Hospital, so they would not be without income, he told himself. But it was impossible to enjoy the bucolic Napa setting at that moment. He asked himself whom he could call to see if there was any chance of his starting work at the newly absorbed Wildfire. A few moments later, he received a call from an HR person at Wildfire—Phillips could hear the noise of a raucous party in the background—who assured him, "Don't worry about it; you still have a job; obviously, we're going to Google now, but we'll see you next week." He had not even experienced a first day of work in his new tech career and he had already gone through an acquisition.

Initially, Google kept the Wildfire group intact and separate, and when Phillips arrived for his first day of work, he discovered that many of his new colleagues had also traveled from majors and occupations that were distant from tech. By then, the company had grown to about 350 people, and Phillips was a member of a group of about thirty newly hired sales associates who composed that month's cohort. Years later, Davis recalls that after Phillips's group finished orientation, the head trainer called Davis's attention to the standout: "Andrew Phillips is just brilliant."

What Davis saw for himself was that Phillips was the most devoted student in the organization. Davis held weekly office hours, inviting the sales associates, about forty-five people, to come by; he would field questions or, if none were brought in, he would share his own sales experiences and lessons learned in the field. Usually, only three or four people would show up, different ones each week except for one: Phillips, who came without fail every week.

The sales associate program that Phillips was in was highly evolved: training took the successful hires through three levels, after which they were eligible for appointment as an account executive if there was an opening. As fast as Wildfire grew, its sales associate program had grown even faster, creating far more account-executive-ready trainees than there were open positions. So even though Philips was a Google employee, and could enjoy the prestige that the association conferred, he was still stuck, one year after being hired as an associate, doing the grunt work of the behind-the-scenes helper who set up the appointments for the actual salesperson. He could see that he would have to put in much more time before he would be given an opportunity to move up.

Phillips wanted to be the person with his own book, the one closing sales, and he began looking around the Valley for the next opportunity. He looked for a company like Wildfire: fast-growing, venture-backed, with a strong team and likable, respected founders. He found what he was looking for in Bizo, a venture-backed software startup that offered targeting and measurement tools to advertisers who addressed businesspeople and professionals instead of consumers.

Phillips started at Bizo in October 2013, and only ten months later, Bizo was acquired by LinkedIn. At the time of this acquisition, he was a member of a startup team of 150 and had been there long enough to feel that he had contributed to the success that had caught the interest of LinkedIn. In his short professional life, he had had two jobs and had experienced two acquisitions by Valley powerhouses. A friend of his who had just founded his own startup joked, "I want to hire you and I don't want you to do anything. I just want you to sit in the front and drink beer all day and then as people come in, they have to rub your belly for luck."

When Wildfire hired Phillips, the company was not looking for students with business degrees; the positions were open to all graduates from all schools. The company sought candidates with certain qualities that could be demonstrated in a myriad of ways that were unrelated to what was imprinted on a student's diploma. When Davis was asked, years later, whether Phillips's Master of Commerce program had made him a more attractive applicant to Wildfire, Davis said, no, it had made zero difference. Then he offered a small qualification: if it mattered at all, it was just additional validation of Phillips's capacity for work, his being well-organized, his ability to remain undistracted in pursuing his goals. The content of the academic program was not relevant to Wildfire; what mattered was what his choice revealed about character.

CHAPTER 12

A MANIA FOR TESTING

AT THE TIME THAT LEWIS TERMAN was testing the "general intelligence" of subjects, mostly children, and refining the scales for the Stanford-Binet, the business world was reconsidering how it went about selecting new hires. A new department, personnel, appeared in many large firms, and personnel managers advocated adoption of "scientific" methods that were to replace the hunches of line managers.

What fell under the rubric of "scientific" depended on intellectual fashions. The use of physiognomy and phrenology in guiding personnel decisions in the nineteenth century—face shape, hair color, curve of the nose, shape of the skull—continued, even as the new personnel departments were set up. In 1916, on the eve of World War I, Robert C. Clothier, the employment manager of the Curtis Publishing Company in Philadelphia, a media giant of its day that published the *Saturday Evening Post* and *Ladies' Home Journal*, avowed that much could be gained from phrenological examinations; their usefulness was limited only because phrenology was "still a science in its infancy."[1] Another personnel manager at Curtis, Katharine Huey, said she obtained vital information by closely examining an applicant's clothes and by interpreting the handshake when first meeting, judging "the firmness or flabbiness of the grasp."[2]

Curtis personnel used interviews to judge which one of five "mentalities" was assigned to each applicant: super-alert, alert, average, slow, or dull. Applicants may not have realized that being perceived as super-alert was to be avoided. The staff at Curtis had devised the designation for "that type of mind which is too active— almost effervescent; a type of mind which is seldom accompanied by the stability and saneness which are requisites in most positions."[3]

The interviews, the universal mainstay of the application process, gathered impressions that no two personnel managers would necessarily interpret in the same way. The absence of clearly defined tools for measuring ability vexed academic experts who looked out upon the landscape of workplaces and saw haphazard judgments made by individuals. Guy Montrose Whipple, a professor of education at the University of Illinois, said general intelligence tests, like the Stanford-Binet, could not be used by personnel departments because the tests were for subjects who were no more than ten or eleven years old; general intelligence tests for adults had yet to be developed. In their absence, Whipple recommended tests of narrow scope for gauging specific abilities for particular occupations. He admitted that for the most part these too had yet to be developed, and he had little to offer for illustration beyond mentioning a test for color-blindness for those seeking to join the Navy or the merchant marine. He criticized academic research that used artificial settings like a campus laboratory for testing, leading to what he saw as a laughable absurdity, a "coed" who scored the highest points on a test that was to determine who was best suited for sea-captaincy.[4]

Walter Dill Scott, a psychologist at Northwestern University, was the pioneer who worked with actual business firms to develop and apply new tests for applicants.[5] In 1914, he offered to members of the National Association of Corporation Schools the services of himself and his Northwestern colleagues as constructive critics, if the companies would be willing to send him information about their methods of selecting employees. He said "the time is ripe" for psychologists like himself to help improve hiring practices because "psychologists have during the last few years made distinct

advance[s] in Mental Tests."[6] The invitation led to consulting en-
gagements that were also opportunities to advance his research; the
American Tobacco Company, for example, asked him to work on
using psychology in the selection of salesmen.[7] In 1916, Scott published descriptions of the tests that he had developed that sought to
determine the extent of "Native Intellectual Ability" that supposedly
could not be learned.[8]

One of his tests demanded that the applicant present mock sales
pitches for products that were assigned.[9] In another, candidates had
to match English proverbs with African proverbs.[10] He also directed
that the candidate's handwriting be analyzed, a test that he apparently thought was placed on a sound scientific basis because it would
be evaluated not idiosyncratically but by the Ayres scale for handwriting quality.[11]

In addition to the tests, Scott had a candidate distribute a highly
detailed questionnaire to the candidate's previous employers, going
as far back as three earlier jobs.[12] His methods seem relatively be-
nign, however, compared with those of his contemporary, William
Fretz Kemble, author of *Choosing Employees by Mental and Physical Tests*
(1917), who coolly provided employers with sample employment
tests that delved into the candidate's most sensitive personal and political opinions. Here is a swatch from a list that a candidate was to
mark up, crossing out items that he did not believe in and underscor-
ing those that he did:

> I believe in—The Democratic party, Republican party, Inde-
> pendent party, Progressives, Labor party, prohibition, socialism,
> anarchy, the initiative, referendum, recall of judges, high tariff,
> low tariff, free trade, woman suffrage, popular election of senators,
> peace at any cost, strong restriction of immigration, government
> ownership, compulsory education, old age pensions, alimony even
> without children, easy divorce, vice crusades, Sunday blue laws,
> the death sentence, more laws, less laws, eugenics, reincarnation,

Christian Science, Christianity, hell, heaven, the devil, Jonah and the whale; in charms, palmistry, vivisection; in unions, trusts, and in government regulation of—private wages, newspapers, plays, marriages, and amusements.[13]

Kemble believed that his "Personal-Opinion Test" was important for classifying individuals "very distinctly according to their mental calibre." The job candidate's answers were to be compared with the answers of "ten very high-class executives."[14]

Suddenly, "mental testers" found their expertise in demand, not by the odd consulting client here and there but by the U.S. military. The United States declared war on Germany on April 6, 1917, and the next month Congress passed a compulsory draft that required all males, initially from the ages of twenty-one through thirty and soon expanded, to register immediately.[15] Determining who should be placed in what position presented an immediate administrative challenge. Professors of psychology, the "mental testers," were called to Washington to devise a solution, quickly. Lewis Terman was a member of the seven-person committee assembled in summer 1917 to begin planning for testing on a mass scale.[16] It was charged with classifying men according to "mental capacity"; separating out the "mentally incompetent"; and identifying the men most qualified to assume "responsible positions."[17] Later, a larger working group of civilians—academic psychologists and personnel managers—would be set up for the Army: the Committee on Classification of Personnel, which initially included Terman, Edward L. Thorndike at Columbia, Robert Yerkes at Harvard, and Edward K. Strong, at George Peabody College for Teachers in Nashville (who would move to Stanford after the war). Walter Dill Scott was the committee's director.[18]

Before the war, Terman had felt scorned by what he would call "old-line psychologists" who looked askance at "mental testing." He had not even joined the American Psychological Association. But when he spent the summer of 1916 teaching at New York University, he started to appreciate that there were other like-minded psychologists with whom he had much to share. The next year, after war was declared, he taught at Columbia that summer and worked with other psychologists on the plans for mass testing. "I no longer felt isolated," he later wrote. "I could return to my work with more confidence than ever that, in the long run, contributions in the field of mental tests would receive the recognition they deserved."[19]

The advisors viewed the Binet intelligence tests, and the various revisions such as the Stanford-Binet, to be too time-consuming. What the Army needed was an intelligence test that was expressly designed for handling a high volume of examinees and rapid processing of results. Arthur S. Otis, one of Terman's doctoral students at Stanford,[20] had in manuscript form an intelligence test that was close to what the advisors were looking for, and it formed the basis of what the Army used in trial tests in the fall at four locations.[21]

The psychologists wanted the test to be made "as completely independent of schooling and educational advantages as possible."[22] But this desideratum remains elusive, even today, with many decades of refining the most widely used successor to the Army's tests, the Scholastic Aptitude Test, and it is a goal that arguably can never be achieved. It certainly was not possible to devise in the short space of mere weeks that they had to finalize a test and procedures. So the test consisted of arithmetic problems, sentences that had been disarranged and needed to be put in logical order, number series that needed to be extended, analogies, synonym-antonym tests, a category called "practical judgment," and, finally, a category that could not have been more closely dependent upon education: "general information."[23]

Here is a sample of some test questions that were used in the final version of the test:

How many are 30 men and 7 men?

Are cats useful animals because they catch mice, or because they are gentle, or because they are afraid of dogs?

Is leather used for shoes because it is produced in all countries, or because it wears well, or because it is an animal product?

Do these two words mean the same or opposite: wet-dry?

Do these two words mean the same or opposite: in-out?

Do these two words mean the same or opposite: hill-valley?

Re-arrange these groups of words into a sentence and tell whether it is a true or false statement.

lions strong are.

houses people in live.

days there in are week eight a.

leg flies one have only.

Write the next two numbers in this series: 3, 4, 5, 6, 7, 8.

In this series: 15, 20, 25, 30, 35.

In this series: 8, 7, 6, 5, 4, 3.[24]

Each correct answer earned a point. The testers believed that the questions would reveal this amorphous thing, general intelligence. They were only interested in the total number of points earned. There was no vestige of interest in "faculty intelligence"; no one attended to niceties such as noting high scores on certain kinds of problems and low ones on others. Men would be tested in groups as large as five hundred at a time, filling out examination sheets that, afterward, staff could score quickly with stencil overlays. The written test was at first called Examination Alpha, and the consulting psychologists claimed that its correlation with Stanford-Binet was .80 to .90. (Its correlation with officers' ratings of their men was only .50 to .70.)[25]

The testers recognized that many men did not speak English well enough to understand the questions or were native English speakers who were illiterate, so men who did poorly on the Alpha were given Examination Beta, with maze tests, picture-completion challenges, and other self-explanatory exercises. About 30 percent of the men needed to take the Beta.[26]

Solely on the basis of the point total, the man was assigned a letter rating, ranging from A to E. Those with A's and high B's would be sent to officers' training school. Those with B's and upper C's were viewed as well-matched for clerical work. The average private scored in the C range. Those with D's and F's were deemed so lacking in intelligence as to be ineffective in the Army, if not deserving to be, in the words of the Army's official history of the program, "inmates of institutions for the feeble-minded."[27]

In a historical blink of an eye, the Army's intelligence exam was given to more than 1.7 million men. It served not only to make intelligence testing a mainstream tool for personnel management but also to sanctify the notion that word problems or mazes and the like unveiled an immutable intelligence that could be expressed as a single number.[28] Doggerel in one military base's newspaper, *Camplife Chickamauga*, preserves the sense of how important the intelligence testing was in the judgment of the military's leadership, even if not by the rank and file:

> "The March of the Psychos"
> (Air: Chopin's Funeral March)
> The valiant, bespectacled psychos are we
> Prepared to assign every man his degree
> Add the place he's best fitted for in the armee
> By psychologee, psychologee.
> Bill Kaiser will shake in this throne 'cross the sea
> When he feels the earthquake of our efficiency
> Pencils up! Forward march! to the great victory
> Of Psychologee in the Army.[29]

At the war's conclusion, these newly prominent experts, the psychologists, offered a method of selecting students or employees that did not attempt to plumb what the candidate had learned but something else, intelligence, which by its nature was presumed to be useful for school or work in any context. Intelligence testing was poised to spread far and wide.

In 1919, Columbia University made the Thorndike Intelligence Examination a requirement for applicants.[30] Created by its own Edward L. Thorndike, the test embodied most of the subtests in the Army's Alpha (and anticipated those on the SAT): reading comprehension, sentence arrangement, arithmetic problems, synonyms-antonyms, syllogisms, recall of drawings and numbers, truth and falsity of statements, and a category that would seem difficult to measure with precision: "judgment."[31]

The Thorndike test embodied a contradiction. Thorndike named his test an intelligence exam, intelligence being an attribute unaffected by education, but the exam's questions were expressly designed for high school students who, by Thorndike's own admission, had enjoyed "good educational advantages." In an instruction booklet he prepared for college admissions offices in 1921, he wrote, "The expectation from equally intelligent graduates of poorly equipped high schools and from equally intelligent foreign students will be less."[32]

Columbia's adoption of the Thorndike did represent a departure from existing practice, which was to rely upon the subject-matter tests published by the College Entrance Examination Board, which had been formed in 1900.[33] By moving to the Thorndike, Columbia's admissions office could cull Jewish applicants who were viewed as "grinds" and "overachievers," earning superior grades in high school beyond their "natural intelligence" by dint of above-average effort.[34]

Other universities followed Columbia in adopting the Thorndike in admissions. When the University of California did the same, giving the exam for the first time in January 1921, it saw more clearly than others that the exam included questions closely tied to high school subjects. When referring to the Thorndike Intelligence Examination for High School Graduates, the faculty committee overseeing it made up its own name for it, the "Thorndike College Entrance Test," without mention of "Intelligence."[35]

Stanford took notice when the University of California introduced the Thorndike,[36] and the faculty invited Lewis Terman to brief it on the experiences of other colleges and universities with intelligence tests. Not surprisingly, Terman advocated vigorously that Stanford adopt an intelligence test for admissions, arguing that it would block applicants who were admitted and then ended up being ejected for poor grades. By his calculation, if the cost of what Stanford had spent teaching students who had been suspended were added to the cost of teaching those who were disqualified, the total spent on students who had been "officially labeled unsatisfactory or doubtful" was equivalent to about one-third of the university's instructional budget.[37]

A few months later, Stanford's Academic Council voted to require the Thorndike of all undergraduates, initially as an experiment without using the scores to determine admission, and then, experiment concluded, as the basis for a minimum score required for matriculation.[38] Once it was in place, Terman cheered when "the requirement had the desired effect of scaring away some of the dullards who would otherwise have reached us, and of attracting a goodly proportion of high-scoring candidates." In two years, the average score of entering students increased by ten points. He urged the university to publicize that Stanford was "in the market for brains" and predicted that by the university giving more weight to the "intelligence score" when evaluating applicants, the average score of the student body would equal what before had defined the top decile of the student body.[39]

Test scores and broad generalizations went hand-in-hand. As soon as the scores were collected from Stanford students, generalizations about subgroups were drawn. The university reported that swimmers, debaters, and actors were among the students that got above-average scores; daughters of faculty members and alumni scored below average.[40]

Just as Terman was pushing Stanford into adopting intelligence testing, he was securing funding to launch the study of one thousand high-IQ children in California, the study that would turn out to be longitudinal and the subject of four of his books. It would occupy him for the rest of his life, as well as the professional lives of his successors.[41]

Terman coined the phrase "gifted children," but he was not occupied exclusively with the study of them. In 1922, he published a scholarly paper titled "Adventures in Stupidity: A Partial Analysis of the Intellectual Inferiority of a College Student."[42] One less-than-bright Stanford student, referred to as "K," had been brought to Terman's attention by a colleague who taught art and who told Terman that he had never seen a student who had made such absurd mistakes when asked to draw simple objects. Terman gave the student, who had been admitted to Stanford before intelligence testing had arrived, the Stanford-Binet test, which assigned him a "mental age" of twelve. K would fail all of his classes in the first term and be dismissed from the university, but not before agreeing to take many other tests given by Terman, who was fascinated by what he called "the psychology of stupidity" and sought to measure it precisely.

K's father owned a general store and headed a bank in a small town in California, and the young man returned there after his short stint at Stanford, working in his father's store as a clerk. "It is unlikely that he will ever be able to manage a business of any considerable importance," predicted Terman. K's intelligence, as captured in the Stanford-Binet, would determine his professional course. He could be a baker, barber, bricklayer, butcher—Terman listed thirty possible trades, in alphabetic order—but Terman maintained that the only way K would become a successful businessman would be by relying on the capabilities of others, either lieutenants or a wife.[43]

Even here, in a study of the measured general intelligence of ostensibly a single person, K, who was white, Terman used intelligence test scores to issue supposedly scientific decrees that stratified whites by trade and consigned non-Anglo-Saxon populations to positions inferior to those occupied by Anglo-Saxon whites:

> It will be well to note that the degree of stupidity with which we are here concerned is really not extreme. K is in fact only moderately less dull than the average of the genus homo, judging from the intelligence scores made by nearly two million soldiers. His intelligence is probably not equalled or exceeded by more than 70 per cent, of our white voters, by more than 50 to 60 per cent, of semiskilled laborers, by more than 40 to 50 per cent, of barbers or teamsters, or by more than 20 to 30 per cent, of unskilled laborers. It is probably not equaled or exceeded by more than 30 to 40 per cent, of our South Italian or by more than 20 to 30 per cent, of our Mexican immigrants. Compared to the average American Negro, K is intellectually gifted, being equaled by probably not more than 10 to 15 per cent of that race.[44]

The aura of scientific truth protected Terman and the "mental testers" from being questioned. So in 1922, when Walter Lippmann in a series of articles in the *New Republic* took on Terman and the intelligence-testing movement, Lippmann did so alone. He was a journalist, without advanced degrees, and yet he was able to expose major shortcomings of the tests and the ways in which they were being used.

Lippmann began his critique by looking at Alfred Binet, whom Lippmann noted had started out with the ambition to define intelligence and then had had to abandon the project without an answer. In its place, Binet devised questions and puzzles and "stunts," in Lippmann's phrasing, that Binet hoped would reveal something about intelligence, and then he tested Parisian schoolchildren. If about 65 percent of the children of a given age passed the test, then that test was, ipso facto, a test of intelligence for that age. But the psychologist still didn't know what intelligence was.

When Lewis Terman brought Binet's questions to California and tested schoolchildren there, the questions did not produce anything close to the same results as they had in France. But instead of questioning the assumptions upon which Binet's tests had been built, Terman simply revised questions until the same 65 percent of an age group passed.[45] Lippmann pointed out that nothing was being objectively measured, other than that some students answered questions differently than others. The answers designated as correct could be hilariously arbitrary—Lippmann noted that Terman counted a correct definition of "justice" as "it's what you get when you go to court" but counted as incorrect "to be honest." But the arbitrariness was hidden by the crisp precision of the distribution: by design 65 percent of the subjects always agreed on the Terman-approved answer.[46]

Lippmann pointed out that "the type of mind which is very apt in solving Sunday newspaper puzzles, or even in playing chess, may be specially favored by these tests." But that does not mean these individuals are necessarily intelligent; it just means they are good at puzzles or games. He believed that genuine intelligence was "the capacity to deal with life," and no one, including the psychologists like Terman, had empirical proof that high IQs were closely correlated with Lippmann's practical definition of intelligence.[47]

The quest to find correlation would take a long time, Lippmann said. He expected that the measurement of "hereditary intelligence" would be shown to have no more scientific basis than "phrenology and palmistry" and "correspondence courses in will power."[48] In the meantime, he was gravely concerned that educators would believe that the tests scientifically revealed "predestined ability" among children, enabling "the more prejudiced" among educators to classify students according to the test results "and forget that their duty is to educate."[49]

The *New Republic* gave Terman space to respond, and he did so with the voice not of a coldly analytical academic but of a feisty political candidate, playing to a sympathetic crowd. He mocked Lippmann, rather unfairly, for tacitly criticizing mental testers who pointed out "that some members of the species are much stupider than others" or that "college professors are more intelligent than janitors, architects than hod-carriers, railroad presidents than switch-tenders." Terman also took aim at Lippmann's questioning of the testers' finding that the offspring of professionally successful parents "have better endowment" than the offspring of the lowly trades.[50] Terman assumed, here and elsewhere in his writings, that higher scores reflected "better endowment," and that the differences between classes and races were primarily hereditary in their nature.

Lippmann's objections did not halt the advance of "mental testing." The Thorndike Intelligence Examination filtered high school students seeking entrance to universities, but once they passed and began their college studies, another test would be needed to complete the logical next step: determining which occupation students would enter. The test that would become most widely adopted nationally was the Strong Vocational Interest Blank (today called the Strong Interest Inventory). The "Strong" in the name does not modify "Interest"—it happened to be the last name of the Stanford psychologist who developed it, Edward K. Strong, Jr. In 1922, Stanford's administration asked Lewis Terman to move from the Department of Education to chair and expand the Department of Psychology. Having worked with Strong during the war, Terman recruited him from the Carnegie Institute of Technology to join the department.[51]

Just as Binet and Terman had abandoned attempts to determine the components of intelligence and had settled for using answers obtained from a majority of subjects to set a baseline, Edward Strong had abandoned attempts to determine the components of aptitude for a given vocation. Instead Strong surveyed a sample of practitioners in a field about professional and nonprofessional interests to use their answers as a baseline. One version of the exam had four hundred questions, which included inquiries into the subject's interest in things that seem to have been selected at random: "Do you like making a speech? Do you like window shopping? Do you like people who chew gum?"[52] Strong said that the questions were chosen for their ability to prompt similar answers among practitioners in one occupation and different answers from those in others.

He began his surveys by administering them to doctors, lawyers, and engineers. He then asked male students—a version for female students would not arrive for ten years[53]—the same questions about their own interests. Depending on how closely the students' answers correlated with those of practitioners in a profession, a letter was assigned to represent the match between student and prospective profession: A, B, or C, representing the entire gamut, from close match of interests to look-for-another-line-of-work.

Did a college student who, for example, thought he wanted to become a doctor need to take the Strong test? Lewis Terman believed the answer was most emphatically yes. He said that vocational interest was "not readily discoverable by introspection and self-observation." Instead, it was uncovered as a close match between the interests of the student and those of successful members of the profession. Reliance on a test also would protect students from being misled "by parental bias, by the personal influence of a favorite teacher, by incomplete or inaccurate knowledge of vocations," or by other factors that Terman did not enumerate.[54]

When Strong and the assistant registrar Karl M. Cowdery attempted to administer the test to every male student in Stanford's Class of 1927, they discovered a minority of "hard-boiled fellows" who knew little "about the subject of psychology" and who did not treat the test with due seriousness.[55] They asked that the students not use the occasion to "demonstrate their collegiate humor," as in the history class where one wit, when asked to route the passage of a ship from Duluth to New York, had written that the ship was sunk just out of Duluth. "That is very funny but is of no value in Vocational Interest Tests," they said.[56]

Even when students filled the Strong test out soberly, it produced results that were almost comically predictable. "Certified public accountants score most like executives, bankers, office workers, and life insurance salesmen and they score least like artists, ministers, doctors, authors and lawyers," said Strong, in the *Journal of Educational Psychology* in 1927. He himself was mystified. "The explanation of all this is not clear."[57]

Having collected questionnaires from the men in the Class of 1927 (Strong ignored the women), Strong sent follow-up questionnaires in 1928, 1929, and 1932, attempting to determine the predictive power of his vocational interest test. Half of the graduates had followed their original career plan; one quarter changed plans radically; and the remainder had had no idea what they were going to do after graduation.[58] Strong tested Stanford freshmen in 1930, sent out follow-up questionnaires in 1931, 1939, and 1949, and came up with this utterly unremarkable finding: 77 percent had the same vocational interest nine years after the freshman survey and 76 percent still had the same interest nineteen years later.[59]

The Strong Vocational Interest Blank was published by Stanford University Press for many years, then licensed, and later sold, to CPP, the publisher of the Myers-Briggs Type Indicator test.[60] It lives on but outside of the lives of today's Stanford students, whose post-graduation plans are not shaped by a vocational interest test.

Stanford students are affected, or at least were affected before arriving to campus, by the offspring of the Army Alpha test: the SAT. The Scholastic Aptitude Test is, essentially, the Alpha with harder questions.[61] It also rests on the premises that guided the preparation of the Alpha, that the questions reveal general intelligence that cannot be increased with education or coaching, premises that by now have been exposed as fallacious. But just as the Army needed to process many draftees quickly, and the test that was developed was built for mass deployment, so too the SAT is built to handle millions. Convenience trumps science. But its wide use does serve as a strong bulwark against aptitude or discipline-oriented tests, which would push students into narrow tracks early and prevent them from benefiting from a liberal education.

CHAPTER 13

THE STRENGTH OF WEAK TIES

ELISE GRANGAARD was an American Studies major, one of the earliest of the many multidisciplinary majors that have proliferated since it was introduced in the 1940s.[1] By 2012, a multidisciplinary major was the choice of one-third of Stanford's undergraduates.[2] Grangaard's choice of major was not much on her mind when she graduated and looked for work, however, because she graduated in 2009, the first class to emerge in the midst of the Great Recession. Market demand for new college graduates was weak, and she experienced many travails during a dark period following graduation. She did find a way out, however.

Grangaard had come to Stanford from Edina, Minnesota, a suburb of Minneapolis, where she had gone to a French-immersion school. Both of her parents had gone to Stanford: her mother had majored in English, her father in economics.[3] In high school she had most enjoyed classes in history and English, and American Studies, being a superset of both and offering multiple disciplinary perspectives on a single historical time, immediately drew her interest. She took an entrancing introductory seminar, "Visions of the 1960s"; the class read *The Autobiography of Malcolm X* and *The Electric Kool-Aid Acid Test*, among other works, and discussed *The Graduate*. Outside of classes, she joined Stanford's largest student-run theatrical group, Ram's Head. She also played trumpet in the Band—the Leland Stanford Junior University Marching Band, or LSJUMB—

and was a member of the Band's core group that traveled to play at away basketball games.[4]

After her freshman year, Grangaard returned to Edina for the summer. She had not arranged an internship and spent the summer working as a nanny and spending time with friends from high school. The summer did not advance her professionally, and she resolved to arrange an internship in the Twin Cities the next summer following her sophomore year. Her father, who was the chief executive of a shoe manufacturer, inquired on her behalf with a friend of his who worked at Target Corporation, headquartered in Minneapolis, and that friend contacted the human resources department, which, in turn, got in touch with her about an internship in human resources. Grangaard would be one of more than one hundred summer interns spread across the company.

It was summer 2007, and Target had not yet done much to utilize the Internet to spread word on college campuses of its job openings in management. It would put job postings up on its corporate website but not do much else. For her summer internship project, Grangaard was assigned the task of figuring out how Target could use the web more effectively to reach students at the schools it wanted to reach. Not only did Silicon Valley's elite, such as Google and Facebook, restrict their recruiting to a handful of campuses, so too did Target. In fact, the term that Target used to refer to the twenty or twenty-five favored colleges and universities was *target schools*—lower-case *t*. One of its principal targets was local, the Carlson School of Management at the University of Minnesota; most of the others were in the Midwest; a few were distant. Stanford was one of Target's targets.

Grangaard enjoyed working on the project. She did research on the online alumni job boards for the targeted schools and developed a procedure for the HR department to get Target's openings posted on those school-based job boards. She did well and was invited to return the following summer for another internship in a different department.

She spent spring quarter of her junior year studying in Paris. She remembers telling herself, again and again, to savor each moment of the experience, even meals, because she did not know if she would ever have the opportunity to return.

After Paris, she returned to Target headquarters in Minneapolis for her second summer internship. Assigned to Merchandising Operations, she was asked to work on "clearance pricing" for babies' and children's merchandise, studying price and sales data and optimizing the schedule for progressively reducing the prices of items from, say, regular price to 50 percent off, to 70 percent, and then to 90 percent.

Grangaard was one of five interns in her group that summer; the majors of the others were business and economics. But no one challenged her ability to learn how to do the analysis. It speaks well of the humanities that this not-yet-a-senior American Studies major and French minor could take on data crunching, learning on the fly. Target was pleased by the quality of her work, and in the fall of her senior year the company offered her a full-time permanent position in Merchandise Operations for when she graduated the following June.

Accepting the offer would have relieved her of the great worry about what was to come after graduation, a worry that she knew would grow exponentially as the countdown to graduation progressed. It was November 2008. Lehman Brothers had collapsed in September; the Emergency Economic Stabilization Act of 2008 had been rushed through Congress and enacted in October. The college seniors at Stanford could see that their Class of 2009's job-search cycle was not going to be a normal one. The investment banks, usually a ubiquitous campus presence in the fall, failed to appear. Consulting companies had also scaled back their recruiting drastically. Even Google did not seem to be hiring, at least in nontechnical positions. But as ominous as the clouds overhead were, Grangaard could not summon excitement about the offer from Target. She loved theater and music and did not want to return to Merchandise

Operations, whose work she did not love. Without any alternative opportunity in sight, she turned Target down.

Grangaard aspired to obtain a job of some kind, any kind, in the arts. Or maybe a position in book or magazine publishing. During her senior year, she applied for editorial assistant jobs in New York, Boston, Los Angeles, and Minneapolis. Looking back on that experience, she says she did not know that merely sending in her résumé online was "not how you do it, that's not how you're going to get a job."

In her freshman year, Grangaard had formed close friendships with seven others; not one of that group had a professional job lined up as they arrived at graduation. Grangaard, longing to return home to Edina and be with her younger siblings and friends from high school, nonetheless resisted the temptation to return. She decided that she would spend the summer in Palo Alto and see if she could find a job in the arts. The first task, though, was to get a job to support herself. Two weeks before graduation, she took a part-time job as a hostess at a restaurant and pub, Gordon Biersch, in downtown Palo Alto.

She moved into the house of a friend's grandmother for which she didn't have to pay rent, so her part-time job—the hostess job soon became a server position—was enough to cover her expenses. She spent daytimes sending off her résumé, running, and continuing to play trumpet in the Band, which had weekly rehearsals in the summer, as well as occasional events.

By the end of the summer, she had applied to about two hundred jobs and nothing had come of it. She resolved to remain and continue the search. She had to move out of her rent-free house and ended up renting a room in a four-bedroom house in Palo Alto occupied by four other young women. Grangaard's room was what a realtor would euphemistically call a "bonus room"—the laundry room. Her housemates, acknowledging that it wasn't ideal, had her pay less than a one-fifth share of the house's rent. She says that once she set ground rules that forbade her housemates from starting a new load of wash after a certain hour in the evening, the situation was not so bad.

One of her housemates was at Autonomic Technologies, a medical device startup in Redwood City, and worked the long hours demanded of all at startups. Autonomic needed a temporary office manager for two weeks, and Grangaard was hired. The hours were conventional daytime hours and didn't interfere with her evening shifts as server at the restaurant. Grangaard ended up working there for three months as the company searched for a permanent replacement. She oversaw purchase orders and shipment requests, and worked with a CPA to go over the office's accounting. The experience helped shore up her self-confidence, even if it was not a job that she wanted to have on a permanent basis.

When the stint as interim office manager ended, Grangaard had to increase her shifts at the restaurant to earn enough to cover her still-modest expenses. She worked three or four nights a week and double shifts on the weekends. Her exercise routine disappeared. She was bowed by stress, but she did not know what else she could do.

During the summer, her parents had been supportive of her decision to stay in California, and they hoped for the best. But when summer turned into fall, they were not able to maintain a worry-free facade. When Grangaard spoke with them by phone, she often could not keep back tears.

Her father thought that holding on to a waitress job was not the best way to pursue her job search. He did not want to apply pressure on her or lecture her, so he had Grangaard's mother deliver his advice secondhand, in the form of a gentle suggestion for her consideration: your father thinks it would be better if you took a regular nine-to-five office job, even if it was nothing more than a receptionist position in a dentist's office. Grangaard did not agree. She wanted to have her days free for job interviews, which her nights-and-weekends work schedule at the restaurant provided. She did not accept the suggestion.

Her father also set up a meeting for her with the head of the Stanford Alumni Association, someone who had been in his class at

Stanford and who could give her some career advice that would not be tainted by coming from a parental unit. She told him about the jobs that she had been applying for and confessed to feeling discouraged and run down. He told her parents that he did not understand why she was looking for just any job rather than focusing only on the jobs that she would love. He also said that she sounded passionless, which, when her parents relayed this to her, came as a shock. She thought of herself as buoyant, energetic, full of passion. It was hard for her to hear this, but it impelled her to start looking hard for a job in the arts. She worked her personal network; did informational interviews; and, eventually, one year after graduating, got a toehold, an unpaid internship working in the office of San Francisco Performances, which put on music recitals and dance performances. As the internship concluded seven months later, an officemate there mentioned that the Cypress String Quartet was looking for a part-time, two-days-a-week coordinator, and she got that position, which was also in San Francisco.

Grangaard was "working in the arts," but it was office work, not creative work, and the pay was so low that she had to continue to work nearly full time at the restaurant to supplement. When she was not at one of the two jobs, she looked for a full-time job in the arts.

The coordinator position for the Cypress String Quartet entailed fundraising, public relations, and marketing, and quickly expanded to four days a week, so she found she was working seven days a week at either one job or the other or sometimes both. On top of the hours, driving back and forth between her office job in San Francisco and her restaurant job in Palo Alto was exhausting. After five months of long daily commutes, every day of the week, she decided it was unsustainable and gave notice at the restaurant. She had been there for two years and seven months, but it was work experience that was not going to lead to a job that would put her college education to good use.

Just after she gave notice, she was offered a full-time position at the Cypress String Quartet. When Grangaard had started there she was one of three who composed the tiny staff of the Cypress Performing Arts Association. But the executive director had died and the associate director left, and only she remained. The catch was this: promotion to full time did not bring a significant increase in pay or recognition. The Quartet simply added more hours to her schedule, while keeping her minimum-wage hourly rate intact. She gulped: she was making less than a babysitter. It was not enough to live on.

What kept her going was her belief that the position would give her connections in the art world that would lead to something better—something that would actually provide a subsistence wage. Everyone had said, "Once you get a foot in the door—" but her foot had been jammed in the Quartet's door for more than a year and a real job had not materialized.

The closest she got to a job that she wanted, or at least it seemed tantalizingly close, was a dream job: at Pixar. She got an interview not from being at Cypress, however, but from working a network chain that began with meeting someone who knew one of her father's former colleagues who put her in touch with someone at Pixar who was willing to do an informational interview with her over the phone. That led to a referral to someone else at Pixar, with actual authority to hire, who set up a phone interview with her. The phone interview apparently went well: Grangaard was invited to Pixar for an on-site interview. This is when her hopes climbed. "I really wanted it. I would still work for Pixar in a heartbeat," she says. "But there are a lot of people who'd work for Pixar in a heartbeat." She did not get a job offer.

With the distance of four years separating the present from this moment in her job search history, she says she was not nearly as close to getting the job as she had thought at the time. She thinks she was given the on-site interview "because I was a young, passionate, smart person from Stanford—that was probably 40 percent of it"—but the other 60 percent was because of the referral from the manager with whom she had done the informational interview. Getting help from a referral is instrumental if you are the perfect candidate for a job.

But if you're not the perfect person for the position, she says, "you probably weren't as close as you thought you were."

In summer 2012, more than three years after she had graduated, Grangaard realized that the time had come when she should start looking outside of the arts. One night she went to dinner at the apartment of an old Stanford friend, where the conversation with the friend and with his girlfriend that evening would result in a life-changing turn for Grangaard. The friend was a year ahead of Grangaard, Class of 2008, an engineering major with a specialization in architectural design. She says she would never have met him at Stanford were it not for the Band. He was the drum major and part of the same traveling unit that went to basketball games. Grangaard remembers, years later, the shared experience in which the two got to know each other well, on a Band road trip to Texas, leaving at midnight and not stopping until the next night. The long conversations in the car were their bonding moment, she says.

When he graduated, he had gotten a job with an architecture firm but decided to leave the field. After resigning, he traveled a bit, and then, unemployed, he moved into the house where Grangaard was renting. Both were looking for work. They followed a routine together, anchored by their doing a Sixty-Day Workout as workout buddies: upon waking up, they'd do the day's workout together, make lunch, and then park themselves at their laptops and look for jobs for the next five hours. In 2011, the housemates went separate ways.

When Grangaard went over to the apartment where her friend now lived with his girlfriend in 2012, the friend was no longer unemployed. He had gotten a job at Meraki, a small startup that sold Wi-Fi systems that could be used to cover large areas with interconnected Wi-Fi hotspots; the Meraki networks were managed remotely, in the cloud, a then-novel arrangement.[5] He had gotten the job with the help of a friend connection from the Band who was already working at Meraki. Grangaard's friend now was a manager, overseeing a team of support engineers.

Grangaard had no thought of seeking a job at Meraki herself when she arrived for dinner that evening. But when her friend-hosts asked her about how her coordinator job with the Cypress Performing Arts Association was going, she told them that she was frustrated for many reasons and had recently resolved to look outside of the arts world for a new job. Here, serendipity enters. Or, as labor economists say, she learned of a job vacancy by informal methods. The team at Meraki in which her friend worked was growing rapidly, and he had heard his immediate boss say that it was reaching the point where it needed a coordinator to help manage the team's hiring. Her friend offered to speak with his boss and see if a position might be available.

The dinner was on a Sunday evening. On Tuesday, her friend emailed Grangaard a job description; Grangaard wrote back, sending her résumé and expressing her interest in an emailed cover letter. On Thursday, she was invited for an interview the next day. She went in for the interview and was offered the position on the spot. She had the offer letter in hand the next Monday to start immediately. This is how quickly the hiring process can go at a startup. For the new hire, it's a whirlwind. The only drawback is that *immediately* does mean immediately. Grangaard gave Cypress two weeks' notice, but after her last day there, she had to start at Meraki the very next work day.

It was August 2012, and Grangaard was Meraki employee #286.[6] Her title was team coordinator for the Technical Support Team, which was the group that provided phone support when a user had trouble with the Meraki Wi-Fi network.

At the time she was hired, her boss, the director of support, was handling the recruiting for the group, but he could not give it the attention it needed. As coordinator, Grangaard was charged with creating a process for, and then overseeing, the recruiting. She experienced déjà vu: she set up procedures for posting job openings on a selected set of college job boards—precisely what she had done four years earlier at Target, as a summer intern who had been given, it was clear now, real responsibilities.

The team at Meraki that she joined fielded calls from customers who were themselves not technical people and who were using Meraki's free trial offer. Unlike the network engineers at Meraki, who had no contact with civilians, the support team's free-trial-support engineers had to be able to translate networking vocabulary into easy-to-understand language for these customers. The team also had to be more "sales-y," as Grangaard phrases it, than the network engineers because her team also was expected to convert the free-trial users into paying customers. The conversion rate was the primary yardstick used to measure the team's performance.

Grangaard found that she worked well with the support engineers. She knew she had a natural facility with language, but she also credits her humanities courses at Stanford for giving her an ear for how words come across, helping her contribute to improving the ways in which the technical team worked with its nontechnical constituents. "The engineers don't always, in my experience—" she pauses, "it's a very blanket generalization," and then resumes, "Their communication style is a little bit different; they're not really thinking in the same way about communication or about words as I am."

Four months after Grangaard started, networking giant Cisco announced that it was acquiring Meraki for $1.2 billion.[7] Her life at work did not change after the acquisition, however. A few months later, seeking a role that would expand her repertoire of skills beyond the recruiting function, she secured a program manager position, handling technical training programs for Cisco Meraki resellers, and then more senior positions.

She felt fortunate for having landed at Meraki when she did, early enough that the company's continued growth opened up opportunities for her to rise quickly. Two-and-a-half years after she joined, the company had grown to such an extent that it felt to her that she was among the longer-tenured employees.

Grangaard also felt fortunate that she happened to visit her old friend from the Band when she did, and the opening at Meraki came up organically. She says she would not have contacted him to see about openings because on her own she did not imagine that there might be a place for her in the tech world. The story of her gaining the entry level position at Meraki ultimately should be traced back to the friendship she had developed in the Stanford Band years earlier.

Grangaard's story nicely illustrates the continued importance of a decades-old finding made by sociologist Mark Granovetter, who investigated in depth how personal contacts did or did not help individuals get new professional, technical, or managerial positions.[8] In research undertaken in 1969, Granovetter (who later joined the Stanford faculty in 1995) found not only that his subjects' networks of social contacts—relatives, friends, and acquaintances—were the way a majority of the new jobs in those professional occupations were found,[9] but, more surprising, it was the acquaintances, not closest friends, who were most useful in job searches because the acquaintances were the ones who were "more likely to move in circles different from and beyond our own."[10] He called the phenomenon "the strength of weak ties."[11]

Elise Grangaard found her job not from closest friends, and not from posted job notices, but from someone who would seem unlikely to be helpful: a friend she hadn't seen in a while. For humanities majors seeking work in a marketplace that fails to evince interest in their majors, the ties to acquaintances can prove to be not just strong but a godsend. But obtaining an entry-level job is nothing more than obtaining an opportunity to do well. Genuine success requires, once on the job, learning quickly, the ability strengthened by the courses taken to complete a humanities major.

CHAPTER 14

THE SHINY NEW THING

THE ASCENSION OF COMPUTER SCIENCE in recent years may seem foreordained, the perfect expression of "a practical education." But its rise to the preeminent position at Stanford—it is now the most popular undergraduate major—has been rather sudden. In 2009, only 75 graduates majored in computer science, and the multidisciplinary human biology was the favorite major, with 227. But by 2012, the number of declared computer science majors eclipsed those in human biology, and in 2014, 214 graduates majored in computer science, almost triple the number of five years earlier.[1] Enrollment has continued to swell since then, catching the department by surprise and forcing the faculty to scramble to provide enough course sections to handle demand.[2]

This state of affairs contrasts starkly with the years when the university was first getting acquainted with computers and no department of computer science existed. The beginning was in 1953, when Stanford acquired an IBM Card Programmed Electronic Calculator and established the "Computation Center" to serve everyone at the university who wanted to use the machine. The programming was accomplished by physically rewiring the machine, connecting short patch cords into the sockets of a plug board.[3]

The Computation Center acquired a second machine in 1956, and the next year, the mathematics department appointed as professor George Forsythe, an applied mathematics PhD who had had

wide experience with computers at Boeing and at the National Bureau of Standards. Forsythe had cut his computing teeth on a machine that had a capacity of only 256 words and was so unreliable
that every program had to be run twice—the results were accepted
only if the two runs produced identical output.[4] But Forsythe could
see what the machines would be capable of one day and was an energetic proselytizer of computing.

In a talk that Forsythe gave in 1961 at a meeting of the American
Association for the Advancement of Science, he said,

> Those of us who work with automatic digital computers suffer from
> a certain megalomania. We consider that we are not merely work-
> ing in an area of great importance—we insist that we are instru-
> ments of a revolution—the Computer Revolution. We consider
> that the revolution is destined to exceed the Industrial Revolution
> in its impact, and that moreover it is coming off a whole lot faster.[5]

Occupations that entailed little more than information-gathering
and routine decision-making would disappear as computers took
over those roles, Forsythe foresaw. Higher education was called
upon to provide specialized training that would not be susceptible
to automation. Courses should also be developed, he proposed, in
"computer appreciation," which "would be designed to acquaint
nontechnical students with the meaning of computers in today's
world, without making them technical experts."[6]

The course in computer appreciation did not materialize, but the
department of mathematics expanded course offerings in the new
field.[7] In 1961, the department established a separate division of
computer science, which enjoyed autonomy in deciding on new hires;
it was headed by Forsythe.[8]

In the early years of computer science, some faculty members,
including Forsythe, believed a good case could be made to leave
computer science in the same school that serves as liberal education's
home. In his 1961 talk, Forsythe noted "the abstract nature" of com-

puter science that "makes it attractive to students who are attracted by Mathematics, by Physics, and by Philosophy."[9]

When Forsythe sent the dean of the School of Humanities and Sciences, Robert R. Sears, the text of his talk, he said that computing should serve "to bring the sciences, social sciences, and humanities together." This potential had not been fulfilled, he observed, and the impact of computing on the humanities in particular was still slight. Forsythe saw opportunities to use computers in linguistics and musicology, but a Stanford colleague, a professor of modern European languages, told him that most of his humanities colleagues "prefer 'stone age tools.'"[10]

In 1962, Forsythe proposed a new course, Computing for Non-science Students (Computer Science 139). He wrote the dean, "Too many students of the humanities and even social sciences are frightened by computers, and especially by science students taking Computer Science 136 [Use of Automatic Digital Computers]. We need a way to isolate the non-science students and make computers accessible to them."[11] The university made clear that it was in no hurry to plan for a bachelor's degree in computer science because it was then viewed as a form of "professional" education, which did not fall within the bailiwick of the School of Humanities and Sciences.[12]

As long as computer science remained housed in a sub-department division, it could award a doctorate only in mathematics. Forsythe lobbied the administration to upgrade the computer science division to a department. He knew the administration would not want to be seen as falling behind other institutions, and he let everyone within hearing know which universities were adding such departments or were rumored to be contemplating doing so.[13] Finally, the administration acquiesced, and the division was spun off into a separate department in 1965.[14] It remained in the same school as mathematics: Humanities and Sciences.[15]

In this nascent stage of the field's life, computer science had not been appropriated by engineering. Nor was CS competing with other disciplines for majors: when Stanford created the department, it could only grant master's degrees and doctorates; there were no CS majors. CS was not a pipeline to a profession—it was a field that would serve all others.[16]

In the meantime, Stanford students flocked to the early courses, even though the courses did not belong to a professional track.[17] By 1965, the introductory CS course was described by Forsythe as having grown into "one of the most popular courses at Stanford,"[18] which is all the more remarkable considering the absence of a CS major. In 1969, Forsythe estimated that 40 percent of Stanford's undergraduates took at least one CS course, and he wondered aloud how the university could get the other half of the undergraduate student body acquainted with computing.[19]

What the advent of computers would mean to life at Stanford was much on the mind of the provost at that very moment. The provost's computer committee was investigating the computing needs of humanities departments for the next three to five years and toward that end had distributed a questionnaire for faculty members in those departments. In the Department of History, it fell to an assistant professor, Lyman Van Slyke, to attempt to persuade his colleagues to fill it out.[20] (In the cover letter that Van Slyke sent them, he explained, "An injudicious opening of the mouth at a recent Department meeting left the questionnaire in my hands.")[21]

"Most faculty members in the humanities react to computers in terms of *1984*," Van Slyke said, or as machines for accounting or arithmetic operations, of no use to historians. He explained that they were general-purpose information-handling machines that could do many things, such as storing research notes, substituting for 3-by-5 note cards. The machines could make certain kinds of research feasible that had not been practical before. They could also help with instruction, going well beyond merely drilling students to providing introductory courses in languages, mathematics, and other disciplines.

Van Slyke knew that his appreciation for the capabilities of the machines, though greater than that of most of his departmental colleagues, still paled compared with that of colleagues in the computer science department and at the university's Computation Center, where one found "a kind of missionary zeal toward the lesser breeds," he said. "Without trying to associate myself with their effort to propagate the faith," he continued equably, "it seems clear to me that if you are having problems with control of information—any kind of information—then the computer may be able to help."[22]

When George Forsythe died in 1979 at the age of fifty-five, the university lost the forceful voice of one of the national pioneers in computer science education. In Forsythe's absence, support for a CS major at Stanford sprang up in an unlikely place on campus: the admissions office. In 1983, Fred Hargadon, the dean of admissions, suggested in an internal memo to the dean of Humanities and Sciences that Stanford establish an undergraduate major in CS so that it did not lose strong applicants who indicated an interest. "Many of our brightest applicants (and by that I mean exceptionally able *across the board*) are, when asked, now indicating a 'major' interest in Computer Science. . . . Presumably such applicants have read our bulletin and know we do not offer an undergraduate major in Computer Science, but given Stanford's reputation in the field, they may have in mind either (a) taking what they can in that field if admitted, or (b) having us as a second-choice option to one or another other college to which they have applied and which does offer such a major."[23]

Hargadon did not envision moving the computer science department out of Humanities and Sciences. "I think our engineering is as attractive as it is at least in part because it is set within a liberal arts University. I think an undergraduate major in Computer Science would be equally attractive for the same reason," he wrote.[24] Hargadon soon got his wish—the major was introduced in 1985— but only after the department was moved over to engineering.

The new major did not immediately attract large numbers of students. Ten years after the move, in 1995, only fifty-one students majored in CS, about the same number as in history and half the number that majored in English. With the dot-com boom in the late 1990s, the department's enrollment grew—in the graduating class of 2001, it more than doubled to 127—but when the tech bubble burst, enrollment fell back.

The idea that an undergraduate should major in computer science became mainstream only recently: in the wake of the financial crisis of 2008. Finance lost its allure, and the beneficiary was computer science. But the shift could be said to have been prepared by a secular decline in the social science majors. Over the course of thirty years, social science majors at Stanford declined in number from about 37 percent of bachelor's degrees in 1986 to 14 percent in 2016. During the same period, engineering majors increased in number from about 28 percent in 1986 to 37 percent in 2016. (Among males alone, the percentage in 2016 reached an astounding 48 percent.)[25] This was far higher than the corresponding average of 10 percent of their cohorts that engineering majors occupied in 2014 at the Ivy League schools and others that Stanford viewed as its peers, leaving aside the two engineering-centered institutions of MIT (60 percent) and CalTech (54 percent).[26] At a meeting of the faculty senate in 2016 in which he presented this data, Russell Berman, a professor of German studies and comparative literature, remarked about the 37 percent figure, "Right now we are effectively half way to Caltech from Princeton, which is one way to think about it." He had heard colleagues describe this position as a "sweet spot," but without agreeing or disagreeing, he pointed out, "I think this implies a change in how we think about ourselves as an institution."[27]

The growth of engineering majors was primarily made up of computer science majors.[28] The attraction of computer science was not only visible in the number of CS majors but also in the growth of a smaller interdisciplinary major, which had been established in 1986, called symbolic systems. SymSys, as students called it, centered on the human-computer relationship and on artificial intelligence, and required a number of CS classes. It also incorporated classes in linguistics, philosophy, psychology, communications, statistics, and education. In the class of 2016, Stanford had 277 CS majors (compared with 215 the year before and 51 twenty years earlier in 1995) and 65 in SymSys (compared with 38 the year before and 16 in 1995).[29]

A contemporaneous decline on the humanities side over twenty years should be noted to provide a sense of proportion, even if not as severe as the drop in majors in the social sciences. In 2016, there were 46 English majors (compared with 104 in 1995) and 37 history majors (50 in 1995).

What grew even more dramatically than the number of CS majors was the number of students who took the introductory CS courses. The Programming Methodology course, CS 106, had been renamed CS 106A and became the most heavily enrolled course on the entire campus: approximately 90 percent of undergraduates took the course.[30] "It felt really cool to be a part of something so big," said a freshman student interviewed by the school paper in 2013 who had taken the course. The same student also recalled the first day of class, when every seat in the room, the second largest classroom on campus, was occupied and students who had failed to get seats stood along the walls and others were seated in the aisles, until the fire marshal arrived and ordered those without seats to leave.[31]

In a quarter in which 650 students were enrolled in CS 106A, as in fall 2012, the department had to arrange sixty-five small-group sections to complement the lectures.[32] Staffing so many could not be done by relying on graduate students alone; undergraduates who were CS majors were hired for this purpose as well. These arrangements for teaching on a mass scale also had to be made for a second computer science course, which was almost as popular: Programming Abstractions, CS 106B, which was the course that followed in the introductory sequence.[33]

Mehran Sahami, a professor of computer science,[34] argued that the hordes of Stanford students that his department was attracting each quarter were well-served. "It's somewhat of a misnomer to say that an education in computing is not a liberal education," he said in 2013. "I think the fact that everyone needs to know something about computing these days makes them a well-rounded person. If you didn't know anything about computing, that'd be a little bit odd in the 21st century."[35]

In 2015, the Stanford alumni magazine published an essay by Marisa Messina, a Stanford student who had just completed a double major in symbolic systems and French. The essay was titled "Content to Code? Straddling Silicon Valley's Techie-Fuzzie Divide." Messina arrived at Stanford without any programming experience. When she heard fellow students talking incessantly about "CS" during freshman orientation activities, she did not know what the letters referred to until she asked. She went on to take a number of CS courses for her symbolic systems major, and though she said that "I can't say I have found that experience particularly enjoyable," and she does not imagine that she will be a professional programmer, she does credit the courses for instilling the ability to decompose a problem into smaller, manageable subproblems, an ability that "has boundless applications well beyond the technical." Computer science taught her how to think clearly when tackling a stubborn problem. "When the going gets tough," she said, "the answer is often to reframe the problem."[36]

Messina was not comfortable, however, with the way the people she met at Stanford and in the San Francisco Bay Area seemed to her to value highly her technical major, symbolic systems, but not her nontechnical one, French. "When I introduce myself as a 'sym syser' [symbolic systems major] to fellow students and local professions, the smiles are warmer and the conversations more respectful than when I mention only my French degree," she wrote. "Is being tech-savvy becoming synonymous with being seen as a worthy human?"[37] Dylan Sweetwood, an English major who graduated in 2015, had even stronger criticism of the CS-centric campus:

> Everyone does CS 106A, everyone knows at least how to code this much. There's not "everyone does Phil 100, everyone does Fem Studies 101." Everyone should—those are important classes that teach you really important basic concepts for living your life as a decent person.[38]

Sweetwood elected to take a nonprogramming computer science class, Introduction to Computers (CS 105), to fulfill the one-course distribution requirement in some area of engineering. He was skeptical that he would need to know the Java programming language for any job that he anticipated wanting after graduation. One could say that even if he had taken 106A, the one course would hardly have made him a software developer in the eyes of a prospective employer. The Department of Computer Science viewed Programming Methodology CS 106A as so elementary that the course did not fulfill any requirements for the major. A student had to reach the successor course, Programming Abstractions CS 106B, to get started on the requirements.

If knowing "something about computers these days" is an indispensable component of a liberal education, would it be sufficient if the "something" was simple web-page design, which was covered in the Introduction to Computing class that Sweetwood took? Or did it require programming? And if programming was essential, how many concepts and how many programming problems needed to be solved before the student gained the proficiency that Marisa Messina spoke of in breaking down large problems, of any kind, into smaller, more tractable ones?

In 2015, New York City Mayor Bill de Blasio threw his office behind the notion that computer science, encompassing coding as well as web design and robotics, should be in the curriculum at all levels of K–12 education. He announced a new initiative that promised to provide all 1.1 million students in the city with "computer science education."[39]

The announcement drew a derisive response from Jeff Atwood, a professional programmer who is well-known to software developers for, among various accomplishments, cofounding Stack Overflow, the much-visited question-and-answer website for programmers. In an opinion piece that he published shortly after the de Blasio announcement, he took aim at the foundational assumptions underlying the case for computer science for everyone. His target was de Blasio's initiative for K–12 education, but the same criticisms could apply to the contention that programming should be treated as an essential element of a college education:

> If someone tells you "coding is the new literacy" because "computers are everywhere today," ask them how fuel injection works. By teaching low-level coding, I worry that we are effectively teaching our children the art of automobile repair. A valuable skill—but if automobile manufacturers and engineers are doing their jobs correctly, one that shouldn't be of much concern for average people, who happily use their cars as tools to get things done without ever needing to worry about rebuilding the transmission or even [changing] the oil.[40]

Atwood said he had no objection to giving students some exposure to computer science, but he could not advocate making room for that exposure if it meant less attention to fundamental skills. "I've known so many programmers who would have been much more successful in their careers if they had only been better writers, better critical thinkers, better back-of-the-envelope estimators, better communicators," he wrote. He did not use the word *humanities*, but the most direct way to prepare college students to be better writers and thinkers and estimators and communicators is to have them spend more time studying the humanities.

Stanford's deans and some of its faculty members in the humanities would say that Stanford students need not choose one over the other. In 2014, Stanford's computer science department reached out to the humanities and inaugurated in 2014 a program, "CS+X," to offer students the option of jointly majoring in computer science and in a humanities discipline, with slightly reduced degree requirements in both majors. Backers of the initiative pointed to the results of a survey conducted by the computer science department in 2012–13 that showed students would be more likely to double major if the number of classes required for each major was reduced by two classes.[41] Before CS+X, some students with an interest in both a humanities discipline and computer science could pursue a double major with symbolic systems taking the place of computer science; SymSys required fewer units than CS, making the double major more attainable.[42]

Another option for students with dual interests in the humanities and CS that preceded CS+X was spending a fifth year at Stanford "coterming," in which the student simultaneously worked on the requirements for both a bachelor's degree and a master's degree. Jess Peterson, Class of 2013, who majored in history and cotermed in CS, may have seemed on paper to fit the profile of the ideal student candidate likely to be interested in the CS+X joint degree program, had it been in place when he was an undergraduate. But Peterson disliked the program's assumption that CS and the humanities should be brought together. To Peterson, history and CS had distinct ways of thinking about the world; the CS+X capstone course would only force a synthesis that diminished what was distinctive about history, a domain of unstructured, real-world information to which he was unapologetically attracted. He would cheer the CS+X initiative on if it led more students to take regular humanities courses, rather than hybrids. He also granted that it might help some students blunt the objections of parents to their majoring in the humanities, but that was praise of the faintest sort.[43]

The computer science department did not want anyone to mistakenly think that the requirements for the CS+X joint degree were no greater than that for a single degree, expecting only half of the normal requirements for CS and half for the humanities portion. "It's more like 90 percent of one and 90 percent of the other," Jennifer Widom, the department chair, said in 2014.[44] When the capstone project was included in the accounting, CS+X did not greatly reduce the work that would have been entailed had the student opted for dual, separate majors in the two areas. And CS+X did not address the other, larger deterrent to a dual major entailing CS and a humanities major: the scarcity of students who are able to enjoy working in two disparate realms, handling their heavy demands simultaneously. Coterming permits a sequencing—first the one, then the other—that removes the problem of drilling deeply in two widely separated shafts at the same time, using entirely different tools.

In the Class of 2014, among the fifty-five students who majored in English, eleven, or one out of every five, did a dual major, which suggests the workload alone was not so onerous. But six of the eleven of the dual majors encompassed the humanities—one in art history, one in art practice, one in French, one in drama, one in history, and one in American studies. Four were in the social sciences (one each in sociology, economics, international relations, and psychology), and one was in the sciences (biology). None encompassed computer science or engineering of any variety. The forty-five history majors that year show a similar pattern: twelve did dual majors, the majority were in the humanities, and none were in computer science or engineering.[45]

The English department did not dwell on the dearth of students who were comfortably bilingual in the languages of both the humanities and CS. The department's website presented prospective CS+English students with a brassy declaration that made the very notion of different realms seem quaint: "Left-brained, right-brained, techie, fuzzy—these are less and less terms for the world or for life. Stanford is excited to be launching a new CS+English joint major for students who want to think across the divide and create projects that fuse science and the humanities."[46]

The question is not whether students exist who would *like* to think across the divide but whether there are students who will be able to do so if they have not done so all along, beginning well before they arrive at college. And if they are not able to handle advanced coursework in both realms, is that as unfortunate as it is made out to be? As well-meaning as the backers of CS+X are, their advocacy also tacitly embodies a criticism of students who major in a single humanities field. A line has been drawn by CS advocates that assumes that facility with computer science is what prepares college graduates for this unquestioned desideratum, "the twenty-first century." But there is nothing new about invidious comparisons between the apparently practical and the apparently impractical. In the 1890s and early 1900s, Stanford students who chose English, history, philosophy, languages, and other humanities fields for their majors over engineering could have been painted as ill-prepared for the twentieth century. The difference between then and now is the erosion of what might be called the self-confidence of the liberal arts, the humanities in particular, worn down by the dramatic rise of computer science.

CHAPTER 15

FIRST GEN

MIKE SANCHEZ grew up in Jacksonville, North Carolina, a small city of seventy thousand that sits near a military base and the coast. Neither of his parents had gone to college, and Sanchez gently ignored their advice for him about the schools he should look at. When he was admitted to Stanford, his parents knew nothing about the university's reputation, but Sanchez had no hesitation in accepting. When he graduated in 2012, having majored in East Asian Studies, he moved through several jobs, at each one determining it was in his interest to move on when his parents counseled him to stay where he was.

Sanchez arrived at Stanford thinking of a future in medicine. During spring break his freshman year, he went to Guatemala to work on an international health project. That summer he spent five weeks in India working on a leadership-training project with emergency medical technicians. In the summer following his sophomore year, he worked in the MBA office at Stanford, thinking that the administrative experience would look good on his medical school applications. It was that summer, however, that his plans blew up: he realized he did not want to go to medical school. But if medicine was not his future, what was? He had no idea—and only two years of college remaining in which to prepare. He took a leave of absence from Stanford the fall quarter of his junior year to figure out what to do.

For the new plan, Sanchez decided to study what he called a "critical" language: either Arabic or Mandarin. In the end, he decided to study Mandarin, figuring that there would be business opportunities in addition to government jobs. No one seems to have told him that a smattering of Mandarin would not open up to him future business opportunities—anyone knowledgeable about Sino-U.S. business ties would have told him that only genuine fluency in Mandarin could possibly be competitive in the labor marketplace, filled with bilingually fluent speakers. But decisions about career paths are not always made with perfect information.

Sanchez also composed this plan before he had taken a single quarter of Mandarin. His parents thought this was a strange plan. His father spoke Spanish, but Sanchez did not. Why not learn Spanish, his parents suggested? He pushed on, undeterred. He wanted to major in Chinese, but that would require three years of language study, and he had less than two years at Stanford to do so. So he declared East Asian Studies as his major, which only required two years' equivalency of language study and could be accomplished by doing first-year Mandarin in an intensive program the following summer: five weeks on Stanford's campus, then four weeks in Beijing. In his senior year he continued with Mandarin, and in his final quarter he returned to Beijing for the study-abroad experience required by the major that the earlier visit did not fulfill.

East Asian Studies was an interdisciplinary major that did not draw many students. It allowed students to assemble an assortment of courses that pertained to either China, Japan, or Korea, but without great depth. Only six students in Sanchez's graduation cohort chose it.

Sanchez applied for post-graduate jobs while in Beijing. He started off applying for translator jobs but soon realized his language skills were well short of what would be required. He was not well-positioned to pursue other opportunities, however. Seeking jobs in the United States while living in Beijing was not ideal, even if he could use Skype for job interviews. He did not have personal networks or family connections that would be helpful. He had not been a member of a fraternity whose network he could draw upon. And his prior internship had not been with a prospective employer. He had to rely upon the jobs aggregator site Indeed.com and Stanford's own job board. He received two offers: one was to be a program assistant at a nonprofit in Washington, DC, and the other was to be an administrative associate in Stanford's Office of Government and Community Relations. The nonprofit job paid less than the Stanford job and moving expenses would have been entirely his to assume, so he took the job at Stanford. Upon hearing the news, his parents were delighted: "It's at Stanford!" Sanchez did his best to explain that it was not the plum job that they thought; it was nothing more than a lowly administrative assistant position.

Sanchez got an apartment in San Francisco and took the train down to Palo Alto, coming in to do undemanding office work, tinkering with PowerPoint presentations or printing out paperwork. After three months, he was determined to look for something else; living in the Bay Area, he could not help but search for a way into tech. While at Stanford, he had not taken Programming Methodology CS 106A, the introduction to programming class. He had instead taken CS 105, Introduction to Computers, a course whose only prerequisite was "minimal math skills." He knew, however, that tech companies had non-engineering roles, and he hoped to secure one for himself. The first step he took was to pull out his phone and ask himself what apps he used the most. Those tech companies would be where he started his search for entry-level jobs in tech: Google, Facebook, Quora. He also applied at an education startup for a position as a "recruiter coordinator," which handles scheduling and other assistant-like chores for the recruiters, who are the ones who actually contact prospects. He did not know anything about recruiting and did not get the job. But afterward the recruiter emailed him, complimenting him for the enthusiasm he displayed in the interview and offering to teach him how to "source," if he'd like to work for the startup she was working on in her spare time. Sanchez was interested and sat down with her for about ninety minutes, learning the rudiments of sourcing—finding the candidates that recruiters contact—and how to assemble complexly worded online searches.

Sanchez would not end up working for her because he found an opening elsewhere. He had recently done an Airbnb stay, so Airbnb had been added to his list of possibilities. When he visited Airbnb's website and discovered that Airbnb had a three-month internship program, he applied and swiftly got an interview. He talked about his international travel experiences, which included travel in China after his Stanford summer-language program ended, and said he wished he had been able to use Airbnb instead of student hostels. He got the internship, and much later his supervisor told him the reasons she had selected him: "You come from North Carolina, you're the first person in your family to go to college, you learned Chinese, and you went to Stanford. You're obviously smart. You could pick up the skills for an internship."

Sanchez's parents were not pleased about his decision to do the internship. They urged him to stay at Stanford, where he earned a decent salary and had university-provided benefits, including health insurance. Why give that up for a short internship, which paid less, provided no benefits, and replaced the security of a job at Stanford with uncertainty? "Sometimes, you've got to take a step down to take a step up," Sanchez told them, a maxim he would repeat to himself and follow more than once.

When he arrived at Airbnb, he was assigned to a group in sales that was charged with expanding the number of properties listed on Airbnb's site. Sanchez was asked to search online for prospective properties, find the owners' contact information, and pass on the information to the salespeople who would make calls. It was a form of sourcing that did not involve evaluating humans and did not require much time to master, and for the same reason was work that was not intrinsically interesting. But it provided Sanchez with a way in, and, with luck, an opportunity to be noticed and offered a permanent position in the company.

As his three-month internship neared the end, he became increasingly nervous, wondering if he would be "converted" into a regular employee. He did not foresee what would turn out to be the opportunity that changed his professional life. One Saturday, he was eating at a restaurant when he received an email message, which had gone out to everyone in the company, asking if anyone was free to fill in at a recruiting event for LGBT undergrads that Airbnb was participating in with other tech companies later that day.[1] One of the Airbnb volunteers had just gotten sick and a replacement was needed. Sanchez texted the organizer immediately: "Oh, my God! I'd love to help." The companies at these events were recruiting engineering majors, and Sanchez knew nothing about the technical qualifications that Airbnb would be looking for. But he offered to talk about LGBT issues and Airbnb as a workplace where employees could be their authentic selves. He was invited to come along.

The Airbnb team set up its table, and Sanchez honed a short spiel: "I don't know anything about our engineering stack, but I can talk to you about the culture of Airbnb." Looking back, he says that the students with whom he spoke seemed receptive. At the end of the event, the head of the Airbnb contingent, who was a recruiter who had worked previously for Google in that role, complimented Sanchez for working well with the prospects. "Have you ever considered recruiting?" she asked him. He told her he would very much like to explore any suitable openings. He went home, checked Airbnb's jobs website and found openings for a recruiter and a sourcer, and asked his new patron on the recruiting team whether he would be suitable for either. She said he might be best for sourcing and was about to show him the basics of sourcing when he interrupted her— "I learned a little bit about sourcing before"—and presented her with profiles of ten candidates that he had found. "Do these look good to you?" Impressed, she had Airbnb hire him as a sourcer on a trial basis for three months to see whether his work would lead his employer to at least one candidate who would be hired. His sourcing did land one new hire, and he was given a permanent position, as one of three sourcers who worked with six recruiters, the team that did technical recruiting at Airbnb.

This group recruited software engineers, but none of the sourcers had a degree in computer science. This was typically the case in Silicon Valley companies. The professional background of the recruiting team's most experienced members was simply recruiting at other tech companies or for agencies whose clients were those same companies. Sanchez describes what companies look for when hiring recruiters: "People that can pick it up and that have a good personality and can talk with candidates."

When Sanchez joined Airbnb in spring 2013, there were fewer than two hundred employees, a size that still felt intimate. Airbnb was not yet well-known, and persuading engineers to join the startup, or even persuading them to spend a few minutes on the phone to talk about the opportunities at Airbnb, was a challenge. In those days, Sanchez says, the only way Airbnb was able to hire the software engineers it most wanted was for the recruiter to find an Airbnb engineer who would serve as the company's liaison, whose professional interests matched perfectly with those of the candidate, and who had a personality that would put the candidate at ease. As time passed and Airbnb's valuation increased, prospects did not need to be sold on Airbnb; they thought of stock options that likely would be worth a great deal of money and were eager to talk, too eager, their attention focused on personal enrichment rather than the match of the open position to their skills.

Sanchez's position at Airbnb was at the sourcing end, and he was frustrated that he did not get to personally meet the candidates and engage in conversations with them when they came in for interviews, the end stage that makes recruiting more satisfying work than sourcing. By fall 2014, Airbnb had about twelve hundred employees, and Sanchez missed the intimate feel of the earlier days. When an offer to join a tiny startup came along, where he could do "full-cycle recruiting," that is, everything from sourcing to recruiting to presenting an offer letter, he jumped again. "A mistake!" his mother said. "I just heard mention of Airbnb on the news. You should stay there!"

He indeed should have stayed at Airbnb, he would later think, looking back. The startup he joined was Nextbit, a tiny software company that only had sixteen employees. It had been founded by engineers that had worked on the Android operating system and had raised an impressive sum, $18 million, at conception, to produce "mobile" software that it declined to describe publicly.[2] Sanchez was hired as its first and only recruiter. He got his wish to have his hands on all stages of the recruiting process. Just a year and a half after graduating—with an East Asian Studies major—he got to build an applicant tracking system, set up interview processes, and take on whatever challenges came up in the daily life of a startup, none of which he had had the opportunity to tackle before. He was increasingly disturbed by the company's apparent lack of direction, however. It seemed to him that no one knew what the company was doing. The elaborate recruiting apparatus that he built was ready for high-volume hiring, but Nextbit did not need many new bodies: over the course of eight months, it only grew from sixteen to twenty-one employees. Early on, Sanchez began to look around for a new job.

Just as he began to be restless, Google and Facebook simultaneously contacted him, asking about his interest in recruiter positions that they had for someone like him, who was now deemed an experienced recruiter. These companies had found him, he thinks, with a simple search on LinkedIn, where they looked for people that went to Stanford who had sourcing experience.

Google's hiring process was notoriously protracted. Once Sanchez had the initial phone interview, two months of follow-on phone and on-site interviews and lots of waiting passed before he received an offer. He had initially been offered a position on the sourcing team as a contractor, which was standard for Google. But Sanchez had demurred. A week later, Google got back in touch, telling him that a regular position was now open and he could apply to come on board as an employee, not as a contractor. When he joined the team, he discovered that he was the only member who had not had to pass through a probationary period as a contractor. "So when I came on, it was a little awkward," he said, a few weeks after starting. "It's still a little awkward. My manager told me two days ago, 'We really need you to prove yourself in the next month or two because people are really looking at you.'" "Ohhhh-kay!" he laughed.

Sanchez observed that his career as a sourcer had followed an unconventional sequence, beginning at a medium-sized tech company (Airbnb), followed by the short stint at a tiny startup (Nextbit), which, in turn, led to a leap to a giant company (Google). His parents, finally, were pleased. He teased his mother, "Do you like saying, 'My son, the Google person' or 'My son, the Airbnb person'?" Her reply: "Google!"

Sanchez could see why some Google employees found the organization too large to be amenable to change. He was used to work environments in which "you do whatever it takes to get the job done" and suggestions for improving processes were welcomed. At Google he felt as if offers to help others or suggestions for doing anything differently than it had been done were frowned upon. As he tried to settle in at Google, he looked back at his time at Airbnb with nostalgia and realized that his earlier dissatisfaction with what then had seemed Airbnb's large size—twelve hundred employees—reflected his lack of experience with truly large companies.

At Google, Sanchez no longer got to do "full-cycle" recruiting as he had at the startup; once again, he did only sourcing and handed off promising prospects to recruiters. He also faced long commutes to work. He lived in San Francisco and had not had to commute south when he worked at Airbnb and then at Nextbit. When he joined

Google, the trip down to Mountain View on the Google bus was a daily grind, forty-five minutes going down early in the morning and up to two or three hours on the return trip, depending on the vagaries of highway congestion. What he most enjoyed at Google were the introductory technical seminars for the recruiting team that Google provided, such as a one-hour presentation on cloud computing he attended, which told the team what to expect to see on résumés, enabling Sanchez to ask better questions when speaking with engineering prospects.

When he started at Google, Sanchez told himself that whenever he left Google, his résumé would get him in the door at the fastest-growing startups in the Valley. When at Nextbit, before he had added the Google association to his professional identity, he had applied for a position at Uber—and gotten nowhere. The fastest-growing startups, the Ubers, the Dropboxes, the Pinterests (Sanchez's boyfriend worked at Pinterest), simplify their search for people on their recruiting teams by considering only candidates who worked at Google or Facebook. It was also true at Airbnb, where Sanchez had been an inexperienced exception; the other recruiting team members had come from Google. The hot startups in San Francisco not only offered pre-IPO stock options, they also could eliminate, for the many employees who lived in San Francisco, the long commutes down to Facebook's campus or, even farther south, to Google's.

As soon as he joined Google, he heard from Stanford acquaintances whose career paths led them to places where they did not want to stay and who were searching for career advice. An acquaintance he met in his freshman year sent him an email with the opening, "I don't know if you remember me—" He had been at a startup, which had sunk, and now asked if they could get together for a chat. Sanchez met with him and kept in touch, offering him advice as the acquaintance faced job interviews.

Eight weeks after starting at Google, Sanchez had dinner with an old friend who was at Airbnb and, as it happened, had worked at

Google earlier. She knew why Sanchez was looking fondly at his ear-lier time at Airbnb. "Why don't you come back?" she asked. As soon as she said it, he felt like she had put into words what he was feeling without consciously realizing it. He then set up a coffee chat with his old manager at Airbnb, who was then the head of recruiting, and then with that manager's manager, and in a blink he was offered a position and accepted. Asked if his parents were sorry, he said, yes, at first. "'You're at Google! Why would you leave?' But then, when I told them the salary difference, they're like, 'OK, never mind,'" he said, laughing.

When Sanchez rejoined Airbnb in March 2015, he was a sourcer, just as he had been at Google, but he was able to do side projects, developing training programs for new hires, for example, and work-ing on a new program to promote greater diversity in tech. After a while, he became a full-cycle recruiter. After about a year, he real-ized Airbnb was becoming "more corporate," asking employees to stick to the responsibilities assigned in their core roles. It was what he had seen at Google, and at first it felt constraining to him. But he came to understand that he was asking work to be fulfilling in ways it shouldn't be, and he adjusted his expectations.

Sanchez was a liberal arts major at Stanford and proved agile in finding work in tech companies, beginning with a medium-sized one, then in the space of ten months trying out small and very large, and then returning to the medium-sized one. He undoubtedly was the sole East Asian Studies major among the recruiting teams he worked on. In college, Sanchez had done a crash course in Mandarin. After college, he undertook a self-directed crash course in software-engineering-speak, meeting with engineers to learn how to ask about front- and back-end systems, about Java and C++. In neither case did he approach fluency. But he picked up enough of the tech world's vocabulary to be able to work as a professional searcher of those who were fluent.

CHAPTER 16

THE ART OF LIVING

AT STANFORD, the Golden Age for the humanities in the contemporary era was in the 1960s, when more than a third of the undergraduates selected a major in the humanities. By 2011, the percentage had shrunk to 17 percent, about half of what it had been.[1] At that point, the humanities faculty stared at the approach of a most unhappy event: history and English were poised to drop out of the top ten list of majors, which would mark the first time in the university's history that a traditional humanities discipline was not on the list.[2]

At the department level, faculty members cast about for ideas to recapture student interest. The history department launched a new track, "Global Affairs and World History," offering students a set of courses that the department marketed as helpful to those planning on a career in business, government, or nongovernmental organizations. Stanford's umbrella division for several European and Latin American languages[3] and comparative literature, the Division of Literature, Cultures, and Languages, dangled research funding in front of students, offering to provide anyone who majored in any of its constituent departments financial support to go abroad and conduct research. Such was the desperation that the offer was extended to students who were merely minoring in one of the departments.[4]

Philippe Buc, a professor of history, publicly asked whether Stanford wished to be "CalTech North" or more like "our East Coast peers," such as Harvard, Yale, and Princeton, where humanities majors could be found aplenty. In a *Stanford Daily* opinion piece published in 2011, Buc wrote that Stanford's humanities departments "should stop moping about declining enrollments" and stop trying to increase numbers with ineffective gimmicks like throwing open houses for prospective majors. What was needed, he said, were more students who arrived at Stanford with an interest in the humanities. He had heard that only 15 percent of the university's high school applicants intended to major in the humanities, an abysmally low number that was "an iron barrier to higher enrollments." Buc proposed that the university's admissions office adjust its selection criteria so that 40 percent of the entering class, rather than 15 percent, were headed for a humanities discipline.[5] Some of his Stanford colleagues thought more matriculating students would have a strong interest in the humanities if Stanford simply recruited more aggressively on the East Coast, where more such students could be found, they believed.[6]

The humanities faculty knew that their departments were besieged by the same forces that ringed their colleagues at other universities. The principal one was the conviction that had taken hold of students and their parents that majors linked to professions were the only viable choices. But why had the once-wide appreciation of the usefulness of liberal education evaporated? It could not be fully explained as the expected reaction to the recession and the slow recovery that had followed; the decline in humanities majors had predated the recession and had been disturbingly steady over the decades since the Golden Age. The percentage of humanities majors at Stanford had drifted downward from the apogee of more than 33 percent in the 1960s to 24 percent in 1989.[7] During that time, increasing numbers of students were enrolling in engineering courses, particular in computer science. In 1983, Ralph Gorin, the director of the main computer facility for Stanford students, was reluctant to declare the shift permanent and advocate for shifting university resources to expand computer science. "We do not know if it is a long-term switch, or if the bubble will burst tomorrow and all students will want to major in history," Gorin said. "The University does not want to waste money on fads."[8]

Interest in computer science proved not to be a fad, however, and history and the other humanities continued to report declines in the number of majors. Only 21 percent of graduates in 1994 were humanities majors, and the percentage shrank to 17 percent in 2012.[9]

Some of the professors in the humanities expressed concern about the shift in student interest. In 2013, Jack Rakove, a historian who had won the Pulitzer Prize in history in 1997, said, "If you're a humanist, you really worry that we're churning out a large number of people who don't really know how to read a book and are historically ignorant of the relationship between present and past." He was not happy to see students who "spend an awful lot of time programming and doing problem sets and are really in some fundamental sense ignorant about some things they probably ought to know."[10] Dan Edelstein, a professor of French and a resident fellow of Stanford's Humanities House, said, "I hear from a lot of freshmen in particular just how hard it is to be a student interested in the humanities when everyone else on your floor is excited about 106A or has just declared CS."[11]

Some of Stanford's computer science professors were no less alarmed about the campus's shift away from the humanities. Jennifer Widom, the chair of the computer science department, expressed concern about the growth of computer science enrollments that was hard to distinguish from Rakove's:

> There's a major question of, what does Stanford want to be? Does Stanford want to be a school comprised 40 percent of engineers and half of those in computer science? That's fine if that's what Stanford wants to be, but Stanford has always been such a broad school. If half the students are majoring in engineering or some large fraction, I just think it will change the character of the University a little bit, and I'm not sure if that's a good thing."[12]

Eric Roberts, who had been CS+X's primary advocate, was concerned as well about the impact of students stampeding into computer science courses.[13] "We don't want to be in a position at Stanford, which is a general institution, where everyone somehow associates with Stanford only the technical majors and science and engineering, and increasingly that seems to be happening," he said in 2015. "It's important to me that Stanford be a general intellectual environment, and I think that it's in danger of ceasing to be so."[14]

Faculty members in the humanities deployed different kinds of appeals to prospective students. One line of argument was that a bachelor's degree should not be viewed as a terminal degree. Debra Satz, a professor of philosophy who was the senior associate dean for the humanities and the arts, told students, "You can major in French and still have a completely different career."[15]

Another tack was to describe the all-purpose utility of what was learned with deep study of the humanities. When Karen Wigen, the chair of the history department, asked students to look at her department's new "Global Affairs and World History" track, she made a case for it that could have been adapted for other humanities subjects: "Acquiring deep knowledge about multiple parts of the globe, learning to ask probing questions and construct arguments, evaluating evidence and writing and speaking effectively are all timeless skills in a globalizing world."[16]

As well-crafted as this rationale was, it did not answer the question that students and parents wanted answered: Did employers value these things, too? The faculty hoped that employers did, but had varying success in showing that this was so. In 2011, Richard Martin, the professor of classics who had taught Andrew Phillips's freshman seminar, told the *Stanford Daily* that students majoring in the humanities "can do a liberal arts degree and still get a job. And I don't mean like working in a library or going to grad school and wasting five years of your life." It was well-intentioned but lacked illustrative details. Martin may have been including himself when he went on to say, "Professors don't like to deal with the idea of having to market their field," but they had been forced into this uncomfortable position. "We're fighting an anti-intellectual and vocational mentality," he explained.[17]

The most well-prepared—and philosophically provocative—response to the vocationalism that was destroying student interest in humanities majors was delivered by Joshua Landy, who was a professor of both French and comparative literature. It came in December 2010 at the tail end of the last class meeting of his The Art of Living class. Though he was speaking nominally just to the class's students, the mini-lecture was captured on video, and it was a riveting performance.[18]

"I want to give you a piece of advice straight from the heart," Landy opens. "Don't major in economics." He pauses, while the students laugh uneasily. "Let me rephrase that: *do* major in economics if you love economics," he said. "But *don't* major in economics if it's because your parents told you to, or if it's because you think you can't get a good job without it." Professors of economics agreed with him, he said, and if anyone doubted this, they should go ask them.

Everyone in his class would end up with a good job, Landy said, even those who were majoring in history, psychology, or French studies. "In certain fields, it turns out, a background in the humanities is a positive advantage," he said. "Whether rightly or wrongly, folks out there think we humanists have good communication skills, rich imaginations, intellectual agility, and flexibility."

He showed a slide of Nicholas Negroponte, the founder of MIT's Media Lab, with a Negroponte quotation: "Many engineering deadlocks have been broken by people who are not engineers at all. The ability to make big leaps of thought usually resides in people with very wide backgrounds, multidisciplinary minds and a broad spectrum of experience." Below, Landy had added, "NB: We love engineers. Especially double majors," with a smiley-face emoji.

Landy asked students to note that he was not saying that they *should* become humanities majors, only that they should feel that they could do so, if that is what held their interest. "I hereby give you permission to study something you are actually interested in, including economics," he said.

"If you're a humanities major, there's one question that people always ask you: 'What are you going to do with that?' And what they mean by this is, how are you going to make money?" Landy allowed that this was "a thoroughly fair question." But he pointed out that he wanted to ask the students who did not major in the humanities a question: "When *you* make money, what are you going to do with that? . . . How are you going to spend it? What would be the best way of making yourself happy and fulfilled?"

He flashed a picture of Paris Hilton dancing in a nightclub as an illustration of life choices that did not show money spent wisely. He asked the students,

> What is actually going to make you happy? Are you going to avoid making mistakes that you'll regret for a very long time and you're at least going to learn to learn from your mistakes? Are you going to be able to stave off that midlife crisis? To quote W. E. B. DuBois, "The function of the university is not simply to teach bread-winning. It is, above all, to be the organ of that fine adjustment between real life and the growing knowledge of life, an adjustment that forms the secret of civilization. The true college will ever have but one goal: not to earn meat but to know the end and aim of that life which meat nourishes."

Landry closed by imploring students, "Please don't waste your four years of freedom; don't waste them on learning breadwinning when you could be learning the aim of life." Should their parents give them a hard time about this, "send them to me."

It was a bravura performance, but students continued to pick fewer majors in the humanities and more in engineering. Five years later, Persis Drell, the dean of the School of Engineering, reported to Stanford's Academic Council on the state of her school. In her presentation, she opposed the suggestion to put "gateway" courses in place to restrict the inflow of students seeking an engineering major. Unlike many schools of engineering at other universities, which could control enrollment by raising standards for high school students who had to apply for admission to the engineering school, Stanford admitted students through a single, centralized process, and once admitted, they were free to choose whatever major they wanted, which was good. She wanted her school to provide the students who chose engineering or other STEM disciplines with the best course experiences possible.

Yet Drell did confess to uneasiness about the day that seemed to be coming ever closer when the percentage of students at Stanford who majored in engineering would exceed 50 percent. She worried aloud that too many of those majors were selecting engineering for the "wrong reasons," that they thought, erroneously, 'I have to do a certain route because that's the route to a job and my passion will be my hobby.'" This orientation toward future employment, in turn, prevented students from taking advantage of what she said were "so many interesting things to do at Stanford." Hans Weiler, the academic secretary who recorded the meeting's minutes, drily noted, "She agrees that Engineering is interesting, she doesn't think that it's *that* interesting (*an observation to which the Senate reacts with some amusement*)."[19]

Joshua Landy had given his blessing to a double major encompassing the humanities and engineering, and Persis Drell also advocated for an undergraduate experience that encompassed the two areas, but she did not press for the major in engineering. She suggested that students consider taking, say, CS 106A, the introductory course to programming, and then, perhaps, a second computer science course, then go on to do a "computational track" in political science, which would be the student's sole major. Such a plan would free students from feeling stuck in a predicament, forced to choose "between getting a job and following their passion."[20]

A defense of the increase in the number of engineering majors that went well beyond what the dean of engineering or the engineering faculty voiced was presented by a professor of microbiology and immunology in the School of Medicine, Philip Pizzo. A specialist in pediatric infectious diseases who had recently concluded twelve years as the dean of the School of Medicine, Pizzo had no professional connection to the School of Engineering. And when he had been an undergraduate at Fordham University, he had spent more time taking humanities courses than many of his future medical-school peers: he majored in philosophy as well as in biology.[21] But when Stanford's Academic Council took up a discussion after Drell's presentation of what to do, if anything, about "the 50 percent problem,"[22] Philip Pizzo made a case for what he knew was a contrarian view, for *more* engineering education, not less.

"We shouldn't get trapped into thinking that we're doing something wrong if our students want to do Engineering," Pizzo told the faculty. He mentioned that he had been speaking recently with many professionals who were in mid-life—after leaving the deanship, Pizzo had founded the Stanford Distinguished Careers Institute that brought to campus cohorts of resident fellows with twenty to thirty years of achievements—and had been amazed at how many of them had engineering backgrounds even though their careers had spanned diverse fields.[23] Engineering prepares students for many areas, not just engineering, he argued. Given that students themselves choose their major, and engineering is what they care about, then the flow of students into engineering should be viewed as a positive trend for the university and not something to be contained or curtailed.[24]

Following Pizzo's remarks, Persis Drell said politely that she appreciated his argument, but she returned to her concern that students were choosing to major in engineering for the wrong reasons. Pizzo granted that it was possible that students were choosing the major for reasons that they, the faculty, might see as the wrong reasons—that is, without genuine interest in engineering. But that should not be concerning, he argued, because the degree may equip the students "for things that they may not be able to envision for many years to come." He had the last word, at least for the day, as the discussion ended there. But had he not co-opted the best argument for a liberal education, to equip students for the not-yet-envisioned?[25]

At the same time that the humanities were losing majors, they also suffered a blow that, while not quite as visible, was no less impactful. This was a change in 2012 made in Stanford's general education requirements, removing the three-course Introduction to the Humanities that all freshmen had taken since it was put in place in 1997. The end of Introduction to the Humanities marked another victory for the advocates of professionally oriented education.

Perhaps its end should be seen as another step taken to return Stanford University to its founders' definition of a "practical education." David Starr Jordan had taken pride in barring, with the sole exception of an English composition course, the imposition of any general education requirements. He viewed these as a vestige of the older "aristocratic" tradition from which he wanted to distinguish Stanford. To Jordan, general or core courses were only for personal cultivation, a project in which he had no interest. He did not want the Stanford graduate to end up as a "stoop-shouldered grammarian" but as a "leader of enterprise, the builder of states."[26]

General education came to Stanford in 1920, only after Jordan had retired. Before then, students were admitted to a major department, which dictated the coursework for all four years. In 1920, Stanford adopted the system that state universities had put into place, designating the first two years as the lower division, a time for those who were not certain of their choice of major to explore, and a time for every student to take broadly preparatory courses, which Stanford now prescribed. The specialization of the major was postponed until the junior year.

Ray Lyman Wilbur, a medical doctor by training and the university's president at the time,[27] wanted to eliminate the lower division and to move Stanford to a two-year upper-division-only curriculum for undergraduates. He believed that "other institutions"—high schools or junior colleges—should teach the classes of the lower division, leaving Stanford to handle the upper division and, immediately following, graduate studies.[28] In 1927, Wilbur managed to persuade Stanford's Board of Trustees to agree to restrict admission of freshmen to clear room for transfer students, but the initiative would fade, leaving no enduring traces.[29] Wilbur understood that he faced opposition from students, who did not want to give up what Wilbur called "four years of so-called college life."[30] And he recognized that, student opposition or no, the odds of success in changing a long-established curriculum would be long in any case. "There is almost as much conservatism in changing the social phases and the curriculum of a college as there is in moving a cemetery," he wrote in 1930.[31]

When Stanford introduced general education in 1920, the new requirements included math, English, foreign languages, physics or chemistry, and history, some of which could be fulfilled at the high school level, and the course Problems of Citizenship, which would be required of all first-year Stanford students.[32] The *San Francisco Chronicle* described the bundle of requirements as the broad foundation designed not only for the university education that would follow but also for "later in business or professional life."[33] The faculty committee that made the recommendations said that the university was not retreating from the university's founding grant, with its invocation of the commitment to "direct usefulness," but merely finding a better way to fulfill that purpose. "There never was a time when the advantages of liberal education were so vigorously proclaimed as today," the committee wrote. "The engineering societies vie with the bar associations in asserting the importance of a broad liberal education as a foundation for the most useful professional careers."[34] (Perhaps 1920 should be deemed the Golden Age of the Humanities!)[35]

Problems of Citizenship evolved into the sequence Western Civilization, eventually becoming the three-course Introduction to the

Humanities, or IHUM, which offered students many options. The
university catalog for 2008–09 listed these among the two-quarter
thematic sequences: Epic Journeys, Modern Quests; Mass Violence
from Crusades to Genocides; World History of Science; Rebellious
Daughters and Filial Sons of the Chinese Family: Present and Past;
The Fate of Reason; Art and Ideas; and A Life of Contemplation or
Action? Debates in Western Literature and Philosophy.[36] How far the
curriculum had traveled from the days of Problems of Citizenship.

What had been created was beautiful, at least on the pages of the
course catalog. Alas, many students disliked IHUM—strongly—and
as the years passed, the ranks of the unhappy grew to the point at
which the faculty was pressured into dismantling the program. What
did the students dislike? It seems the answer was, just about everything. They did not like being required to take any courses. They especially did not like being required to take courses whose immediate
utility was not evident. Even though the students also were required
to fulfill communications requirements (Program in Writing and
Rhetoric),[37] those were not resented the way the humanities courses
were because they were focused on writing, research, and speaking
skills explicitly, making them appear to students to be more practical.

Students also did not like the large class sizes of IHUM's thematic lecture courses—typically 150 to 250 students—an un-
derstandable complaint.[38] Attendance at lectures was spotty. But
students also had complaints that grading was not as generous as
they wished, and they expressed their unhappiness with low course
evaluations. They also coined a phrase of derision, "IHUM kid," for
their few classmates who were genuinely excited by what they were
learning in their IHUM courses and were so foolish as to bring the
subject matter up in casual conversation outside of class.[39]

The Stanford students who could not abide three humanities
courses in their freshman year were influenced, no doubt, by the
location of their institution, in the center of the entrepreneur's
dreamscape, Silicon Valley. "It's in the air we breathe," said David

Kennedy, a historian and Pulitzer Prize winner specializing in twentieth-century U.S. history. "It's an atmosphere that can be toxic to the mission of the university as a place of refuge, contemplation, and investigation for its own sake."[40]

Even before the students had arrived at campus, however, they had absorbed what Lanier Anderson, a professor of philosophy, called in 2012 "an overly instrumental attitude toward what their education should be about."[41] But Anderson, who was a member of the faculty task force that reviewed IHUM and proposed its replacement in 2012, was also sympathetic with students, whom he could see were squeezed by majors, some of which had implicit course prerequisites as well as explicit ones. He said, "The real change over the last fifteen years has been that lots of majors have expanded. . . . They're reaching down into the freshman year."[42] The freshmen attempting to keep pathways to two or more possibilities for majors open must attend to prerequisites. "Freshmen get here, and we tell them it's a liberal education, you're supposed to explore, and they feel they have zero degrees of freedom."[43]

At the urging of the task force, the university replaced Introduction to the Humanities, requiring three quarters of humanities courses in the freshman year, with a new program called Thinking Matters, consisting of a single one-quarter introductory course, in any discipline, not just humanities. When the new program began, students signed up in greatest numbers for the non-humanities courses. The historian Jack Rakove expressed frustration in 2013 about the position of the humanities faculty: "We're being whittled back to kind of a marginal position."[44]

Some of his colleagues were sanguine, however. When Lanier Anderson, the professor of philosophy, defended Thinking Matters, he sounded genuinely excited about the prospect of offering non-STEM students the chance to take a Thinking Matters seminar in a STEM field, a field in which the student might not ever take another course. "You're trying to show them what a particular way of thinking has to offer people in general about a particular type of question," he said.[45] That appreciation for the multiplicity of particular ways of thinking is exactly what humanities confers. But here it was used to rationalize the arrival of a new STEM-centered world, in which the humanities has been deemed insufficiently useful for all students.

CHAPTER 17

BILINGUAL

LIAM KINNEY arrived at Stanford in the fall of 2012 without any experience in directing his own education. "I had the *helicopter-iest* parents there are," he says. His family home is in Aspen, Colorado, but for high school he had gone to Philips Exeter Academy in New Hampshire. There, he had taken whatever his parents told him to take, which included many courses in both Latin and Greek. The sole course he had been permitted to choose for himself was Ecology.

Kinney permitted himself to be directed because his parents said that their directions would secure a place in a good school. They also said that the moment he was accepted, they would get off his back, a promise that he thought they would not honor. "There's no way they're going to keep up their end of the deal," he cautioned himself.

And yet they did keep up their end. Completely. He was thrilled to have earned complete freedom to take whatever he wanted at Stanford, but he also felt ill-prepared to make choices on his own. He likened his situation to that of a prison inmate who, upon release, lacks the skills to cope with freedom.

On the basis of his advanced placement exams, he had placed into Stanford's intermediate Greek course and advanced Latin. He started off with the Greek course in the fall, enjoying the thought that he would be seated among third-year philosophy doctoral students. But he viewed it as a lark. The first week of school, he told a friend, "If I declare classics as my major, punch me in the face." He did not see any practical application for classics; he could not see how it would lead to a future. But he had no particular alternative vision for his future major. In winter quarter, he took a Latin class, which was taught by Christopher Krebs. Krebs's passion for classics got Kinney's attention: he describes Krebs's enthusiasm for all things classics as greater than he'd seen in anyone else, about anything. Kinney decided to make Krebs his advisor. He did not think he would make classics his major, but he was fascinated by Krebs's passion and wanted to plumb why Krebs was so attached to the subject.

In the meantime, Kinney thought he would be a product design major, which was an engineering degree. It was not until he was a sophomore that he learned that in the job market, product design majors were not taken seriously, that it was mechanical engineering (ME) majors who got the choice positions in product design. Fine, I'll switch to ME, he thought. But as so many other students discover to their chagrin, setting course for a new major in the sophomore year, even for one closely related to the one that had been pursued in the freshman year, may prove too late, practically speaking. In Kinney's case, there was one requirement for ME that he had failed to take, and which was the prerequisite for other requirements, so he was effectively four quarters behind the ME majors in his cohort. ME was out of reach.

Stanford's "disciplinary breadth" requirement was light. Every undergraduate had to take at least one course in each of the five disciplinary areas: engineering and applied sciences, humanities, mathematics, natural sciences, and social sciences. In Kinney's sophomore year, a friend living in the same house who had yet to take a course in engineering and applied science said he would take CS 106A to meet the requirement. Kinney did not need the course for any particular purpose, but he recalled he had taken a programming and public policy course at Exeter, which had been light on the programming and heavy on the public policy and had been fun, and he decided to take CS 106A.

Kinney liked the course a lot and decided he'd take the second course, CS 106B. That too was fun. He told himself he would continue taking computer science classes until they were no longer fun. He had continued to take a classics course every quarter, too, and a double major was taking shape in his mind: classics and symbolic systems. It was too late to consider computer science as a major instead of symbolic systems: his 106A class did not even count toward fulfilling any of the requirements for a CS major, so he would have only completed a single requirement by the end of his sophomore year. His classmates had knocked out the six core requirements for CS—taking a programming class and math class every quarter—by the end of their freshman year. Again, woe to the student who takes a little while to decide upon a major that has onerous requirements. Symbolic systems, however, seemed to offer CS Lite, with its mix of CS and humanities—and it counted his CS 106A. To a late starter like Kinney, symbolic systems seemed like a practical alternative.

Kinney soon made a dismaying discovery, however: prospective employers in tech were not interested in symbolic systems.[1] They wanted CS majors and only CS majors. The realization came when he attended an on-campus career fair for all technical majors and visited the Oracle booth. He handed over his résumé, and before the Oracle recruiters took a close look, he got the conversation off to what seemed like a promising start, talking about his enjoyment of computer science. But when he mentioned that his major would be symbolic systems, not computer science, and when he talked about his enjoyment of classics and of writing, he saw the smiles disappear. The Oracle recruiter said, "We'll be in touch," but the body language said, "You're clearly not the person we're looking for." He did not hear back from Oracle.

In the spring of his sophomore year, Kinney sent out about thirty email inquiries about summer internship opportunities to tech companies in Silicon Valley. The few that responded wanted to know what symbolic systems was. He explained its interdisciplinary blend, and how it required fewer units than CS, enabling him to pursue the double major with classics. But his double major failed to attract interest; not a single company offered him an interview for a possible internship.[2]

Meanwhile, Google's Laszlo Bock was dispensing encouraging words about double majors to *New York Times* columnist Thomas Friedman. In a column that Kinney's parents read, Friedman asked Bock, "Are the liberal arts still important?" Bock responded,

> [They are] phenomenally important, . . . especially when you combine them with other disciplines. . . . I think a lot about how the most interesting things are happening at the intersection of two fields. To pursue that, you need expertise in both fields. You have to understand economics and psychology or statistics and physics [and] bring them together. You need some people who are holistic thinkers and have liberal arts backgrounds and some who are deep functional experts. Building that balance is hard, but that's where you end up building great societies, great organizations.[3]

Here, as in so many other instances, an executive near the top of an organization expressed a welcome to the liberal arts that did not translate into visible expression at the bottom.

Kinney decided to use the summer to take the next introductory course in computer science, Computer Organization and Systems CS 107. The course delved into the low levels of computing, beginning with the C programming language and then working down to the microprocessor. The teaching assistant was Michael Chang, who was a wizard who could answer, it seemed, any computer science question put to him. He also happened to be blind.

Kinney would later say that CS 107 "changed my life" because he loved the course so much and because it gave him the chance to spend time with Chang, whose enthusiasm for computer science was no less than that of Christopher Krebs's for classics. Kinney marveled at Chang's mastery of the C programming guide, which he appeared to have memorized in its entirety. Kinney anointed Chang, whom he dubbed The Oracle, as his informal, second advisor.

Kinney had never passionately embraced symbolic systems the way he embraced classics—nor with the enthusiasm he was now feeling for computer science. Having seen that SymSys did not open doors for him, he wanted to major in computer science. He told Michael Chang that he wanted to continue with computer science but could not see any realistic way of doing so, and Chang suggested that he finish his classics major's requirements and then he could do a master's degree in computer science. Kinney was skeptical: wouldn't a master's program in computer science only be for CS students who had been programming since they were infants and not for a latecomer like himself? Chang assured him that admission requirements were very straightforward: if, after having taken five CS classes, his GPA, inside and outside of the major, was above 3.7, he would be admitted. Kinney applied in his junior year, before having taken the five, but his record was sufficiently strong that he was admitted.

Landing an internship for the following summer was now possible with his tie to the computer science department as a cotermer and with no longer being burdened with explaining the interdisciplinary benefits conferred by a symbolic systems major. With the help of a friend, he got an internship at DirectTV, working on its "Big Data" team, in El Segundo, California.

When he returned to campus in the fall, Kinney's friends who were CS majors and who were also going to coterm in computer science were envious of Kinney's position. They had to spend their senior year taking courses in math and physics that were requirements for their CS major, courses that Kinney did not have to take. Having completed the requirements for his classics major, he could get started on his coursework for his master's at a leisurely pace, and he could also take courses that served no professional purpose whatsoever. In the fall quarter of his senior year he took a course in improvisational acting, a music class and a separate class in music coding at Stanford's Center for Computer Research in Music and Acoustics, and also his first graduate course, the computer science department's famous CS 221, Artificial Intelligence: Principles and Techniques.

For the final project in his AI class, he wrote a machine-learning program that used a set of historical crime data for San Francisco to predict the likelihood of a given category of crime at any location in the city. It was his biggest CS undertaking, and he was still sufficiently new to the field to feel amazement that his code worked.

More than happenstance was required for Kinney to enroll in a master's program in CS; he had to possess the ability to learn how to program at a pace that many others who came from the humanities side of the campus could not maintain. The housemate who had been the one who led Kinney to sign up impetuously for CS 106A had himself fallen by the wayside almost at the very beginning of that quarter. He could not complete the first assignment. Faced with a zero as his first score, he dropped the course.

In his senior year, as Kinney began looking at prospective employers, his parents reinserted themselves into his planning. His mother had decided that Airbnb should be his future employer, and she urged him ever more frequently to apply.[4] Finally, he did so, applying for an internship for the following summer.

The first stage, the phone screen, seemed to go well. Using a screen-sharing app, Kinney worked on a programming problem supplied by the interviewer. He was given forty-five minutes to complete it. The two used an ordinary phone connection, so Kinney could focus on problem-solving without being distracted arranging himself in front of a camera. Kinney didn't say much at all: he stayed within his CoderPad screen and when he wanted to say something to the interviewer, he simply typed his comment on the screen. After a while, Kinney realized he had not heard anything from the other end for quite a while, so he asked, "Are you following everything?" "Yes, yes," came back the answer, "Keep going." To Kinney, it was easy to maintain the illusion that he was solving the problem without

anyone being present or looking over his shoulder. It was not a stress-
ful experience.

Kinney was then invited to Airbnb's headquarters in San Francisco for the on-site interviews. This was a notable milestone, and
stepping onto the hallowed ground of Airbnb's fabled offices, a
dreamscape for young workers, was exhilarating. The on-site visit
consisted of two technical interviews and a third interview that covered what Airbnb called its "core values."

The technical interviews used the same format as the phone interview: for each, he had forty-five minutes to solve a problem, showing his work as he proceeded. For these, however, the interviewer was
physically present, preventing him from pretending he was working
on the problem on his own. He had never had an on-site interview
before and this was disconcerting. Scared and nervous, he found
himself talking and talking during his first one, previewing aloud
what he was about to do, without pausing to think clearly about how
best to proceed. Looking back on it, he realized that he spent 90 percent of his energy attempting to appear sharp and only 10 percent
on the algorithm he needed to solve the problem. The result was
failure in his first one.

The second technical interview went better, and the core values interview seemed to go extremely well. The Airbnb interviewers never asked about his classics major—if the subject is likely to
come up in any interview setting, a "core values interview" would
seem to be it—and Kinney did not bring it up on his own. He had
decided that evincing any intellectual interest outside of computer
science could be interpreted as a lack of dedication, and he acted
accordingly. In the end, however, nothing apparently made up for
the dismal performance in the first technical interview. He did not
receive an offer.

When he had gotten the on-site interview at Airbnb, Kinney had
allowed himself to think that the position would soon be his and his
summer internship plans were set. When he did not get the position,

he was flummoxed. It was late December and he felt a tinge of panic; would he be left without a summer internship again? He went online and looked for possibilities, applying to a number of places.

The company that he was most interested in was a tiny software startup called SoundHound. It had begun with an eponymous app that recognized any song, like the competing Shazam app did. The company was working on another app, Hound, which answered spoken questions with what seemed to Kinney astounding accuracy. He remembered how much he had enjoyed talking with a person at SoundHound's table at the engineering career fair on campus earlier that fall. Their interests overlapped: the SoundHound person had also gone to Stanford, had also worked on artificial intelligence, had also taken courses at the Center for Computer Research in Music and Acoustics. Kinney had asked then about being considered for an internship for the summer and was told that it would be discussed, but he had never heard back. Now Kinney got back in touch.

Kinney's work in computer science placed him in a position to be considered, but some credit should be given to the career fair. Physical presence continues to give students who go, and find commonalities with a company representative, an advantage over those who may have similar qualifications but have not had the chance to shake hands in person and chat.

"My mom's hilarious," Kinney said during the middle of his senior year, referring to the way she had managed to assert, at the end of every conversation with her son about his job possibilities, that her son and Mark Zuckerberg had so much in common. She would say, "Liam, I really don't understand why you don't just call up Zuckerberg and say, 'Listen. I do CS. I went to Exeter. I did classics.' Why don't you just tell him you're the same person? He'll throw you a bone." It is true that Zuckerberg did have an interest in classical languages, but he was headed for dual majors in computer science and psychology before leaving Harvard.[5] Kinney found himself explaining to his mother that whatever points of similarity she found did not come close to giving him telephone-call access to Facebook's chief executive.[6]

Kinney succeeded in landing a summer internship at SoundHound, where he worked on developing a game utilizing SoundHound's song and lyrics databases. He was offered a permanent position for when he completed his coterm program, but he held off accepting. When he returned to school in the fall, he arranged to take a reduced course load in the fall quarter so that he could work full-time as an intern at another startup, Synack, to see how he liked working in marketing. In the end, he decided engineering was more interesting, and he accepted the offered position at SoundHound.

Kinney's decision to pursue a coterm master's program in CS came from consideration of employment implications, to be sure, but it was also propelled by his enthusiasm for the subject. He liked computer science no less than he liked classics. (He would have been the sort of student whom Joshua Landy, the professor of French and comparative literature, had in mind when he told his The Art of Living students to major in economics only if they genuinely loved economics.)[7] SoundHound's research and development centered on the computer science field of natural language understanding. He looked forward to working on SoundHound's Hound, which fields spoken questions and instructions (not unlike Amazon's Echo), and was intrigued by the challenge of anticipating all of the different ways that a given question could be asked. It involved getting to the roots, which was what study of Greek and Latin also did. Kinney, the classics major, had found a congenial home.

The erosion of course enrollment in Stanford's humanities and arts spurred the Department of Classics to gather links to testimonials on a page at the department's website that addressed the question, "Why Classics?" (The perceived need for such a page was not shared over at the Department of Computer Science.)

One of the essays was by Richard Saller, a historian of Ancient Rome and the dean of Stanford's School of Humanities and Sciences, who said he had been an engineering student when he took a course on Roman history to fulfill a distribution requirement and discovered he was passionately interested in this subject he had known nothing about. "The lesson I would draw," he wrote, "is not that all engineers ought to transfer to the humanities as I did (the world would grind to a halt if they did), but that students should explore a wide range of courses to develop multiple ways of thinking and to find their personal passion, which may turn up in unexpected places."[8]

Saller was a proponent of the same model that advocates of liberal education had been defending since Stanford's founding, of leaving vocational training for graduate school. He argued that humanities majors were strong candidates in graduate programs, and he had a specific suggestion, that these majors consider applying to Stanford's Graduate School of Business's Summer Institute for General Management, the program for nonbusiness majors, for which financial aid was available.

The Department of Classics offered links to other testimonials for studying either the humanities in general (articulated by Lloyd Minor, the dean of Stanford's School of Medicine) or classics in particular.[9] But one link was set apart from the others on the web page. It had its own button, labeled "12 Reasons to Study Classics in the 21st Century," and led to an enumerated brief, five thousand words in length, presenting a much fuller case for classics than did Saller's short essay or the work of the others. It was written not by a dean but by a lowly undergraduate: Liam Kinney.[10]

Before Kinney presented his list, he explained that the ancient Greek word *techne* refers to acquiring a skill, that engineering majors would be *techne* majors, and that *paideia* refers to knowledge for knowledge's sake. What is most remarkable is that Kinney was not content to make his case solely in terms of *paideia*. The first six reasons address classics as a form of *techne* in the modern world.

Kinney opened by marshaling data to show that classics majors are well-positioned to apply to graduate programs. Students who

majored in classical languages scored the highest on the verbal portion of the GRE; those who majored in classics were in second place.
These majors were among the few who accounted for the best ag-
gregate GRE scores. He argued that the connection is more than
correlation. Mastery of Latin or Greek requires a thorough understanding of grammatical concepts, which one obtains only by studying one's native language. He recalled how he was surprised that in
his first year of Latin in high school, the teacher had devoted the
first two weeks to English grammar. "I thought this was silly until
I learned that Latin grammar is so variable and convoluted that it
demands a mastery of one's native language rules in order to study
it," he wrote.

Classics majors do not need to go on to a graduate program
to utilize skills obtained from study of the classics, Kinney argued.
Classics is one path for understanding humans, and is that not what
technology companies need in order to put ever-growing piles of
data to good use? He noted that eBay's databases contain 90 peta-
bytes of information. Engineers amass the data, but it is humanists who should be extracting insights from it. Classics, utilizing the
critical perspective enabled by distance, helps us understand "why
people do what they do."

CHAPTER 18

A HISTORY OF THE FUTURE

IN JANUARY 1969, a reporter for the *Stanford Daily* assembled a collage of predictions that she had collected as she roved the campus, inquiring what her subjects thought Stanford would look like in the next millennium, in 2001. A person in the university's planning office spoke of more reliance on bikes. A teaching assistant in the geology department said the area was due for another major earthquake ("but unless you say that the earthquake is coming on a specific date, no one takes you seriously.")[1]

The predictions of Raj Reddy, an assistant professor of computer science,[2] are the ones that retrospectively stand out. They centered on computer-enabled education and anticipated online courses that would be individualized according to the needs of each student.[3] "Everybody will follow his own individual program, some students finishing a four-year college program in two years," he said. Stanford would not need an academic calendar—"everybody can learn at his own stride." From their computers students could watch lectures, and not just from Stanford, but from anywhere in the world. "The computer would make distances meaningless," he said.[4] Students would watch the day's lecture not when the professor gave it but when they felt like watching it.

Reddy sensed that many people were fearful of computers, and he did his best to offer reassurance. "It would take a whole city block to build a computer with a brain capacity equal to that of a man," he said. "There is no reason to fear computers. The computer is just some clever person who is telling the computer what to do."[5]

Forty-five years later, Stanford attempted to see its own distant future, and this time the exercise was much more ambitious. In 1969, the effort was conducted by merely one student reporter, who did a few interviews. In 2013–14, the contributors were two hundred students and more than sixty administrators, and their eyes were trained on 2025.[6] The project was organized by Stanford's d.school. The "d.school," in lower case and sans separating space, is the informal name that is ubiquitous; the formal name is the Hasso Plattner Institute of Design at Stanford. The "school" in "d.school" is a misnomer; the institute offers courses and workshops to Stanford's graduate students, but it is not a degree-granting unit.

In May 2014, the findings of "Stanford 2025" were presented as an exhibit, not as prognostications but as history seen by those in the far, far future, as if it were a historical exhibit staged in the year 2100, looking back on 2025, the year when a "paradigm shift" had occurred at Stanford, upending most of the familiar features of a Stanford education. Setting it up as a retrospective look *back* at the year 2025 was clever: the exhibits projected the verisimilitude of actual history.

Stanford 2025 did not imagine a Stanford that had gone completely online, without classrooms, the computer-mediated education that Raj Reddy had briefly sketched in 1969 for Stanford's future. It assumed that Stanford undergraduates would have a residential experience on the physical campus. The contributors chose not to incorporate into their vision massive open online courses, MOOCs, recently pioneered by three Stanford computer science professors: Sebastian Thrun, Andrew Ng, and Daphne Koller.

As an experiment, in fall 2011, the three professors had offered online versions of three of the department's popular courses—Introduction to Artificial Intelligence;[7] Machine Learning; and Introduction to Databases, respectively—to nonstudents for free as well to

Stanford students. Thrun expected enrollment of 500; more than 160,000 enrolled. Ng also drew more than 100,000 students to his course, or, as he put it, a number that were he to try to match by continuing with the classroom format, "I would have to teach at Stanford for 250 years."[8]

These enrollments were so unexpected, so thrilling, that for the moment—briefly, it would turn out—these new courses seemed to point to the future of education. "Having done this, I can't teach at Stanford again; it's impossible," Thrun said at a conference in Munich a few weeks after the end of the quarter. "I feel like there's a red pill and a blue pill. And you can take the blue pill and go back to your classroom and lecture your twenty students. But I've taken the red pill and I've seen Wonderland."[9] He told conference attendees that he had resigned his tenured position at Stanford and had launched a startup, Udacity, to bring a free Stanford-class education to everyone in the world.[10] He titled his talk that day "University 2.0." Udacity was soon joined by Coursera, cofounded by Andrew Ng and Daphne Koller, which offered to its partner universities the software technology for operating online courses, sharing the fees collected with its partners if students elected to earn a certificate attesting to satisfactory completion.[11]

When the *New Yorker* published in April 2012 a portrait of Stanford University, "Get Rich U.," Ken Auletta, the author, asked aloud whether online education might "disrupt everything that distinguishes Stanford." He said John Hennessy, Stanford's president, had named online education as occupying the top spot on the list of things that he was devoting his sabbatical, then underway, to thinking about. Auletta wrote, "Stanford, like newspapers and music companies and much of traditional media a little more than a decade ago, is sailing in seemingly placid waters. But Hennessy's digital experience"—Hennessy was a computer scientist and successful Valley entrepreneur—"alerts him to danger." Auletta ended his piece with Hennessy saying, "There's a tsunami coming."[12]

Spring 2012 turned out to be the high-water mark for the excited talk of a university education provided for free to anyone on the globe who had an Internet connection, of single-course enrollments exceeding a hundred thousand, and of imminent disruption to existing institutions of higher learning. With a little more experience, the pioneers soon saw major problems that had been overlooked amid the giddiness in the initial experience with "massive." Thrun saw that fewer than 10 percent of the students who enrolled in Udacity's classes completed the courses, and not all of those did work that was sufficient to pass. Perhaps only five out of every one hundred who enrolled could be said to have learned the subject matter satisfactorily.[13] Students in Coursera's courses seemed to do no better. The University of Pennsylvania's Graduate School of Education looked at the records of a million students who enrolled in sixteen Coursera courses between June 2012 and June 2013 and found that course completion rates averaged 4 percent.[14]

In January 2013, Thrun tried to use Udacity's technology on a non-massive scale, launching an experiment with San Jose State University to offer three courses for credit—entry-level mathematics, college algebra, and elementary statistics—and offering the students the assistance of online mentors who could answer their questions.[15] The results were awful: the students who were in the online sections did worse than the control groups, the students who took the same classes on campus.[16] In the summer, San Jose State tried using Udacity again,[17] but the results failed to show that online delivery was equal to classroom delivery and the partnership ended.[18]

Thrun said he learned from this experience that the online courses he had designed while at Stanford were for extremely bright, highly motivated students. "The basic MOOC is a great thing for the top 5 percent of the student body," he said in 2014, "but not a great thing for the bottom 95 percent."[19] By then he had turned Udacity away from credit-bearing college courses to vocational training. In 2017, it offered only "nanodegree programs" related to software:

Intro to Programming, Artificial Intelligence, Predictive Analytics for Business, Android Basics, and others.[20] All of the excited talk about the Great MOOC Disruption dissipated. The short-lived nature of the euphoria brings to mind the similar euphoria over "universities of the air" that a number of universities set up in the 1920s and 1930s, using campus-based radio broadcasts (and mail).[21]

Although Sebastian Thrun believed that the online college course he had originally developed was only well-suited for students like those he had taught at Stanford, it was not viewed by the authors of Stanford 2025 as pointing the way to Stanford's future. What they saw as sine qua non, extending even to the imagined vantage point of the year 2100, was residential education. The birthplace of so many of the technologies that made it technically and economically feasible to move education online would preserve the physicality of educational interactions: actual human beings gathered in one physical location.

When those human beings would gather would change, however. Stanford in the year 2025 would be an "open loop" university, where students would come for a while, leave, then return, looping back to the campus multiple times over the course of a lifetime. By describing today's present in the past tense, the project made current practices seem benighted:

> Before neurosocial educators fully understood the cognitive processes surrounding human learning, society sent its young people to college for just a few years, early in their adult lives. They were meant to absorb all the information and skills they would need for the rest of their productive lives, and then burst forth fully formed and equipped to succeed—much like the even older myth of Athena born in full armor, springing from the head of Zeus.[22]

Not all students would be admitted to Stanford when they were eighteen. Ten percent of an incoming class would be reserved for "age blind" admission, which would be introduced to add diversity in the mix of student ages on campus. These and the other changes were couched in the past tense, as they would be in a history of the university that was written in the year 2100. "Classroom learning was enriched by both the naive, bold perspectives of younger-than-average classmates, and the wisdom of the experienced, older ones," the project said.[23]

For admissions decisions, in the imagined history of the future, Stanford began relying on a pool of experts to nominate individuals whose accomplishments rather than test scores established their readiness for Stanford, and the selected individuals were invited to come to Stanford without having to apply. In this fictional history, "by 2016, 10 percent of students were admitted via invitation. Six years later, Stanford and twenty-eight other universities were using invites instead of applications for the vast majority of their students."[24]

Beginning in the year 2020, Stanford reorganized the curriculum to emphasize "skills and competencies," such as scientific analysis, quantitative reasoning, social inquiry, moral and ethical reasoning, aesthetic interpretation, creative confidence, and communication effectiveness. Mixing-and-matching disciplines and "competencies" was said to have led "to the creation of some of Stanford's most celebrated fields of study in the mid-21st century: Artificial Intelligence for Social Inquiry, Quantitative Global Affairs, and Right Brain Finance."[25]

Students no longer declared majors. Instead, they declared "a mission," which was a discipline coupled with the purpose underlying the choice. Examples: "I'm learning human biology to eliminate world hunger" or "I'm learning Computer Science and Political Science to rebuild how citizens engage with their governments."[26]

Stanford 2025 said that learning and pacing became highly individualized. Professors offered "bite-size introductions" to subjects to give students a taste of subjects that they could then pursue more deeply in combined "living and learning quarters" that replaced the lecture halls of the Main Quad in 2016. The closer relationships between professors and students contributed to accelerated learning, "often equivalent to a pre-2015 PhD, that students reached in just 18–24 months."[27]

The exhibit showed a student placing her hand on a platen that was called "the hormone mirror," which would be invented by a student and made available in 2020, supplying "cognitive biofeedback" to students so that they could adjust courses and extracurricular activities to "optimize mental, emotional, and physical well-being." The "hormone mirror" was introduced "after it was found that the cortisol (stress hormone) level was so high in the undergraduate population that it was inhibiting the function not only of serotonin (happiness hormone) but also of dopamine (reward hormone), which is a key indicator of learning."[28]

The university's backing of this advanced technology was accompanied with an equal commitment to "meditative modes" and the creation on campus of many "zones of digital silence," which were called "not-spots." The humanities made one tiny contribution to the mental health of students by pioneering something called the "Slow Cognition movement" (which, regrettably, was not described or explained).[29]

Stanford students no longer left the university with a transcript. Its replacement, the "skill-print," showed "competencies." This was the one element of this history of the future that was not a stretch at all. The talk of competencies, which we earlier traced back to the foundations of student testing and industrial psychology in the early twentieth century, has increased in recent years and found expression in Udacity's nanodegrees. It seems more likely that something like the skill-print will replace transcripts before the other predictions will be realized, like an admissions office run like the Macarthur Foundation.

Stanford students in the future were described as being "aggressively recruited for their versatility and their ability to learn and adapt as rapidly as their companies and organizations evolved."[30] Versatility? Ability to learn and adapt? My argument is that there is no need for a skill-print, or an inventory of "competencies," or a d.school reimagining of higher education at Stanford, nor need to wait until the arrival of the year 2025 before students can show employers these attributes. A humanities major with a conventional transcript can show these capacities right now.

In 2015, the *Chronicle of Higher Education* published a long ruminative essay about Stanford's d.school, titled "Is 'Design Thinking' the New Liberal Arts?" It was written by Peter N. Miller, a historian and the dean of the Bard Graduate Center in New York City.[31] The previous semester Miller had taught simultaneous video-linked seminars with Michael Shanks, an archeologist in Stanford's Department of Classics and one of the few tenured professors of humanities who taught at the d.school. Miller had followed with a visit to the d.school, which he praised as "a very important experiment in humanities higher education."

Miller placed the d.school in the European tradition of institutes, which sit outside discipline-based units and provide places where scholars open up cross-disciplinary questions. He had mastered the d.school's vocabulary and methodology and wrote sympathetically of what it did. He said that what the twelve hundred students at Stanford who each year took d.school classes, some without expecting to earn credit, were pursuing "looks like liberal learning at its best." But in Miller's view it was not the new liberal arts, at least "not yet." The d.school methodology lacked historical context, which brings complexity. "If we think hard about what the liberal arts teach, we find that the study of the past achievements of humans, whether history, literature, philosophy, music, or art, provides us with a richly nuanced appreciation for the complexity of human existence," he wrote. Design thinking is "about taking the complexities of life and simplifying them in the interest of problem-solving." He worried aloud that if d.school courses were "to replace the classical liberal arts, we would lose precisely the practical value of classical education: seeing ourselves as existing in time and managing a range of imperfect complexities."[32]

One of the considerations behind the Stanford 2025 project was "the shifting needs and expectations from future employers"—and the expectation that a student who graduates today will have many employers.[33] Stanford 2025 selected an epigraph from a *Forbes* magazine article about job-hopping, which said "the average worker today stays at each of his or her jobs for 4.4 years but the expected tenure of the workforce's youngest employees is about half that."[34] The nature of the job changes was not specified, and the Stanford 2025 authors did not distinguish those who expected to change employers many times but continue doing one particular job from those who expected to change their occupation more than once. It is the latter group who would be most helped by a liberal education, which Howard Swearer, former president of Brown University, describes as "preparation for appointments not yet made."[35]

The idea that undergraduate education will be most practical if it prepares students to be able to hold unknown jobs in the future is nothing new. But we can see a loss of appreciation among many employers for the education that best provides that preparation, the liberal arts, and in particular the humanities. The students whose stories have been narrated here are all fortunate, for they have found opportunities to demonstrate that they had learned how to learn, prepared for appointments not yet made.

In a report to Stanford's faculty senate in 2016, Harry Elam, vice provost for undergraduate education, expressed concern about the "changing educational mindset" he sees in the students who are entering Stanford, who view their education as a means to an economic end only. One of his freshman advisees had recently confided that he was worried that he felt behind in the expected schedule of having his own startup up and running by the end of his sophomore year. Elam was also concerned about the continuing increase in engineering majors. He hoped for an end to "the problematic hierarchy of 'fuzzy' and 'techie.'" He pleaded for a melding of the arts and humanities and technology and science, what he called "new harmonies" that were "more than just artists that can code or engineers and scientists who play music," that were not just interdisciplinary but "post-disciplinary."[36] It may indeed come to pass—by the year 2100. But in the meantime, the humanities deserve to be seen, in this practically minded age, as the most universally useful of the practical arts.

CHAPTER 19

DO-OVER

WHEN DOUG BLUMEYER, a film and media studies major, graduated from Stanford in 2008,[1] he sought work in the world of film. He did not succeed in this quest. But he lived in a historical moment when it was possible to acquire professional training in programming, a field for which there was demand for his services, without returning to a university setting. He got the training quickly without taking on debt, and he remains appreciative of the liberal arts education that he received as an undergraduate.

One hundred years ago, large industrial firms, the high-tech firms of an earlier age, established their own in-house training programs. In April 1929, General Electric advertised in a Stanford alumni magazine its "post-graduate college of electrical science," enrolling four hundred new students annually. "The leaders of the future must not only be born, but made," it said, and the making was to be done by the company, not the university.[2]

The training that a graduate could receive, gratis, could extend for years. In 1934, for example, an insurance company sent Stanford's alumni placement service a request for a man—nothing gender-neutral about the job descriptions—who ideally was an economics major and who would spend three years training in the office as preparation for a sales position.[3]

Computer science did not exist in the 1920s, of course, and we cannot directly compare today with then. But a student who, let us say, wants to get the unabridged version of a humanities education as an undergraduate, using four years for that, and then begin work on acquiring a graduate degree in computer science to supply the unambiguously vocational component of his or her education, would need two more years at Stanford to get a master of science degree.[4]

At least, that was the case until recently, when a new model of post-graduate education emerged for software developers: for-profit schools that provide a curriculum that requires mere weeks, not years, to complete. The schools accept students with little or no coding experience, including humanities majors who never took a computer science course. The programs do not lead to a degree, but the schools claim that by stripping away unnecessary academic coursework, they provide students with the software development skills that prospective employers are clamoring for.

The schools often refer to themselves as "coding boot camps," an apt term for an experience that typically lasts only twelve weeks, at facilities that are appointed with nothing but bare essentials: leased office space filled with inexpensive tables, PCs, and monitors. For San Francisco alone, a census of boot camps in 2015 included the following: Anyone Can Learn To Code, App Academy, Coder Camps, Coding Dojo, Dev Bootcamp, Galvanize, General Assembly, Hack Reactor, Hackbright Academy, Make School, and Rocket U.[5]

One of these, App Academy, began marketing directly to Stanford alumni in fall 2015 with a banner ad—"Over 50 Stanford Grads Hired at Over $105K."[6] The school was founded in 2012 by two friends who had met when both were students at the University of Chicago: Kush Patel, an economics major who found work at a hedge fund, and Ned Ruggeri, a software engineer at Google. They set up App Academy first in San Francisco and later added an office in New York City. After some experimentation, they settled on twelve weeks per term, which was standard. But App Academy stood out from the pack for the way it charged its students. Instead of assessing tuition fees of $15,000 or $17,000, not unusual amounts for boot camps of similar duration, App Academy used a pay-later model, charging 18 percent of the graduate's earnings in his or her first year, payable over six months.[7] If the student remained unemployed for the year following, the obligation to pay the school expired.

This arrangement forced App Academy's cofounders to pay close attention to what the marketplace for novice software developers wanted. At the beginning, they divided the course into two halves: one devoted to learning how to develop mobile apps for Apple's iOS operating system for the iPhone and iPad, the other for developing web applications, that is, the software that runs partly on a distant server and partly within a web browser. App Academy's cofounders found, however, that it was difficult to get the first batch of graduates placed. Providing even minimal competence in developing iOS mobile apps required more than a few weeks, so they decided to drop the mobile portion to focus exclusively on web applications, teaching Ruby on Rails and JavaScript, the technologies that seemed to be most in demand.

App Academy did not offer to make a successful programmer of anyone who applies. While it did not require that its applicants have a college degree, nor did it formally require prior programming experience, it put applicants through a multistage testing process to ensure mastery of basic programming concepts. Initially, it accepted only 5 percent of applicants, but by 2015, the acceptance rate had dropped to 3 percent.

Prospective applicants were encouraged to work their way through practice exercises, preparing solutions in the form of a few lines of code, before taking the forty-five-minute timed test that is the first stage of applying. The exercises in 2015 included writing code that does the following: reverses the order of a string of letters, detects the longest word in a sentence, detects whether a given number is a prime number, returns the greatest integer that evenly divides both numbers, and returns the greatest integer that evenly divides any two given numbers. There was nothing language-specific in any of the challenges, and students could submit code for the written exam in Ruby, Python, JavaScript, Perl, PHP, or Java. "We accept partial solutions, and overall logic is more important to us than exact syntax, so try not to stress if your solution is incomplete or imperfect," it told applicants who were preparing.

Students who passed the written exam, which consisted of three challenges, each of which was to be completed in fifteen minutes, moved on to a second exam, which involved similar problems and time limits. That one was conducted through a Skype call with an App Academy staff member, who watched on a shared screen as the applicant formulated solutions (and tamped down nervousness that comes with being watched in this process). The two levels of exams gave no special credit to those who went to Stanford or any other highly selective school. The only thing that the exams sought to determine was whether the applicant had the ability to solve elementary programming problems.

For those who passed, one more stage of evaluation remained, what App Academy called the "fit interview," which refers to an evaluation of the candidate's comfort working with others. This was important because App Academy's program used "pair programming," in which two students sit at a single screen and keyboard. The two take turns, one typing while the other makes suggestions and checks for errors or alternative solutions. At App Academy, students were given new pairings every day, so they worked with many classmates and had to accommodate their varying personalities and idiosyncrasies.

The enforced pairing in the classroom, the Spartan setting, the waiving of tuition in exchange for a portion of the first year's earnings—none of this resembled the classroom settings and financial demands of Stanford. Perhaps most dissimilar was the absence of a conferred degree at the end, an absence that left App Academy

and the coding boot camps invisible in the rankings of graduate programs assembled by the traditional judges of educational prestige,
U.S. News & World Reports and the professional associations of academic disciplines. Stanford students who heard App Academy's pitch
would naturally wonder, would going to a code boot camp like App
Academy negate whatever impressive associations had attached to
them when they had matriculated at Stanford? Some solace could be
taken from knowing that the humanities major who left Stanford with
a bachelor of arts degree and forewent graduate school for code boot
camp was nonetheless fulfilling the conception of higher education
that defenders of the humanities had constructed in the early twentieth century: undergraduate years would best be used for nothing but
a liberal education, and professional training should come after.

Some professions, such as medicine, require so many prerequisites that students must set off on that track while still undergraduates; making up for lost time once one has graduated can be done
only with additional—and expensive—education after graduation.
But the coding camp model, which requires no prior coursework
or even a degree, offers an open door to everyone, from the newly
minted graduate to the alumnus who got his or her degree years
previously. Doug Blumeyer applied to App Academy six years after
graduation.

When Blumeyer applied, he was not a software neophyte. But he
had suffered earlier at Stanford because he thought he knew more
about programming fundamentals than he did. In middle school,
he had gone to a summer camp to learn programming. There he
had learned BASIC and written some simple text-only role-playing
games. After camp, he had taken more classes in school but had not
developed an interest that was sufficiently strong to lead him to start
programming on his own at home.

Blumeyer did pick up a deep interest in artificial intelligence,
however. He applied to many Ivies, MIT, and Stanford, and got in
every place he applied. He chose Stanford because the school offered

an interdisciplinary major that would let him study AI as an under-graduate: symbolic systems. He wasted no time when he arrived on campus in starting on the required courses in computer science in his first quarter. He decided he did not need the introductory course, CS 106A, and could go directly to CS 106B. And as he had some prior exposure to programming and because, as he self-mockingly recounts his story, the world had always told him he was a very, very smart person—he had applied to nothing but top-tier schools and been admitted to every one, hadn't he?—he decided it would be best that he take the accelerated version of the course, CS 106X.

"I fell flat on my face," Blumeyer recalls. "I failed that class re-ally hard." This came as a bone-jarring shock. He had never expe-rienced failure in his life. The failure dealt a major blow to his plans to study AI. He also found life away from home to be full of distrac-tions. "I didn't get a whole lot of partying and being-a-kid type of things out of my system when I was growing up," he says. So he spent time getting them out of his system now, which did not serve his academic plans well.

Blumeyer backed up and took CS 106A and 106B and a few other CS classes. His first formal class on AI did not go well, how-ever. At the same time, he happened to take film theory 101, and the world of film drew him in. Watching one scene from Andrei Tar-kovsky's *Nostalghia* (1983) was a mesmerizing experience. He decided that film theory offered everything he liked about symbolic systems, and he switched his major to film and media studies, a major that had originated as a concentration in the art history department and was offered for the first time as a standalone major that year.

Blumeyer wanted to make movies of his own. He worked on short films, using resources provided by a workshop associated with the Stanford Film Society. At his advisor's urging, he spent a summer in New York taking a course in film-making at NYU and made more short films. He returned to Stanford and time passed quickly. He found himself graduating, and without a job.

As a high school student, Blumeyer had followed what he speaks of as "rails" that led to elite schools. It was so appealingly simple: work hard, which came naturally to him, and the rails led him to his desired destination. In college, however, film and media studies did not offer clearly laid-out rails that led to what he wanted, making films. Unable to see an alternative career, and itching to spend some time abroad, which he had never done before, he went to Japan after graduation and taught English for a year. He returned. No rails to a future in film had materialized in his absence.

Blumeyer moved back to his parents' house in Illinois and finished a feature-length screenplay. He then moved to New York City to reestablish ties to the film students he had met at NYU, whom he thought he could enlist in producing his screenplay. He looks back ruefully on that time, on how he had expected that "everyone who looks at it is going to fall instantly in love with it and understand that this is The Next Big Thing and drop what they're doing and join the project." When this did not happen, and he realized that he would not earn enough to support himself with the day jobs he had held, he moved back home again, regrouped, and then headed back to the San Francisco Bay Area and tried again, working day jobs, searching for a way to produce his first film, and playing with music and poetry. Years passed, and he was not happy with how his life after college had turned out.

At some point, code boot camps had appeared. When Blumeyer noticed, he realized that they offered him a chance for a do-over. A camp would not even require much time. It would just be *I have no life for three months*, and then he would emerge, magically, as a web developer. And App Academy drew his attention in particular, as he saw he would not have to borrow money for tuition. He applied to App Academy and was accepted in the session that ran from December 2014 through February 2015.

App Academy ran classes from 9 a.m. to 6 p.m., five days a week. Homework assignments filled its students' evenings and weekends.

Students were told at the outset to expect to spend eighty to one hundred hours a week devoted to the class, and Blumeyer found his average was closer to one hundred. He was grateful for the chance to reclaim a part of symbolic systems, the major that had drawn him to Stanford, and treated the curriculum's demands with great seriousness.

Typically, 75 to 80 percent of the App Academy class was male. About half of the students came from STEM fields. No one else from Stanford was in Blumeyer's batch. One of the academy's teaching assistants told him that a smaller percentage of applicants who come from a selective college or university were accepted than those who come from less selective schools. The reason was not known, but the TA speculated that it was because the applicants simply didn't want it as badly, perhaps because they had more options than others.

With his prior computer science classes at Stanford, Blumeyer had more programming experience than most of his fifty-three batchmates. He was not frustrated, however, when he found himself paired with someone with considerably less experience. The academy had a large enough pool from which to pluck students that the 3 percent who were accepted were uniformly able to handle the work; only two members of the batch failed to complete it. And Blumeyer saw that pairing was valuable to the more-experienced or more-skilled member as well as to the less-experienced because the more senior person became a teacher. He cannot remember who originally said, "You don't really understand something unless you can explain it two different ways," but Blumeyer appreciates the wisdom it embodies. "You might be comfortable enough with something that you just sit down and do it, but when you're grilled on every little piece of it and why it couldn't be any other way, that's when you really challenge yourself to understand it to the deepest level," he says.

The first nine weeks of the App Academy term were devoted to the programming curriculum. In the final three weeks, room was made for what the academy called "career support." Some of the support covered generic topics, such as the preparation of a résumé and cover letter. Hiring managers at tech firms may share the view of iFixit CEO Kyle Wiens, who in an essay for the *Harvard Business Review* in 2012 wrote, "Programmers who pay attention to how they construct written language also tend to pay a lot more attention to how they code." Wiens explained his "zero-tolerance approach to grammar errors" this way: "If it takes someone more than 20 years to notice how to properly use *it's*, then that's not a learning curve I'm comfortable with."[8]

Other career-support units at App Academy were tailored to the particular needs of software development: a technical interview workshop; coding challenges; and a workshop that film and media studies majors were unlikely to have taken before, on salary negotiation. Mixed in with these workshops were units on algorithms that were most likely to show up in technical interviews.

Blumeyer posted his credentials on numerous job boards. The largest, fastest-growing startups are inundated with applications from more experienced developers and are generally reluctant to hire the inexperienced.[9] Their recruiters did not pursue Blumeyer, but the universe of software startups is large and there were many startups that were welcoming. He was inundated with inquiries from recruiters. That was a refreshing change from when he graduated from Stanford with the film and media studies major. App Academy had counseled the students not to go straight for the companies on the students' "A list," the ones they were most excited about it. "Blow your first shaky interviews on companies you're not as serious about," he was told (and Liam Kinney had not been told when he leapt for the chance to interview at Airbnb). "So I did that."

Blumeyer was already well-versed in the art of the interview when he went for his interview with Pivotal Labs, a software consulting company that helps its clients build mobile and web apps and other software by training the client's in-house developers with

Pivotal's methodologies. Pair programming is one of the techniques it uses. It's also a company that would be perfectly receptive to inexperienced programmers coming out of a boot camp because Pivotal puts the programmers who work for its corporate clients through a three-month training program, working closely with Pivotal's programmers, modeled explicitly after a military boot camp that is designed to change habits.[10] Blumeyer was offered a job and joined. More than one year later, he says he enjoys the work and continues to learn new things.

During that year following his hiring, Pivotal grew, grew some more, and in May 2016 raised $253 million,[11] an otherworldly sum of money for a company without high capital costs. Blumeyer had not carefully studied the Silicon Valley landscape, looking for fast-growing startups with a certain trajectory, as Andrew Phillips had done. He had simply sought an employer willing to take him and his boot camp training. But he had landed well.

The path to the job would have been much shorter had Blumeyer not, as he self-deprecatingly puts it, "took my time growing up." But he believes that his path did work out for the best: he got a liberal arts education, and then a professional one.

CHAPTER 20

LIBERAL EDUCATION
IS VOCATIONAL

MARC TESSIER-LAVIGNE, a neuroscientist who had been a faculty member at Stanford, a senior executive at Genentech, and then president of Rockefeller University, was as deeply steeped in the values of STEM as it is possible to imagine.[1] Yet when he was appointed as the president of Stanford University and gave his inaugural address in October 2016, he spoke out strongly on behalf of the liberal arts and decried how transfixed both politicians and the parents of college students were by STEM. He said the most important skills that could be imparted to undergraduate students were critical and moral reasoning, creative expression, and appreciation of diversity, and the best preparation was the broad education of the liberal arts.

To Tessier-Lavigne, the "liberal" in "liberal education" referred to "liberating the mind," liberation that was threatened by "the mounting pressure for a vocational focus." Nor was STEM, or specialization in any vocationally related field, helpful in preparing students to adapt over a lifetime. To convey the all-purpose usefulness of a liberal education to a student's future work, he tried out a new tagline: "the liberal is the vocational."[2]

When he met with the faculty a few days later, Tessier-Lavigne observed that the fields that are popular at the moment, led by computer science, had not been so twenty or thirty years earlier. And they may not be the most popular twenty or thirty years hence. The conclusion that he drew was the very one that a professor in the humanities or social sciences would draw: the university must maintain a broad disciplinary base and ensure that student interest extends across all disciplines.[3]

Tessier-Lavigne gave his defense of the liberal arts prominent placement in his remarks to various campus communities, and he did not hedge his position in any way. That he had distinguished himself in his own career in the applied sciences made his defense all the more remarkable: he was not defending home turf. And though he was addressing Stanford in particular, everything he said applied to colleges and universities broadly. All students can be expected to change jobs frequently in their lives, all need to be prepared to fill jobs that will evolve rapidly and to work with people with varied cultures and backgrounds, and all would benefit from his prescription: "a broad-based education."[4]

The one thing Tessier-Lavigne did not do was draw attention to the dispositive role of employers in determining the fate of the liberal arts. "We are fighting against much of society, a society which is driving students to focus rather than broaden," he said. He elaborated: "This focus on immediate prospects . . . comes very strongly from parents but also from students, from peers, and others, as I've heard anecdotally."[5] But parents and students are merely reacting to the signals that prospective employers send out in the job market. If employers were to signal an appreciation of the liberal arts, students and parents would notice.

The humanities majors who were profiled in this book are contrarians. They selected their majors in the face of abundant evidence that they would have considerable difficulty finding professional work upon graduation, and difficulty did come. Their stories were presented not to dispel the notion that the market looks at humanities skeptically but to show that when employers give them the chance, their workplace experiences provide tangible proof of the claimed usefulness made on behalf of the liberal arts—that the liberal is the vocational.

The anxiety undergraduate students feel about what the future holds depends upon the choice of major and the perceived receptiveness to that major on the part of the desired employers. It has always been so. In the first decades of Stanford's history, engineering majors could be confident of finding work if their specialization was not an esoteric one such as mining. Students who majored in pre-law or prepared for medical school also enjoyed the comfort of seeing before them a well-lighted path to a professional career. So too did the graduates who did half a year or a year of post-graduate courses in the education department to earn a teaching credential for high school; one-third of Stanford's graduates in the early twentieth century went into teaching, either temporarily or permanently.[6]

In those same early years, however, students who were not on a professional track were subject to feeling terrified at the blankness of their post-graduation futures. In 1904, a student writer imagined the despair of the graduate who had studied English and history, peering at the framed sheepskin written in Latin and asking "What in the world is the use of it?"

> It hangs above the bookshelf
> In the old mahogany frame,
> And he can't read any blame word of it
> Except his danged old name![7]

About the same time, the student humor magazine at Stanford described well the terror of the senior who would soon be pushed overboard by the university into a depthless sea:

> Step lively now! you beggar,
> What makes you move so slow
> When seven score as good as you
> Are battened down below?
> For Heaven's sake get off the boat
> And jump into the sea!

So we can tidy up the ship

And then step down to tea[8]

Stanford, like other colleges and universities, would come to see itself as responsible for placing its students after graduation, even though, realistically, it lacked the power to determine the one factor that mattered most: what employers sought in students. If liberal arts majors had difficulty, the university would direct the blame to itself.

Was Stanford doing all it should for those students who did not follow a professional track? The question was taken up in 1910 by an associate professor of English, Richard M. Alden. He sent out a questionnaire to a large number of Stanford upperclassmen, excluding those who were headed for careers in engineering, medicine, law, and teaching, and asked about the reasons for their choosing their majors. He found that at least one-half of the students whose major was attached to "non-professional departments" had no "vocational end" in mind. This was especially the case with those who chose English, history, or German.[9]

To Alden, the nonvocational majors encompassed both "undesirable" and "desirable" students. The undesirable ones were those who "come to the University primarily for other than educational purposes" and who chose a major department only because they were required to do so. The desirable nonvocational majors, however, did not wish to specialize in the study of a particular field because either their intended occupation was one for which the university did not offer special preparation or because the preparation would be supplied in graduate training. Alden defended these students' desire to take more introductory courses, explore many branches of knowledge, and receive a liberal education. His only reservation was whether such students even had a legal right to be at Stanford, given that the university's charter specified that the education "fit the graduate for some useful pursuit, and to this end cause the pupils, as early as may be, to declare the particular calling in life which they may desire to pursue." Alden passed up an opportunity to argue that a liberal education could serve as excellent preparation for all fields, or that earning a bachelor's degree should be thought of as the penultimate stage of education, before the professional training in graduate school commenced.[10]

Rather than attempt to persuade the outside world of the virtues of an education that was "non-vocational,"[11] the university instead sought to ameliorate what was seen as the problem: students lacked adequate information about career options. The Committee on Vocational Guidance, initially composed of five faculty members, was established in 1913. It organized talks about particular careers by "men of affairs" (and occasionally by women, for women students), compiled lists of occupations that were matched to majors, and oversaw the expansion of a collection of books related to careers that the university library maintained in the reference room.[12]

The phrase "vocational guidance" was then in vogue in higher education circles, but the committee was aware that the adjective *vocational* was problematic, conjuring images of occupations that did not require a college education. An early pamphlet that was published by the committee explained that its use of the word was different from common usage: "In this bulletin the word 'vocation' is used to mean the occupation which a person adopts as a life work irrespective of the nature or grade of the work." W. M. Proctor, who taught a course in "vocational guidance" in the education department, used the same phrasing in a talk he gave to Stanford students in 1919 on how to choose a life work.[13]

The committee also knew that most undergraduates were inclined to believe that the bachelor's degree was all that they would need to get started in that life work. It was the committee's unhappy task to explain that not all careers would be open to those with merely four years of college. Their pamphlet pointed out how some careers might require graduate work, some might require an apprenticeship, and others could be entered only by taking "a minor position which may ultimately lead to a permanent vocation."[14]

Stanford's Committee on Vocational Guidance offered advice to students interested in business that is refreshing to revisit today. Noting in 1919 that the university did not have a business school, the committee did not urge students with an interest in business to major in economics. It instead said that these students would use their time well by pursuing any interest—in science, language, or literature, for example—it did not matter. "It is not so much the knowledge but the training gained in securing that knowledge that makes the university graduate successful in business," the pamphlet explained. It continued, "This training can be secured by study in almost any field, provided the study is earnest and extended."[15]

The faculty committee did not anoint some careers as more desirable than others; it encouraged students to consider many dozens of possibilities, providing inviting introductions to a number of careers that students might not have heard of or would not have thought of as suitable for a college graduate: "Fruit-growing"; "Scientific drafting"; "Actuarial work"; "Public speaking"; "Health Officer"; "Astronomer and Geodesist"; and, carrying on the committee's good work, "Vocational Counselor."[16]

Nary a negative word was said about any of the many dozens of careers dangled before the students, but one exception was law, which had long been overcrowded, leading to depressed average incomes and the flight every year of "large numbers of men" from the profession. Professional acting was another career that was not encouraged: "The precarious and uncertain life of the stage and the conditions surrounding it at the present time are matters which should receive most earnest and careful consideration before one decides upon the stage as a life work."[17]

Women who were interested in secretarial work—the committee did not use gender-neutral language—and were university graduates would have to compete with "young girls who are lacking in education, judgment and ability, and who wish to work only for the purpose of paying for their own clothes until they are married" and who, "because of their inefficiency and lack of interest in their work, greatly lower the standard of pay received by secretaries and make it more difficult for capable women to get the opportunities they deserve." But should women graduates remain undaunted and think of entry-level secretarial positions as apprenticeships in which much could be learned from "their less-well-educated, but more experienced associates," they could advance to better paying positions.[18] The committee, however, did not supply encouragement to women who were interested in an occupation that was filled with men.[19]

In 1930, a reporter for the student newspaper tried a touch of humor to draw students to a program of speakers arranged by the Committee on Vocational Guidance: "The four-year vacation of the younger generation, commonly called higher education at some college or university, is drawing to a close and in June the large majority of Stanford's graduating class will face the world in stark reality unprepared and undecided as to their life profession."[20] The "large majority" was limited to students with majors in the liberal arts. Another reporter observed that "the doctors, lawyers, and engineers have their future programs pretty well in mind, but the great majority of entering freshmen haven't looked any farther ahead than the next football season or another spring quarter. That is where vocational guidance begins to do its work."[21]

Vocational guidance expanded. C. Gilbert Wrenn, a PhD student in the education department, was appointed secretary of the university's vocational guidance service in 1929[22] and held office hours for students in the afternoons.[23] Wrenn was also appointed as a member of the Vocational Guidance Committee, which had bulked up by 1930 by acquiring three deans and the university registrar in addition to faculty members.[24]

Over time, the faculty and administration representatives stepped back and let the students carry on the arrangements for speakers and publicity for the talks. The work that was done by student volunteers on behalf of this cause, vocational guidance, was extensive. At its organizational peak, the student committee was so diligent that it met once a week.[25]

The career guidance was apportioned into separate domains for men and women.[26] In 1940, for example, when the Men's Vocational Guidance Series invited Edward C. Lipman, an executive with the Emporium department store, to come to campus, the message delivered to students was "All Men Welcome." Lipman's visit was followed by those of representatives of the American Trust Company, Crown-Zellerbach Corporation, and Standard Oil Company of California.[27] If women students got to hear about department store management, it was only when addressed separately by a speaker who offered a list of opportunities specifically for women: "the vocations of drama, writing, personnel work, teaching, and department store management."[28] The speaker who was invited to campus in 1940 to talk about careers in fashion design did not come to address men.[29]

When C. Gilbert Wrenn addressed Stanford women students in 1932, he placed stress on the importance of "developing a pleasing personality." This would make them "indispensable to prospective employers," he claimed.[30] He told the women to "get practice in meeting men; acquire self-confidence; develop personality; expect to make a name for yourself."[31]

The women students episodically pushed back against male paternalism and advice. The nine students who composed the Vocational Student Committee in 1939 were exceptionally independent, rounding up information on not just the four areas that had led in a survey of women students' interests—"personnel, social, education, and business"—but in other areas as well, including forestry, geology, government service, and "any number of other positions in which women's participation is unfamiliar, but not irregular."[32] The committee called attention to folders of career information maintained by Anastasia Doyle, the vocational counselor in the Dean of Women's office, that were available to all women. A folder on careers in law included magazine clippings about women judges and lawyers. In addition, the folder had letters written by former Stanford women students who were engaged in the actual practice of law and who provided "an insight into the problems and advantages of the profession which is seldom captured in a magazine article."[33]

What may be most impressive about these students' volunteer work in vocational guidance was that these women and men, who invested so much time and effort into getting speakers and rounding up students to attend, were willing to help their fellow students with career planning rather than only pursue their own professional interests. The student organizers had not secured their own futures; they were beset by worry about the unknown, too. (We, looking back, can see what they could not: how, for example, Derek Bok, a political science major who would graduate as a member of the Class of 1951 and was an active volunteer on the Senior Vocational Committee,[34] would eventually become the president of Harvard University.)

The distribution of information about careers subsequently became institutionalized and professionalized. "Career planning" formally became part of the name of Stanford's placement center for a while, and the altruism that had infused the earlier era of student-volunteer-led vocational guidance disappeared.

In 2013, Stanford appointed a new director for its Career Development Center, Farouk Dey. Dey, who had been the director of Carnegie Mellon University's Career and Professional Development Center was charged with remaking Stanford's center.[35] After a steering committee was organized and the planning for the center's future, "Vision 2020," was complete, Dey was ready in 2015 to declare, "The days of a 'brick-and-mortar' career services are over."[36] Dey described the new model for career services in grand, if rather indistinct, terms: "Our career educators are connected everywhere on and off campus to help expand and leverage the Stanford ecosystem for our students."[37]

Dey and his colleagues wanted their organizational unit to have a new name to reflect the new mission, but they apparently could not think of a good replacement noun for "Center." What they devised was an acronym, BEAM, a grammatically strange concoction that omitted the final noun: Bridging Education, Ambition, and Meaningful (work).

BEAM's description of its new identity emphasized that "we educate, rather than place people in jobs." Specifically, BEAM would educate students "about the process of cultivating their personalized networks to shape their professional journey and bridging their education and ambitions with meaningful work."[38] The importance of personal networks is a motif that runs through the narratives of the graduates presented in this book. It should be noted that engineering students do not need those personal networks; it is humanities and other liberal arts majors who need them.

Without a "Center" at the center of its name, BEAM might have been expected to shrink considerably in size, as students took on the networking that the university used to handle for them. That did not transpire. A new director, with a new vision and a new name for his program, can lay claim to more resources. Dey, whose group had twenty-six full-time positions when he arrived in 2013, doubled the size of the staff by 2016. BEAM was organized into new subgroups: Career Communities, Career Catalysts, Career Ventures, and Branding and Digital Communities.[39]

The dramatic expansion of BEAM can be seen as reassurance theater, responding to the heightened anxiety experienced by liberal arts students—and, perhaps even more important, their parents—about future job prospects. Like all universities, private and public alike, Stanford must convey to all interested parties that it assiduously helps all undergraduates find work upon graduation, particularly those whose major likely will not attract multiple job offers. The commitment is displayed with an enlarged career-services staff that can project tireless busyness on behalf of students who will soon graduate.

I am skeptical that the makeover of career services will make any difference whatsoever. But I do not fault its staff members. They cannot effect an economy-wide shift in employer attitudes that would open doors to liberal arts majors. I see abundant evidence that students have greatly lowered their own expectations of what career services can do. Institutional help is largely absent in the stories of the students presented here. I can also point to the Stanford students who are pushing full-time career counselors to the side and taking a more active role in career planning by enrolling in great numbers in a two-credit, pass/fail course that Stanford began offering in 2010 titled "Designing Your Life."[40] The course was developed by Bill Burnett and Dave Evans, instructors in the Stanford Design Program. The course description says that it "uses design thinking to address the 'wicked problem' of designing your life and career." *Vocation* makes many appearances in the course description and among the course objectives: "vocation formation throughout your life"; "vocation development, now and in the future"; and in the student's "own vocational vision."[41]

In the earlier era, faculty members and students alike treated "vocational guidance" as, essentially, the process of supplying students with richly detailed information about many vocations. The students did not need to be literally guided; they just needed plentiful information, obtained principally from campus visits by experienced practitioners who could ideally provide "the inside dope," as a *Stanford Daily* article about a speaker's series promised in 1940.[42]

The contemporary form of vocational guidance at Stanford, that is, *vocational development*, as embodied in the "Designing Your Life" course, gives less attention to the particulars about careers and more to the process of selecting, which will be employed not just once but many times. Instead of talking about "the career," the course talks of the transition "from university to first career." The syllabus is a potpourri, including New Age-y psychology (Martin Seligman, *Authentic Happiness: Using the New Positive Psychology to Realize Your Potential for*

Lasting Fulfillment); more serious psychology (Mihalyi Csikszentmih-alyi, *Flow: The Psychology of Optimal Experience*); career planning (Rich-ard Bolles, *What Color Is Your Parachute* and Marty Nemko, *Cool Careers for Dummies*); and job-related oral histories (Studs Terkel's *Working: People Talk About What They Do All Day and How They Feel About What They Do*).

Bill Burnett explained how the methodology essential to design applies to choosing a life work as well: "You prototype, you test, and you constantly change your point of view." Students in the course are required to develop three entirely different five-year plans for themselves—"Odyssey Plans"—and then select one of them as the basis for developing a fully fleshed-out ten-year plan. The exercise is supposed to force students, in Burnett's words, to "prototype differ-ent versions of the you that you might become."[43]

Ten-year plans do not seem suited for humanities majors, how-ever, at least without contemplation of graduate school or other post-graduate education. The stories of the professional paths taken by the graduates told in this book, who were selected partly because they did not head to graduate school, could not have been mapped in advance. When two economists of the Federal Reserve Bank of New York, Jaison R. Abel and Richard Deitz, used data collected in the 2010 census to look at how well college graduates' majors matched their jobs, they found that, after excluding those with grad-uate degrees, only 27 percent of college graduates with only a bach-elor's degree were working in a job that was linked to the graduate's major by the federal government's classification scheme. This en-compasses all disciplines. To be sure, the scheme is not very generous in defining matches: only 1 percent of liberal arts majors were found to be in jobs matched to their particular major.[44]

Some students who themselves are comfortable with the un-known must fend off parents who apply pressure on their wayward offspring to select a major that works like a conveyor belt, delivering the graduate to a destination known in advance. Steven Pearlstein, a professor of public affairs at George Mason University, wrote a piece in 2016 for the *Washington Post*: "Meet the Parents Who Won't Let Their Children Study Literature."[45] It told of a conversation with his students after the class had read and discussed David Nasaw's eight-hundred-page biography of Andrew Carnegie, a book that many of the students thanked Pearlstein for assigning. He learned that of the twenty-four students in the class, an honors seminar on wealth and poverty, none were history majors. Nor English majors. Nor philosophy majors. He asked them, How could this be? Half a dozen of them replied, "Our parents wouldn't let us."

It is not only the parents of students at state universities who direct their children away from the humanities. Jill Lepore, a professor of history at Harvard, told of one student who had come enthusiastically to her home for an event promoting Harvard's history and literature program and who while there received a torrent of urgent text messages from her parents: "Leave right now, get out of there, that is a house of pain."[46]

Amanda Rizkalla, a freshman at Stanford, wrote an essay for the school paper in the fall of 2016 about the difficulty she faces, as a first-generation college student coming from a low-income background, in explaining to her father why she would like to major in creative writing and not follow a pre-med track expected by him. Were she to tell her father about her wish, she expected he would say, "You already know how to write. You don't need to go to school for that. You need to be practical." She was not willing to let him dictate her choice, however. "I am the one who got into Stanford, not my parents," she wrote. She concluded with stirring words: "Yes, I am first-generation. Yes, I am low income. Yes, I lack a safety net to fall back on. And wholeheartedly, unapologetically, I choose passion over practicality."[47]

I hesitate to touch Rizkalla's phrasing, but I would not place "passion" in opposition to "practicality." I see graduates' passion for their chosen majors in the humanities running through the stories gathered in this book, passion that carries over into their first jobs, post-graduation—or, if the jobs were intrinsically uninteresting—passion for learning new things, taking on new projects, finding ways to make themselves useful to their employer outside of the boundaries of their formal job description. Their passion proved to be quite practical.

On the surface, the stories in this book may seem tied closely to one school. In many of the individual accounts, a school-based network was used to get in the door that led, it turned out, to a first destination after graduation. It is only natural that in the process of reading these narratives a dismaying assumption would take shape in the reader's mind, that anyone who did not go to that school would not have access to that network. I would argue that the recurring mention of the role of Stanford's alumni network in the narratives makes it seem more determinative than it deserves to be. I am emboldened to make this argument because of the work of two economists who have done two large, ingeniously designed studies that get as close as anyone has gotten to quantifying an answer to the question, What is the economic payoff to attending an elite college or university?

Stacy Berg Dale, an economist at Mathematica Policy Research, and Alan B. Krueger, a professor of economics at Princeton, looked at applications, transcripts, and earnings into middle age of two cohorts of students at Stanford and other schools, including highly selective schools such as Princeton, Yale, and Williams College, and some less selective schools such as Penn State and Xavier University.[48] Previous studies had found that among students with the same SAT scores or high school grades, those who attended selective colleges that attracted students with high SAT scores or high school grades were likely to end up with higher earnings.

Dale and Krueger were able to look at not only the colleges that the students attended but also the ones that they applied to, being accepted by some, rejected by others, and when that data was analyzed, something unexpected came into view. It turns out that after controlling for similar SAT scores and grades, what most matters in predicting future earnings is not the selectivity of the school a student attended but the selectivity of the most selective school the student applied to, even if rejected by that school. A hypothetical student who applied to both Stanford and Xavier, who was admitted by Xavier and was rejected by Stanford, would earn as much, on average, as the peer who had similar SAT scores and high school grades and was admitted and graduated from Stanford.

Their explanation of the phenomenon is that admissions offices cannot see critically important attributes such as ambition and confidence, which are revealed by where a student chooses to apply, and which are far more important than differences in school's faculties or in the reach of alumni networks. They noted a famous example: Steven Spielberg, who was rejected by the film schools at both the University of Southern California and UCLA, attended California State University, Long Beach, without apparent detriment to his career.[49]

When Alan Krueger was interviewed about these findings, he offered this advice to students: "Don't believe that the only school worth attending is one that would not admit you." Find a school whose academic strengths align with yours, he urged. He added, "Recognize that your own motivation, ambition and talents will determine your success more than the college name on your diploma."[50]

The unifying theme that runs through the stories presented in this book is the overarching importance of character, encompassing an appetite for intellectual challenge, the defiant rejection of the easiest paths, the capacity to work hard, the drive to reach higher. Students at any campus who happen to love studying a liberal arts subject, who are willing to dive deeply and excel, should take heart in the stories here. It is character that shines through. Parents should take heart, too.

As for prospective employers of tomorrow's graduates, I hope that these stories will help to restore the willingness shown in the past to consider the entire gamut of liberal arts majors for entry-level positions that do not require a specialized degree. This requires abandoning the expectation that every new hire can be completely prepared on the first day of work. If formal on-the-job training cannot be supplied, then time for informal on-the-job learning should be. The ability to learn quickly is a hallmark of those who have majored in the liberal arts; for that ability to shine, however, the candidate needs a first chance.

When employers are surveyed, they say they value the very things that a liberal education emphasizes. A 2013 survey by the Association of American Colleges and Universities found that 95 percent of employers agreed that "our company puts a priority on hiring people with the intellectual and interpersonal skills that will help them contribute to innovation in the workplace" and 93 percent agreed with the statement that "candidates' demonstrated capacity to think critically, communicate clearly, and solve complex problems is more important than their undergraduate major."[51]

To put these professed convictions into daily practice, however, the managers and teams who actually do the hiring must shed acquired habits of looking for particular majors when hiring non-specialists and turning away all others. The wisdom captured in that 1919 vocational guidance pamphlet, that "it is not so much the knowledge but the training gained in securing that knowledge," deserves to be appreciated anew. "The training can be secured by study in almost any field"—and students should not forget the final piece—"provided the study is earnest and extended."[52] Opening more doors to students who elect to major in the liberal arts—and who study diligently—would bring a multiplicity of perspectives for understanding a complex world and a well-practiced facility for communicating that complexity to others. Nothing yet discovered is more practical for preparing for the unpredictable future.

ACKNOWLEDGMENTS

I wish to thank Elizabeth Kaplan, my agent, who oh-so-gently imparted a practical education, nudging me away from an ill-conceived plan and back onto solid footing. She also found a wonderful home for this project at Stanford University Press. There, Jenny Gavacs was enormously helpful in guiding me through several iterations of the project's plan, and Kate Wahl supplied perspicacious suggestions that resulted in a much-improved book. Gigi Mark looked after production details with tender care. Stephanie Adams, Kalie Caetano, Ryan Furtkamp, and Kate Templar were assiduous in their preparations to spread word. And Michel Vrana, the designer of the inspired dust jacket, is a master at his craft.

I am indebted to the students who shared their experiences for the project and thank all of them: Kyle Abraham, Mark Bessen, Doug Blumeyer, Amanda Breen, Olivia Bryant, Michael Crandell, Truman Cranor, Magali Duque, Elise Grangaard, Stephen Hayes, Meredith Hazy, Trent Hazy, Gus Horwith, Marie Hubbard, Liam Kinney, Carly Lave, Jessica Moore, Jennifer Ockelmann, Jess Peterson, Andrew Phillips, Steven Rappaport, Mike Sanchez, Arielle Sison, Alexis Smith, Dylan Sweetwood, Brian Tich, Makshya Tolbert, and Judy Wang.

I am grateful for the time Daniel Davis and Derek Draper shared with me, supplying material used in the profile of Andrew Phillips.

For the profile of Doug Blumeyer, Kush Patel of App Academy supplied me with an interview and a tour of the academy, and Jon

Wolverton kindly indulged my request to go through a coding-skills exam (the sweat that poured off me testified to a realistic experience).

At Stanford, I received helpful assistance from Mehran Sahami, professor of computer science; Juliet Charnas, Alice Hu, and Jake Sonnenberg, students; Arthur Patterson, Miriam W. Palm, and Michelle Futornick in the Stanford News Library; Drew Bourn, historical curator at the Lane Medical Library; and the patient staff of Special Collections & University Archives.

As it has done many times, the College of Business of San Jose State University generously provided a leave with financial support to enable me to work on the book.

Earlier versions of the manuscript were transformed after undergoing review by a Dream Team of readers: Gail Hershatter, Leslie Berlin, and Barry Shank. Each was tireless in identifying weak arguments and lazy writing, supplying marginalia that were equal parts incisive, mortifying, and entertaining.

The writing of a book is consuming, but it is not the whole of a life. Ellen Stross is my partner in living fully, making everything, including writing, joyful.

I've dedicated the book to three extraordinary teachers and wise souls, my exemplary guides in the humanities: Emily Rosenberg, Harold Kahn, and Lyman Van Slyke.

NOTES

ABBREVIATIONS

CPPC   Career Planning and Placement Center

DPA   *Daily Palo Alto*

H&S   School of Humanities and Sciences, Stanford University

H&SR   School of Humanities and Sciences, Records 1930–1999 (SCOO36), Special Collections and University Archives, Stanford University Libraries

LSP   Leland Stanford Papers, University matters (Series 6), Stanford University, Stanford Digital Repository, http://purl.stanford.edu/qm411yg8385.

NYT   *New York Times*

SCUA   Special Collections and University Archives, Stanford University Libraries

SD   *Stanford Daily*

SFC   *San Francisco Chronicle*

SU   Stanford University

CHAPTER 1. THE MAJOR DECISION

1. Jaison R. Abel and Richard Deitz, "Underemployment in the Early Careers of College Graduates Following the Great Recession," National Bureau of Economic Research, Working Paper 22654, September 2016. Abel and Deitz, both of whom are on the staff of the Federal Reserve Bank of New York, found that between mid-2011 and mid-2014, employment fell among recent college graduates but underemployment rose to more than 46 percent, a level last seen in the early 1990s. STEM majors and accounting, business analytics, economics, and finance majors fared the best in finding initial jobs that utilized their majors; English, history, art history, and other humanities fields had far higher rates of underemployment following the Great Recession. Occupation-specific majors occupied the two extremes: nursing majors had the very lowest rate of underemployment, and criminal justice majors edged out performing arts majors for the top spot, with the highest underemployment rates. See Figure 4 in the appendix.

2. Debra Humphreys and Patrick Kelly, *How Liberal Arts and Sciences Majors Fare in Employment* (Washington, DC: Association of American Colleges and Universities,

2014), 9–10. If those who earned an advanced degree are excluded and graduates with just baccalaureate degrees are compared, an earnings gap between those with a humanities or social science major and those with a professional or preprofessional degree persists. But humanities majors are more likely to earn an advanced degree than all holders of bachelor's degrees: 42.5 percent compared with 36.3 percent for all BAs. See Norman M. Bradburn and Robert B. Townsend, "Use Data to Make a Strong Case for the Humanities," *Chronicle of Higher Education* (December 2, 2016): A23.

3. "Overcrowding Plagues CPPC Job Interviews," *SD*, February 4, 1981.

4. "Successor to Lyman as Eighth University President, Kennedy Speaks on Advising, Faculty, Humanities," *SD*, August 15, 1980.

5. "New President of Stanford," *NYT*, June 14, 1980.

6. "1979 Senior Survey Results," *SD*, April 22, 1980.

7. Stan Young, "Pity the Fuzzy Study Major," *SD*, January 11, 1980. Young stayed at Stanford to get a master's degree in history and then went to Harvard Law School, getting his law degree in 1985.

8. "Successor to Lyman."

9. *The Major Decision* (Stanford: H&S, 1983), 6.

10. Ibid., 8.

11. "Plastics" refers to the well-known brief scene in the iconic movie *The Graduate* (1967) that exposes the fatuousness of much of the career guidance dispensed by well-meaning parents and their friends. Benjamin Braddock, the new graduate played by Dustin Hoffman, is pulled aside by a family friend, Mr. McGuire:

"I just want to say one word to you. Just one word," McGuire says.

"Yes, sir."

"Are you listening?"

"Yes, I am."

[Dramatic pause.]

"Plastics."

[Confused pause before reply.]

"Exactly how do you mean?"

"There's a great future in plastics. Think about it. Will you think about it?"

"Yes, I will."

"'Nuff said. That's a deal."

12. In his profile of University of Michigan undergraduate William ("Bill") Joy, who was a student at the University of Michigan at exactly the same time as Crandell was at Stanford, Malcolm Gladwell credits the beguilingly responsive nature of the new time-sharing systems that had just been installed at the university for drawing undergraduates into programming. Gladwell, *Outliers: The Story of Success* (New York: Little, Brown, 2008).

13. After earning his bachelor's degree at Stanford, Fazzino earned a master's degree in public policy from Occidental College and an MBA from the University of Washington. He later served two terms as the mayor of Palo Alto. He died in 2012 at the age of sixty. Gary Fazzino, obituary, Palo Alto Online, http://www.paloaltoonline.com/obituaries/memorials/gary-fazzino?o=1882.

14. "Hard to Find: Workers with Good 'Soft Skills,'" *Wall Street Journal*, August 31, 2016. The article referred in passing to results of a survey conducted in 2015.

15. Notable recent works include Fareed Zakaria, *In Defense of a Liberal Education* (New York: Norton, 2015); Michael S. Roth, *Beyond the University: Why Liberal Education Matters* (New Haven: Yale University Press, 2014); and Andrew Delbanco, *College: What It Was, Is, and Should Be* (Princeton: Princeton University Press, 2012).

CHAPTER 2. THE NEW EDUCATION

1. "Seeing Red: Stanford v. Harvard," *Harvard Crimson's Fifteen Minutes Magazine*, October 30, 2014.

2. Ibid.

3. Ibid.

4. Ibid.

5. Ibid.

6. [untitled], *Harvard Crimson*, May 15, 1884.

7. "The Stanford Memorial College," *SFC*, May 23, 1884. The article had originally appeared in the *New York Tribune*.

8. "Stanford Memorial College." The *Argonaut*, a political and literary journal published in San Francisco, used similar imagery when it wrote that Stanford's school would educate students "in such practical industries as will enable them to go out into the world equipped for useful labor, with such knowledge as will be of service to them in the battle for bread." "Editorial Correspondence," *Argonaut* 14, no. 25 (June 21, 1884). The piece is unsigned, but the heading makes clear that Leland Stanford had been interviewed by the editor of the *Argonaut*, Frank M. Pixley.

9. "Stanford Memorial College."

10. "Practical Education," *SFC*, June 1, 1884.

11. Ibid.

12. Thomas Jefferson to George Ticknor, July 16, 1823, Thomas Jefferson Papers Series 1. General Correspondence, 1651–1827, http://hdl.loc.gov/loc.mss/mtj.mtjbib 024710.

13. Daniel A. Wren, "American Business Philanthropy and Higher Education in the Nineteenth Century," *Business History Review* 57, no. 3 (1983): 325.

14. Melissa Stone, "Another Time, Another SSS: A Brief History of the Sheffield Scientific School," *Yale Scientific* 82, no. 3 (November 2008), http://www.yalescientific.org /2008/11/another-time-another-sss-a-brief-history-of-the-sheffield-scientific-school.

15. Roger L. Geiger, "The Rise and Fall of Useful Knowledge: Higher Education for Science, Agriculture, and the Mechanic Arts, 1850–1875," in *The American College in the Nineteenth Century*, ed. Roger L. Geiger (Nashville: Vanderbilt University Press, 2000), 156–157. Geiger notes that Harvard's Lawrence Scientific School departed from the path of applied science taken by others when gifts allowed Harvard's school to hire the renowned scientist Louis Agassiz and orient the curriculum around pure science.

16. Edwin G. Knepper, *History of Business Education in [the] United States* (Bowling Green: Edwards Brothers, 1941). Knepper marks the beginning of the "Business College Era" in 1852, with the establishment of the Bryant-Stratton Chain of commercial

schools. By 1871, a few nonprofit universities, including Northwestern University and the University of Notre Dame, offered what Knepper calls "commercial work of some kind." Knepper, 43–44. Also see John R. Thelin, *A History of American Higher Education* (Baltimore: Johns Hopkins University Press, 2004).

17. The article was published in two parts: Charles W. Eliot, "The New Education," *Atlantic Monthly* 23, no. 136 (February 1869): 203–221; and Eliot, "The New Education II," *Atlantic Monthly* 23, no. 137 (March 1869): 358–367.

18. Eliot, "The New Education," (February 1869), 203.

19. Ibid., 218.

20. In his inaugural presidential address at Harvard, Eliot said, "The endless controversies whether language, philosophy, mathematics, or science supply the best mental training, whether general education should be chiefly literary or chiefly scientific, have no practical lesson for us to-day. This University recognizes no real antagonism between literature and science, and consents to no such narrow alternatives as mathematics or classics, science or metaphysics." *Addresses at the Inauguration of Charles William Eliot as President of Harvard College* (Cambridge: Sever and Francis, 1869), 29.

21. Roger L. Geiger, *The History of American Higher Education: Learning and Culture from the Founding to World War II* (Princeton: Princeton University Press, 2015), 287. Stanford, Cooper, and Cornell would found new institutions; other businessmen gave gifts to existing institutions that changed their names to honor their benefactors. Daniel Wren compiled a list of colleges and universities that acquired the names of businessmen that included other names: Bates, Brown, Bucknell, Carleton, Case, Clark, Colby, Colgate, Converse, Creighton, DePauw, Drew, Drexel, Duke, Hopkins, Newcomb, Peabody, Pratt, Purdue, Rollins, Rose, Simmons, Stetson, Stevens, Tulane, Vanderbilt, Vassar, Wells, and Wofford. He also noted that Queen's College in New Jersey was so pleased to receive $5,000 and a bell from Colonel Henry Rutgers, a wealthy landholder, that in anticipation of being named in Colonel Rutgers's will, the college changed its name. But the Colonel was unmoved and left his fortune to a church. Wren, "American Business Philanthropy," 336.

22. Carl Becker, *Cornell University: Founders and the Founding* (Ithaca: Cornell University Press, 1943), 131; Andrew Dickson White, *Autobiography of Andrew Dickson White* (New York: Century, 1906), 1:371. Ezra Cornell told reporters of his idea to offer a free education to work-study students before he secured White's support. Becker speaks of White's "dismay" when White saw the announcement in the *New York Tribune*.

23. "Practical Education," *SFC*, August 14, 1874.

24. Geiger, *History of American Higher Education*, 290.

25. "Practical Education," *SFC*, February 18, 1886. The article also criticized Ezra Cornell's "mistake" of placing the university in a small town that was not located on a major rail line and his spending "too much money for buildings and general improvements."

26. Early in his planning, Leland Stanford believed that a university alone would not be sufficient to impart the practical education that he had in mind. He spoke of building two preparatory schools, one for boys and one for girls, on the two flanks of a central university campus. The prep schools would take students from the age of twelve and get them started early in their chosen calling. "Stanford's Projects," *SFC*, January 23, 1885.

27. "Governor Stanford's Plans," *Sacramento Daily Record-Union*, May 26, 1884. Yale was not mentioned by name, but Leland Stanford said he would be accompanied by one "Professor Marsh of Yale College" and visit educational institutions of Connecticut, as well as of Massachusetts and Vermont. See also SU, "History of Stanford: The Birth of the University," https://www.stanford.edu/about/history/index.html.

28. Charles W. Eliot to David Starr Jordan, June 26, 1919, David Starr Jordan Papers 1861–1964 (SC0058), General Correspondence 1872–1931, SCUA, https://stacks.stanford.edu/file/druid:zk100zx0318/sc0058_s1a_b98_f870.pdf.

29. "The Stanford Gift," *SFC*, May 15, 1887. The $20 million comprised $5.3 million of land holdings at three scattered sites, including the Palo Alto farm that was valued at $1.2 million, and $14.7 million in other investments.

30. "Stanford's Projects," *SFC*. Cooper Union was erroneously referred to as the "Cooper Institute."

31. "A Public Benefaction," *Sacramento Daily Record-Union*, January 27, 1885.

32. "Pacific Slope," *Sacramento Daily Record-Union*, August 29, 1885.

33. Leland Stanford and Jane Lathrop Stanford, "The Founding Grant," November 11, 1885, in *Stanford University: The Founding Grant with Amendments, Legislation, and Court Decrees* (Stanford: Stanford University, 1987).

34. "Senator Stanford's Address," *Sacramento Daily Record-Union*, November 16, 1885.

35. "The Stanford University," *SFC*, November 19, 1885.

36. "Senator Stanford's Address." At the university's urging, a state law was passed in 1909 that banned liquor sales within 1.5 miles of universities, but it was written in such a way that it only applied to Stanford. The no-liquor zone, which extended into Menlo Park as well as Palo Alto, remained intact until the ban was struck down in a 1990 court case. See "Downtown After Dark," *Palo Alto Weekly*, September 21, 1994.

37. "The New University," *SFC*, May 13, 1888.

38. Ibid.

39. Orrin Leslie Elliott, *Stanford University, the First Twenty-Five Years* (Stanford: Stanford University Press, 1937), 16–17. Elliott said his source was an interview that had appeared in the *New York Evangelist*, February 19, 1891.

40. "Practical Education," *SFC*, February 18, 1886.

41. "The Stanford University."

CHAPTER 3. NATURALLY CURIOUS

1. "First Campus-wide Job Faire to Take Place on Wednesday," *SD*, April 23, 1979.

2. "CPPC Sponsors Job Faire Today in White Plaza; 60 Firms Attend," *SD*, April 25, 1980.

3. Ibid.

4. After Hazy got the job at Twitter, she asked her supervisor if her past tweets had been read as part of the evaluation process, expecting that these had been helpful in her candidacy. But she was told that no, the tweets had not been read.

5. Twitter, which was founded in 2006, did not introduce advertising until 2010, and when it did, it tried a new form of advertising—the "promoted tweet"—to go with the new form of messaging. This was not to be a conventional ad, the company

explained, but rather a tweet that would already exist, an "organic tweet," published by the brand for those who followed it, and it would have to "resonate with users" or it would disappear from view. "Hello World," Twitter blog, April 13, 2010, https://blog .twitter.com/2010/hello-world.

6. "Stripe's Valuation Rises to $3.6 Billion with $70 Million Round," *Wall Street Journal* Digits blog, December 2, 2014. A mere seven months later, when Stripe raised another round of funding, its valuation had jumped to $5 billion. "Stripe, Digital Payments Start-Up, Raises New Funding and Partners with Visa," *NYT*, July 28, 2015.

7. Randall Stross, *The Launch Pad: Inside Y Combinator, Silicon Valley's Most Exclusive School for Startups* (New York: Portfolio, 2012), 64–66.

8. "Online Payments Startup Stripe Raises New Funds at $5 Billion Valuation," *Wall Street Journal*, July 28, 2015.

9. "Stripe's Valuation Nearly Doubles to $9.2 Billion," *Wall Street Journal*, November 25, 2016.

CHAPTER 4. PROPER PROPORTION

1. "The Stanford Gift," *SFC*, May 15, 1887.

2. Ibid.

3. "The Stanford University," *SFC*, May 15, 1887.

4. "Practical Education," *SFC*, February 18, 1886.

5. Jane Lilly, "If These Walls Could Talk: A History of Roble Halls," *Sandstone & Tile* 30.2 (Spring/Summer 2006): 3–5; David Starr Jordan, *The Days of a Man: Being Memories of a Naturalist, Teacher and Minor Prophet of Democracy* (Yonkers-on-Hudson, NY: World Book Company, 1922), 1:367, 385. Originally, the Stanfords planned to admit the first batch of women only after the first class of men had started their studies but changed their minds two years after construction had begun. In 1889, they commissioned the women's dorm, Roble Hall, to be ready by October 1, 1891, the expected start of the academic year for the first class. There was not enough time to complete the women's dorm, however, and its size had to be reduced mid-construction by two-thirds. The dormitory named Roble Hall that stands today on Santa Teresa Street is a different structure; it was completed in 1918, replacing its namesake, which was renamed Sequoia Hall and later demolished.

6. "Meet President Jordan," *Stanford Magazine*, January/February 2010.

7. "Prominent Cornellians," *Cornell Alumni News* 50, no. 6 (May 10, 1899).

8. "Meet President Jordan"; Jordan, *Days of a Man*, 1:354–355.

9. Editorial, *SFC*, March 24, 1891.

10. Ellen Coit Elliott, *It Happened This Way; American Scene* (Stanford: Stanford University Press, 1940), 172.

11. "Waiting Students," *SFC*, September 26, 1891.

12. Jordan, *Days of a Man*, 1:402, 415. Some of the students were over thirty. Jordan told this yarn: "Once when two youths met on a tramp in the hills, one became expansive in regard to his own exploits. Finally, surveying his companion, he inquired: 'Frosh?' 'No, Prof.' 'Oh, Lordy!' said the dismayed freshman."

13. Orrin Leslie Elliott, *Stanford University, the First Twenty-Five Years* (Stanford: Stanford University Press, 1937), 50.

14. "Meet President Jordan."

15. Edwin E. Slosson, *Great American Universities* (New York: Macmillan, 1910), 116.

16. Jordan pursued Josiah Royce, the chair of Harvard's philosophy department; as Royce was born and grew up in California and had earned his bachelor's degree at the University of California, Jordan could couch the offer as a means to return home. According to the *San Francisco Chronicle*, Royce asked for a salary of $5,000, and when Jordan countered with a best offer of $3,000, Royce turned him down. "A Small Faculty," *SFC*, May 5, 1891. But in his memoirs, written many years later, Jordan disputes the charge that he had not been able to offer attractive salaries; he claimed that he had been authorized to offer salaries of $7,000 to senior scholars—including to Royce—but for most it seemed too much of a risk "to join an institution as yet unorganized, with libraries and laboratories still to be developed." Jordan, *Days of a Man*, 1:396–397.

17. Leland Stanford to Professor David S. Jordan, telegram draft, April 13 [1891], LSP. Jordan would later claim that Leland Stanford had him limit the number to fifteen because Stanford "feared that the presumably small number of students the first year would cause a larger group to seem absurd." See Jordan, *Days of a Man*, 1:396–397.

18. Leland Stanford to David S. Jordan, telegram draft, May 26, 1891, LSP.

19. Leland Stanford to David S. Jordan, telegram draft, June 1, 1891, LSP.

20. "A Small Faculty."

21. Elliott, *Stanford University*, 55. At that point, Jordan reported to Stanford that the next searches would be in the following fields: English, Spanish, freehand drawing, the library, gymnasium, music, art, American history, social and municipal institutions, military tactics, and telegraphy. His desiderata were stuffed with applied subjects: in a year or two, he planned to follow with faculty hires in agriculture, agricultural chemistry, horticulture and viticulture, veterinary surgery, forestry and economic botany, entomology and economic zoology, mining engineering, mineralogy, metallurgy, psychology, ethics, and oratory.

22. Jordan, *Days of a Man*, 1:421.

23. "Leland Stanford Junior University: The Opening Ceremonies," *SFC*, October 2, 1891.

24. Leland Stanford to D. S. Jordan, May 10, 1892, LSP. Also see Leland Stanford to D. S. Jordan, May 23, 1892, LSP.

25. Leland Stanford to David S. Jordan, February 17, 1892, LSP.

26. Leland Stanford to David Starr Jordan, telegram draft, February 18, 1892, LSP.

27. "Stanford Interviewed," *DPA*, October 19, 1892.

28. Elliott, *Stanford University*, 114–115.

29. Jordan, *Days of a Man*, 1:479. Jordan faulted Leland Stanford's former business partner Collis Huntington for reneging. Jordan described Huntington's code of ethics this way: "Whatever is not nailed down is mine. Whatever I can pry loose is not nailed down."

30. "Stanford Gets $2,500,000," *DPA*, May 4, 1896.

31. Jordan, *Days of a Man*, 1:479, 496–497, 509.

32. "The Law Department," *DPA*, December 12, 1895.

33. In 1911, Jordan said that he no longer pressed for eliminating "the junior col-

lege" because of better enforcement of liquor laws and the university's attracting "a very different type of student, older students whose influence incites the younger to better work." He declared the most recent class to be "considerably superior to any preceding class." Elliott, *Stanford University*, 520, 529.

34. John Maxson Stillman, "Specialization in Education," *Addresses at the Fourth Annual Commencement, Leland Stanford Junior University*, (Palo Alto, CA: Stanford University Press, May 29, 1895), 11–12.

35. Slosson, *Great American Universities*, 147.

36. "Four Years Retrospective of Stanford University," *DPA*, May 29, 1895.

37. Nell May Hill to Garlin Hill, January 15, 1893, cited in Earl Pomeroy, introduction, "Letters of Herbert C. Hoover," *The Call Number* 27, no. 2 (Spring 1966), 3.

38. "Four Years Retrospective."

39. The author expressed the representation of women not in percentages but as a ratio of women to men. In the first year, 1891–92, the ratio was thirty-three women to one hundred men; three years later, it was fifty-one women to one hundred men.

40. Walter Miller, "The Old and the New," *DPA*, May 25, 1898.

41. David Starr Jordan wanted to see more students pursue graduate studies. He claimed that Leland Stanford had wanted the same. Jordan wrote, "Nothing in the work of the university gave Mr. Stanford greater pleasure than the fact that of its first two graduating classes more than half have remained for advanced work." But Stanford was not sufficiently excited about graduate education that he offered praise for it in the interviews he gave when asked about his plans for the university. David Starr Jordan, "The Educational Ideas of Leland Stanford," *Educational Review* 6 (September 1893), 142.

42. Miller, "Old and the New."

43. "Conferring of Degrees," *DPA*, May 25, 1898; "The New Registrar," *DPA*, May 13, 1896. A longer definition of the term *bionomics* would be experimental biology that used controlled laboratory conditions to simulate natural environments. It originated among British biological scientists, but its leading proponent in the United States was Vernon Lyman Kellogg, an entomologist who joined the Stanford faculty in 1893. See Mark A. Largent, "Bionomics: Vernon Lyman Kellogg and the Defense of Darwinism," *Journal of the History of Biology* 32 (1999): 465–488.

44. Slosson, *Great American Universities*, 133. Edwin Slosson made sure that his readers did not get the impression that he thought that the women were doing academic work that was the equal of what the men did. He wrote that "[in] the humanistic departments, in which the women predominate, the work is easier than in the technological course." He did not comment on the difficulty of mathematics, however, whose majors comprised five women and only one man.

45. J. C. Branner, "Class Day Address," *DPA* May 25, 1898.

46. "Why Mrs. Stanford Restricts," *Chicago Tribune*, June 7, 1899.

47. "Mrs. Stanford's Great Gift," *DPA*, September 12, 1899. Jane Stanford could not abide the thought of automobiles on the campus, or of liquor, or of male and female students spending time together "promenading" in the late evening hours. When reports of romantic couples who were walking on campus reached her, she was so angry

that she asked the trustees to remove women entirely from the university, but was persuaded to relent and let women remain. "Early History Of '500' Told by G. E. Crothers," *SD*, October 13, 1931.

48. When Stanford's board of trustees decided to lift the limit, it proclaimed its everlasting fealty to Jane Stanford's wish to keep women from attaining a majority and directed the admissions office to cap the enrollment of women at 45 percent of the student body, the percentage that women occupied in May 1899 when Jane Stanford had imposed the cap on women's enrollment. "More Women Will Enter as Ruling Spells End of '500,'" *SD*, May 12, 1933.

49. Slosson, *Great American Universities*, 127.

CHAPTER 5. A FOOT IN THE DOOR

1. Stephen Hayes, "From Moderation to Confrontation: African Responses to the Natives Land Act of 1913," *Herodotus: Stanford's Undergraduate Journal of History* 20 (Spring 2010): 5–24.

2. "Walking Backward: A Day in the Life of a Tour Guide," *SD*, March 10, 2010.

3. "Those Who Can, Teach," *SD*, March 10, 2010.

4. Ibid.

5. United's round-the-world ticket permitted seven stops, as long as the passengers continued to move in the same east-west direction as taken in the first leg.

CHAPTER 6. ENGINEERING SUCCESS

1. Only two U.S. presidents to date have been engineers: Hoover and Jimmy Carter. Both were single-term presidents who confronted significant unanticipated challenges while in office; both left with low public approval ratings.

2. Even if Hoover had taken economics, macroeconomics would necessarily have been pre-Keynesian (Keynes had yet to reach the age of twelve when Hoover graduated) and blind to stimulus of deficit spending during a depression. Hoover took very few courses other than in engineering, science, and math: none in his freshman year; elementary French his sophomore year; philosophy in his junior year; and one semester of elementary German, History of the Nineteenth Century, Ethics, and Personal Hygiene in his senior year. All classes were graded pass/fail; he failed German. Transcript in Herbert Hoover Subject Collection, Box 5, Stanford Diploma folder, Hoover Institution Archives.

3. Rose Wilder Lane, *The Making of Herbert Hoover* (New York: Century, 1920) and Will Irwin, *Herbert Hoover: A Reminiscent Biography* (New York: Century, 1928). Lane's book was published in the year Hoover turned forty-six. Hoover's own memoirs came much later, in 1951, when he was seventy-seven and his recall of some experiences during his college years do not jibe with known facts. Herbert Hoover, *The Memoirs of Herbert Hoover* (New York: Macmillan, 1951).

4. Hoover, *Memoirs*, 1:13.

5. George H. Nash, *The Life of Herbert Hoover: The Engineer, 1874–1914* (New York: W. W. Norton, 1983), 13–23.

6. Hoover, *Memoirs*, 1:14–15.

7. Irwin, *Herbert Hoover*, 33.

8. Ibid., 33–35.

9. Lane, *Making of Herbert Hoover*, 105.

10. The inheritance was one-third of $2,500, split among Hoover and two siblings and held by a county-appointed guardian, Lawrie Tatum. Nash, *Life of Herbert Hoover*, 10–11.

11. David Starr Jordan, "Why Do Eastern Students Come to Stanford University?" *SFC*, May 2, 1897. Some respondents did cite the relatively low cost of attending Stanford. One example: "By personal observation I found that I could attend Stanford 3500 miles away from home as cheaply as I could Princeton, Yale or Harvard, carfare included. I have therefore the education and pleasure of travel thrown in."

12. "Waiting Students," *SFC*, September 26, 1891.

13. Irwin, *Herbert Hoover*, 44–45.

14. Lane, *Making of Herbert Hoover*, 105.

15. Leland Stanford to D. S. Jordan, August 30, 1892, LSP.

16. Irwin, *Herbert Hoover*, 46.

17. Herbert Hoover to Nell May Hill, August 30, 1892.

18. Irwin, *Herbert Hoover*, 44–45.

19. "College Man in the Business World," *Stanford Illustrated Review*, April 1933, 214.

20. "Quad," *DPA*, April 20, 1894.

21. Nash, *Life of Herbert Hoover*, 35.

22. Hoover to Nell May Hill, November 9, 1894.

23. "The Three H's Elected," *DPA*, April 24, 1894.

24. Irwin, *Herbert Hoover*, 38–39.

25. Ibid.

26. Jordan, *Days of a Man*, 1:490.

27. Lane, *Making of Herbert Hoover*, 161.

28. In Hoover's Class of 1895, the self-anointed Pioneers, only 16 percent of the graduates were engineers; 23 percent were in science and math and 42 percent were in the humanities. Economics, law, hygiene, and a smattering of other fields were the choices of the remainder. Edwin E. Slosson, *Great American Universities* (New York: Macmillan, 1910), 147.

29. Lane, *Making of Herbert Hoover*, 180. Initially, Hoover worked the night shift. E. B. Kimball to John Branner, November 13, 1895, John Casper Branner Papers, Series I (SC034), Box 26, Folder 104, SCUA. Kimball, who was a classmate of Hoover's and also a geology major, found work at the same time in another underground mine. After finishing his stint, he wrote Branner about the experience, "Those who are under thirty seem to be over fifty. Yet I do not bewail the time as lost that I have devoted to the work for I believe that without it one cannot become a good practical man, that he cannot form an idea of the amount of work a miner should perform, that he will not appreciate the difficulties that the men have to contend with and that he cannot direct the men unless he thoroughly understands what he wants done. I don't agree with Hoover when he says that such work is not necessary, for the results of the workings of college men in many cases have been disastrous to those that have employed them." E. B. Kim-

ball to John Branner, April 1, 1896, John Casper Branner Papers, Series I (SC034), Box 26, Folder 104, SCUA.

30. Hoover, *Memoirs*, 1:27; Lane, *Making of Herbert Hoover*, 183.

31. Hoover, *Memoirs*, 1:27.

32. Ibid.

33. Lane, *Making of Herbert Hoover*, 184–185; Irwin, *Herbert Hoover*, 71.

34. Hoover, *Memoirs*, 1:20.

35. "College Man," 214.

36. Lane, *The Making of Herbert Hoover*, 185–186; Irwin, *Herbert Hoover*, 72. Lane places the salary raise after the report was completed, and his chronology seems more credible than Irwin's, which has the salary raise before. Hoover's *Memoirs* has still another order: a first field assignment in Colorado that came before the court case. Hoover, *Memoirs*, 1:27.

37. "Quads," *DPA*, March 17, 1896.

38. John C. Branner to Herbert Hoover, April 27, 1896, John Casper Branner Papers, Series I (SC034), Box 5, SCUA; Lane, *Making of Herbert Hoover*, 195–196.

39. Lane, *Making of Herbert Hoover*, 198–199. In Lane's telling, Bewick, Moreing said that the candidate should be no more than thirty years old because "a man over thirty can't stand the Australian climate and living conditions." But George Nash presents convincing evidence, including Hoover's misrepresentation of his age when sailing to Australia, that Bewick, Moreing, in fact, had a minimum age of thirty-five for the position. See Nash, *Life of Herbert Hoover*, 605n97.

40. Lane, *Making of Herbert Hoover*, 212–213, 220–221.

41. "Gold in China Is All a Myth," *SFC*, October 24, 1901.

42. "College Man," 214

43. Herbert C. Hoover, "The Training of the Mining Engineer," *Science* 20, no. 517 (November 25, 1904): 717.

44. Ibid., 718.

45. Ibid.

46. "Theodore Hoover, '01, to Organize New Mining Dept.," *SD*, April 16, 1919; Jas. Perrin Smith, "The Stanford School of Mines," *Stanford Illustrated Review* 20, no. 7 (April 1919): 332.

47. Hoover, "Training," 719.

CHAPTER 7. THE DIFFERENT PERSPECTIVE

1. Jennifer Ockelmann, "'Don't Fuss, Mother, This Isn't So Fast': Flappers and the Struggle Between Modernity and Modesty," *Herodotus: Stanford's Undergraduate Journal of History* 20 (Spring 2010): 43–64.

CHAPTER 8. A GENERAL UNDERSTANDING

1. "Program of Tomorrow's Exercises," *DPA*, March 8, 1894; "Founder's Day," *DPA*, March 9, 1894.

2. "Founder's Day."

3. Jane Lathrop Stanford, "Mrs. Stanford's Address of October 3, 1902," in *Stanford*

University: The Founding Grant with Amendments, Legislation, and Court Decrees (Stanford: Stanford University, 1987).

4. Guido H. Marx, "The Making of the Stanford Engineer," *Stanford Alumnus* 9, no. 4 (December 1907): 130.

5. George Elliott Howard, "The American University and the American Man," *Second Commencement Address, Leland Stanford Junior University* (Palo Alto, CA: 1893), 13–14.

6. "What Stanford Lawyers Are Doing," *Stanford Alumnus* 6, no. 8 (May 1905), 51.

7. Ibid. The rank ordering of the first seven law programs was Harvard, Columbia, Chicago, Northwestern, Pennsylvania, Cornell, and Michigan.

8. Charles Henry Huberich, "The Stanford Law Department, Its Aims and Needs," *Stanford Alumnus* 9, no. 9 (May 1908): 327–328.

9. Ibid. In the 1907–08 academic year, the law department represented nearly 18 percent of the total number of students at Stanford.

10. "From the Editor's Private Files," *Stanford Alumnus* 10, no. 9 (May 1909): 364.

11. Barton Warren Evermann, "George Archibald Clark," *Science* 48, no. 1235 (August 30, 1918): 213–214.

12. "Stenography," *DPA*, September 15, 1893.

13. "Shorthand," *DPA*, September 19, 1895.

14. George A. Clark, "Education 19," *Stanford Alumnus* 13, no. 5 (January 1912): 149.

15. "Heald's Business College [advertisement]," *Stanford Chaparral* 2, no. 5 (November 7, 1900): 94.

16. Rakesh Kurana, *From Higher Aims to Hired Hands: The Social Transformation of American Business Schools and the Unfulfilled Promise of Management as a Profession* (Princeton: Princeton University Press, 2007), 109–110.

17. "Academic Secretary Will Talk to Women," *DPA*, December 2, 1913.

18. Clark, "Education 19," 149–150.

19. Unlike Heald Business College, Peirce School was a nonprofit institution.

20. Clark, "Education 19," 151–152.

21. Ibid., 149.

22. Ibid., 151.

23. "George A. Clark, Secretary Dies After Long Illness," *DPA*, April 29, 1918.

24. "Typing, Shorthand to End," *DPA*, July 30, 1926.

25. "Committee to Outline Three New Courses," *SD*, May 19, 1937.

26. "New Courses Instituted for Defense," *SD*, January 6, 1942.

27. Harris Weinstock, "College and the World," *Stanford Alumnus* 9, no. 1 (September 1907): 8. "College and the World" was the editor's heading that appeared above Weinstock's article, but it referred to a planned three-part reprinting of articles that had appeared in the September 1907 issue of *Overland Monthly*, one of which was Weinstock's. The actual title of his essay was "A Business Man's View of College Training."

28. C. J. Randau, "For Better Business Graduates," *Stanford Illustrated Review* 2, no. 1 (April 18, 1917): 323.

29. "Graduate School of Business Opens in Fall Quarter," *DPA*, June 23, 1925.

30. J. Hugh Jackson, "Business Administration," in *University Training and Vocational Outlets* (Stanford: Stanford University Committee on Vocational Guidance, 1935), 12.

31. Jackson, "Business Administration," 13–14.

32. The degree totals were obtained from online searches of Stanford's alumni directory.

33. "School Launches Undergrad Institute," *Stanford Business*, February 2004, 5.

34. "Undergrads Brake for Summer Biz School," *Stanford Business*, February 2005, 5.

35. Stanford Graduate School of Business, Summer Institute for General Management, https://www.gsb.stanford.edu/programs/summer-institute-general-management, accessed January 5, 2017.

36. In 2017, the institute's curriculum would touch upon—enumeration will take almost as long as attending the program itself—finance, accounting, statistics, economics, operations, strategy, talent management, and marketing. It also would cover negotiation, ethics, organizational behavior, and leadership for good measure. Stanford Graduate School of Business, Summer Institute for General Management, Academic Experience, https://www.gsb.stanford.edu/programs/summer-institute-general-management/academic-experience, accessed January 5, 2017.

37. Ibid.

38. "Prepare Your Son or Daughter for a Career in Business" [advertisement for the Summer Institute for General Management and the Summer Institute for Entrepreneurship], *Stanford Business*, November 2005, 15. The business school continued to pitch parents in 2016. See "Parents, Help Your College Students Launch Their Careers" [advertisement for the Summer Institute for General Management], *Stanford Business*, Autumn 2016, 60.

39. "Humanities Career Resources Expand," *SD*, December 4, 2013. The administrator quoted was Katie McDonough, humanities and arts initiatives coordinator for Humanities and Sciences. The university extended the financial-aid offer to majors in "humanities and arts"—I have never understood phrasing that implies that "arts" is not encompassed by "humanities"—and those in some of the interdepartmental program majors: Asian American Studies, African and African American Studies, American Studies, Chicana/o-Latina/o Studies, Comparative Studies in Race and Ethnicity, Jewish Studies, Native American Studies, and Feminist, Gender, and Sexuality Studies. Stanford University, Undergrad, Summer Institute for General Management (SIGM) Funding, https://undergrad.stanford.edu/opportunities-research/humanities/summer-institute-general-management-sigm-funding, accessed January 6, 2017.

40. "Class Profile," Stanford Graduate School of Business, Summer Institute for General Management, https://www.gsb.stanford.edu/programs/summer-institute-general-management/academic-experience/class-profile, accessed January 6, 2017. The remaining categories that made up the class profile: social sciences, 21 percent; natural and life sciences, 15 percent; law, 2 percent; and (the puzzling presence of) business, 4 percent. The number of humanities majors from Stanford, though not specified, could not have been large: the session's 125 participants in 2016 represented more than eighty-two undergraduate institutions.

CHAPTER 9. UNDEREPRESENTED

1. "Stanford University Common Data Set 2008–2009," Stanford University Communications, https://ucomm.stanford.edu/cds/cds_2008. The percentage of African-Americans in Stanford's undergraduate student body would fall steeply, from 10 percent in 2008, when Moore arrived, to 6.4 percent in 2016. "Stanford University Common Data Set 2016–2017," Stanford University Communications, https://ucomm.stanford.edu/cds/pdf/stanford_cds_2016.pdf. The percentages were calculated using the "Black or African-American, non-Hispanic" figures and excluded "Two or more races, non-Hispanic," a category in the 2016 data set but not in the 2008 data.

2. Estelle B. Freedman, *Redefining Rape: Sexual Violence in the Era of Suffrage and Segregation* (Cambridge: Harvard University Press, 2013), 355n12.

3. Jessica Moore, "'[Rape's] Seriousness Ought Not Be Affected If Both Are Colored': Intraracial Rape Cases in the *Baltimore Afro-American*, 1920–1929," *Herodotus: The Stanford University Undergraduate History Journal* 21 (Spring 2011): 18–27.

4. Apparently a majority of fellows do not pursue the PhD. The program's website states, "As of 2016, nearly 5000 students have been selected as fellows, more than 580 of whom have earned the PhD and over 100 of whom are now tenured faculty members." Mellow Mays Undergraduate Fellowship Program, About page, http://www.mmuf.org/about, accessed January 2, 2017.

5. Management Leadership for Tomorrow was founded in 2002 and is based in Washington, DC.

6. Requirements taken from a description for a BOLD intern position for Summer 2017, https://www.google.com/about/careers/jobs#!t=jo&jid=/google/bold-intern-summer-2017-1600-amphitheatre-pkwy-mountain-view-ca-1749620159&, accessed January 1, 2017.

7. Steven Levy, "Marissa Mayer Has a Secret Weapon," *Wired*, July 23, 2012.

8. One may wonder why Google would invest in the skills development of managers who were not bound by any cultural expectation of staying with one employer during their career and who were in Silicon Valley, where frequent job-hopping was the norm. Marissa Mayer, the senior Google executive who created its training program for associate program managers, anticipated that participants would not stay at Google and averred that their departure would be good for Google because "they're going to take the Google DNA with them." Steven Levy, *In the Plex: How Google Thinks, Works, and Shapes Our Lives* (New York: Simon & Schuster, 2011), 5.

9. "Laszlo Bock '99, VP People Operations, Google," Yale School of Management, News, February 20, 2008. Shortly after Bock arrived at Google, the number of job seekers that his group vetted surged. In 2006, 1.2 million résumés were fielded; in 2007, the number jumped above 2 million.

10. "Google VP Says Liberal Arts Leads to Lifetime Success," Ursinus College, News, April 1, 2014.

11. "In Head-Hunting, Big Data May Not Be Such a Big Deal," *NYT*, June 19, 2013.

12. Thomas L. Friedman, "How to Get a Job at Google," *NYT*, February 22, 2014.

13. "Google VP Says."

14. Friedman, "How to Get a Job at Google."

CHAPTER 10. NORMAL

1. Later, when Terman looked at the 1921 edition of J. McKeen Cattell's *American Men of Science*, he found that his family was the only one among one thousand cases that had "twelve or more" children. Lewis M. Terman, "Trails to Psychology," in *A History of Psychology in Autobiography*, ed. Carl A. Murchison, (Worcester, MA: Clark University, 1930), 299, 331.

2. Terman, "Trails to Psychology," 301.

3. Ibid.

4. Ibid., 302.

5. Ibid., 302, 305, 306.

6. Ibid., 305–306.

7. With only a bachelor's degree, Bryan had been appointed as an instructor of English and Greek at the university as a replacement for a faculty member who had resigned amid scandal. He was soon promoted to the position of "acting professor of philosophy" by Indiana University's new president—none other than David Starr Jordan—and began work on his master's degree at Indiana, and then his PhD at Clark University. Terman would not have had the chance to study under Bryan had Jordan succeeded, when he was appointed as president at Stanford, in recruiting Bryan with the offer of a substantial increase in salary. James H. Capshaw, "The Legacy of the Laboratory (1888–1988): A History of the Department of Psychology at Indiana University," *Psychology at Indiana University: A Centennial Review and Compendium*, ed. Eliot Hearst and James H. Capshaw, 1–83 (Bloomington, IN: Indiana University Department of Psychology, 1988), 9, 13.

8. Indiana University sent many students to obtain PhDs at Clark, in addition to Bryan: in 1905, Terman and James P. Porter would be the tenth and eleventh Indiana alumni to earn PhDs in psychology there. See the table "Indiana Students at Clark University" in Capshaw, "Legacy," 21.

9. Terman, "Trails to Psychology," 312.

10. Ibid., 315–316.

11. Ibid., 318.

12. Lewis M. Terman, "Genius and Stupidity: A Study of Some of the Intellectual Processes of Seven 'Bright' and Seven 'Stupid' Boys," *Pedagogical Seminary* 13 (September 1906): 314.

13. Ibid., 372.

14. Terman, "Trails to Psychology," 322.

15. Lewis M. Terman, "Commercialism: The Educator's Bugbear," *School Review* 17, no. 3 (March 1909): 193.

16. Ibid., 195.

17. "Professor Dies After Long Illness," *SD*, February 28, 1910.

18. Huey would die young, too, just three years later, at the age of thirty-three. "News and Comment," *Psychological Clinic* 7, no. 9 (February 15, 1914): 264.

19. Terman, "Trails to Psychology," 323.

20. Ibid.

21. Edwin E. Slosson, *Great American Universities* (New York: Macmillan, 1910),

vii–x. The top three spots were occupied by Columbia, Harvard, and the University of Chicago.

22. Ibid., 122–123, 125.

23. Ibid., 127.

24. Slosson scolded, "The students of Stanford have acquired the esprit de corps of Yale and Princeton, but they have not learned the proper use of it as well as have the students of those universities." Ibid., 144–145.

25. Ibid., 114.

26. Another thing that could not have been predicted when Terman and his family arrived was that his son Frederick—who was only ten years old in 1910—would one day bring about a complete reversal of David Starr Jordan's policy forbidding faculty members from undertaking paid outside work. Frederick Terman would turn out to be the person who, more than anyone else, created the tight symbiotic bonds between university and surrounding industry that would become a defining feature of Silicon Valley. For that to happen, however, Frederick had to first grow up; attend Stanford, earning a bachelor's degree in chemistry in 1920 and a master's in electrical engineering in 1922; and then, after earning a doctorate in electrical engineering at MIT, return to Stanford in 1925 to join the engineering faculty. He would go on to serve as dean of the School of Engineering, as the provost, and as the university's vice president.

27. Edwin G. Boring, *Lewis Madison Terman, 1877–1956: A Biographical Memoir* (Washington, DC: National Academy of Sciences, 1959), 437.

28. Slosson, *Great American Universities*, 114–115. The student editors at the University of Illinois took evident delight in highlighting Slosson's criticisms of Stanford's faculty. The *Daily Illini* reprinted excerpts of Slosson's Stanford report under a subheadline that read, "Conditions at Far Western University Are Hardly in Keeping with Its Remarkable Advantages." See "Unfavorable Remarks on Leland Stanford," *Daily Illini*, April 3, 1909.

29. Lewis M. Terman, *The Teacher's Health: A Study in the Hygiene of an Occupation* (Boston: Houghton Mifflin, 1913), which was a brief summarizing monograph; Lewis M. Terman, *The Hygiene of the School Child* (Boston: Houghton Mifflin, 1914), which was a four-hundred-pages-plus textbook intended for use in teachers colleges; and Ernest Bryant Hoag and Lewis M. Terman, *Health Work in the Schools* (Boston: Houghton Mifflin, 1914). Terman's coauthor, Ernest Hoag, was a medical doctor and the Director of School Health for the State Board of Health for Minnesota.

30. Terman, "Trails to Psychology," 321.

31. Such was the interest in the Binet-Simon Scale that a validity study of a single "normal" child by a doctor in Vermont was deemed worthy of scholarly publication. Arthur Dermont Bush, "Binet-Simon Tests of a Thirty-Nine Months Old Child," *Psychological Clinic* 7, no. 9 (February 15, 1914), 250. Bush criticized the methods that Binet and Simon used to collect their data: "Binet and Simon state that all their norms were determined in those primary schools in Paris which are located in the poorer quarters. It would seem that such norms must be under a normal average—as Binet and Simon tacitly admit. Then, too, the original tests were made but once and by a stranger—all of which conditions must inevitably produce a mean lower than a reasonable average;

as, no doubt, investigations among children more fortunately circumstanced and by investigators well known to the children tested will continue to show."

32. Lewis M. Terman, *The Measurement of Intelligence* (Boston: Houghton Mifflin, 1916).

33. Ibid., 49–50.

34. Terman dedicated *The Measurement of Intelligence* to Binet: "Patient Researcher, Creative Thinker, Unpretentious Scholar, Inspiring and Fruitful Devotee of Inductive and Dynamic Psychology."

35. Terman, *Measurement of Intelligence*, 40–43.

36. Ibid., 68.

37. Terman, "Trails to Psychology," 324.

CHAPTER 11. INTERESTING THINGS HAPPEN

1. Before Andrew Phillips spent the summers at the law firm, when he was finishing his freshman year a family friend asked him if he would be interested in a summer internship working for a blog that focused on Silicon Valley startups that was run by someone the friend knew. Phillips knew nothing about the universe of startups but was willing to learn, and the internship was arranged. On the first day he was to report, he drove to the address he had been given but was confused: it was a house in Atherton, a posh residential suburb, not an office building. Without knowing its importance to Silicon Valley at that moment, he had landed at the house of Michael Arrington and the blog was TechCrunch, the most influential chronicler at the time of Valley startups, even though it was still being run in Arrington's home.

2. "Former Senator Ted Stevens Killed in Plane Crash," *NYT*, August 10, 2010; "K Street Mourns Loss of Colleague Bill Phillips," *Roll Call*, August 20, 2010.

3. The master's in commerce program was forty credit-hours, consisting of seventeen units of, basically, everything, and then fifteen units in one of three tracks—Phillips chose management-and-marketing. The remainder was a "global immersion experience," which took Phillips to China for about six weeks, his first trip to Asia.

4. "Andrew Phillips, M.S. 2012 in Commerce," https://www.youtube.com/watch?v=vTgBi-uh7AU. The video was embedded on the web page of the University of Virginia, McIntire School of Commerce, MS in Commerce, in February 2016 but not in January 2017.

5. Electronic Arts also promoted this same game on its own website with an amusing short video that promised "mom will hate Dead Space 2. See real Mom's reactions to watching clips from the upcoming game." Electronic Arts, "Dead Space 2: Your Mom Hates," January 20, 2011, http://www.ea.com/dead-space-2/videos/your-mom-hates, accessed January 7, 2017.

6. "Facebook's fbFund Names Winners of $225,000 Grants," TechCrunch, December 9, 2008.

7. "The Spark That Fuels Wildfire Interactive," TechCrunch, June 29, 2011.

8. Although the two cofounders of Wildfire, Alain Chuard and Victoria Ransom, would both later acquire MBAs—Chuard at Stanford, Ransom at Harvard—the two were uncommonly adventurous. The first successful startup they began even before

business school was, in fact, an adventure travel company, teaching clients surfing, snowboarding, and mountain biking. Chuard had been a professional snowboarder for two years after high school. "Spark That Fuels Wildfire"; "The Winding Road to Wildfire," *Macalester Today*, Winter 2013.

9. Davis's career in sales had begun at Fisher Investments, a place with a large army of account executives who required an even larger army of "sales associates," the junior people who made unsolicited phone calls to prospects, setting up appointments for the account executives. Davis saw that success in the sales associate role required punishing effort. He had to speak with two hundred people each day; unanswered calls did not count. That required reaching twenty individuals an hour, ten hours a day. Of the twenty, usually ten would hang up on him, angrily. Four would be idle retired people all too happy to engage in a long conversation. Davis was pleased if he succeeded in setting up two appointments from among the twenty reached each hour. Sixty percent of those appointments would actually happen; 25 percent of the meetings would result in a sale. The experience imparted a lesson: more than anything else, sales entailed brutally hard work that brought constant rejection.

10. "Google Acquires Wildfire, Will Now Sell Facebook and Twitter Marketing Services [Update: $350M Price]," TechCrunch, July 31, 2012.

CHAPTER 12. A MANIA FOR TESTING

1. Robert C. Clothier, "Employment Work of the Curtis Publishing Company," *Annals of the American Academy of Political and Social Science* 65 (May 1916): 98.

2. Katharine Huey, "Problems Arising and Methods Used in Interviewing and Selecting Employes[*sic*]," *Annals of the American Academy of Political and Social Science* 65 (May 1916): 213.

3. Clothier, "Employment Work," 98–99.

4. Guy Montrose Whipple, "The Use of Mental Tests in Vocational Guidance," *Annals of the American Academy of Political and Social Science* 65 (May 1916): 195–197.

5. Scott's first consulting engagement, for Butterick Publishers, led to his first book: *The Theory and Practice of Advertising: A Simple Exposition of the Principles of Psychology in Their Relation to Successful Advertising* (Boston: Small, Maynard, 1903). Magazine articles spread his name and more consulting assignments followed.

6. "Executive Committee Meets," *National Association of Corporation Schools Bulletin* no. 1 (March 1914): 48. The association's declared functions were "to develop the efficiency of the individual employe[*sic*]; to increase efficiency in industry; to have the courses in established educational institutions modified to meet more fully the needs of industry."

7. Edmund C. Lynch, "Walter Dill Scott: Pioneer Industrial Psychologist," *Business History Review* 42, no. 2 (Summer 1968): 156.

8. Walter Dill Scott, "Selection of Employees by Means of Quantitative Determinations," *Annals of the American Academy of Political and Social Science* 65 (May 1916): 183.

9. Five minutes were provided to pitch sporting goods to one pretend wholesale buyer, then five minutes for another, hawking office supplies, life insurance, or fountain pens. The "buyers" would then assign a single grade to the performance; then the

grades would be averaged, yielding a single number, which Scott viewed as "expressive of the personality of the applicant." Ibid., 191–192.

10. The English rendering of the proverbs was not consistently clear. What was a test subject to make of the following: "If the boy says he wants to tie the water with a string, ask him whether he means the water in the pot or the water in the lagoon"? Ibid., 187.

11. Ibid., 188.

12. Scott requested that each employer think of ten men filling sales positions and give a numerical ranking of the former employee, indicating his relative rank among the ten. Ibid., 183–184.

13. William Fretz Kemble, *Choosing Employees by Mental and Physical Tests* (New York: The Engineering Magazine Company, 1917), 61.

14. Ibid., 33.

15. "H.R. 3595. An Act to Authorize the President to Increase Temporarily the Military Establishment of the United States," Sixty-Fifth Congress, Session I, Ch. 15, 1917, 80, http://www.legisworks.org/congress/65/publaw-12.pdf.

16. *Army Mental Tests*, ed. Clarence S. Yoakum and Robert M. Yerkes (New York: Henry Holt, 1920), x–xi, 2. The committee was chaired by Robert M. Yerkes, and the other members, aside from Terman, were W. V. Bingham, H. H. Goddard, T. H. Haines, G. M. Whipple, and F. L. Wells.

17. Ibid., xi.

18. Edward Strong, "Work of the Committee on Classification of Personnel in the Army," *Journal of Applied Psychology* 2, no. 2 (June 1, 1918): 137–138.

19. Lewis M. Terman, "Trails to Psychology," in *A History of Psychology in Autobiography*, 297–331, ed. Carl A. Murchison (Worcester, MA: Clark University, 1930), 325–326.

20. Otis earned all of his degrees at Stanford: AB, in 1910, majoring in psychology; AM, in education, in 1915; and PhD in education, completed in 1920.

21. *Army Mental Tests*, 2.

22. Ibid., 3.

23. Ibid., 16.

24. Henry Herbert Goddard, *Human Efficiency and Levels of Intelligence* (Princeton: Princeton University Press, 1920), 31–32.

25. *Army Mental Tests*, 16, 20.

26. Ibid., 12, 16.

27. Ibid., 8–9, 16.

28. Ibid., 12.

29. *Camplife Chickamauga*, clipping, Yerkes Papers, Box 94, file 1782. Reproduced in *Joanne Brown, The Definition of a Profession: The Authority of Metaphor in the History of Intelligence Testing, 1890–1930* (Princeton: Princeton University Press, 1992), 113–114.

30. M. C. S. Noble, Jr., "Standardized Group Intelligence Tests as a Basis of Selection of Students for Admission to Colleges and Universities," *High School Journal* 9, no. 2/3 (February/March 1926): 32.

31. *The Thorndike College Entrance Tests in the University of California*, comp. J. V. Breitwieser (Berkeley: University of California Press, 1922), 3.

32. Edward L. Thorndike, *Thorndike Intelligence Examination for High School Graduates: Instructions for Giving and Scoring, Series of 1919, 1920, 1921 and 1922* (New York: Teachers College, Columbia University, 1921), 12.

33. Nicholas Lemann, *The Big Test: The Secret History of the American Meritocracy* (New York: Farrar, Straus and Giroux, 2000), 28–29.

34. Robert A. McCaughey, *Stand, Columbia: A History of Columbia University in the City of New York, 1754–2004* (New York: Columbia University Press, 2003), 268–269. Columbia discarded the Thorndike exam in 1934.

35. *Thorndike College Entrance Tests*.

36. "U.C. Faculty Asks to Take Intelligence Tests with Students," *SD*, January 24, 1921.

37. Lewis M. Terman and Karl M. Cowdery, "Stanford's Program of University Personnel Research," *Journal of Personnel Research* 4, no. 7 and 8 (November/December 1925): 263.

38. Ibid., 263–264.

39. Ibid., 264.

40. "Fall Students Brightest," *SD*, April 1, 1924.

41. The study ended up with 1,528 subjects. Edwin G. Boring, *Lewis Madison Terman, 1877–1956: A Biographical Memoir* (Washington, DC: National Academy of Sciences, 1959), 429. When Terman died in 1956, the study was taken over by Robert Sears, a Stanford psychology professor who himself was one of the subjects, a "Termite," as they were called. Near the end of Sears's life, in 1987, Albert Hastorf, another Stanford psychologist, took over, maintaining the project archives and vowing in 2000 that the study would continue until the last Termite had died. Hastorf died in 2011. Mitchell Leslie, "The Vexing Legacy of Lewis Terman," *Stanford Magazine*, July/August 2000; "75 Years Later, Study Still Tracking Geniuses," *NYT*, March 7, 1995; "Albert Hastorf, Professor Emeritus of Psychology, Former Vice President and Provost, and Former Dean of the School of Humanities & Sciences, Dead at 90," *Stanford Report*, September 27, 2011.

42. Lewis M. Terman, "Adventures in Stupidity: A Partial Analysis of the Intellectual Inferiority of a College Student," *Scientific Monthly* 14, no. 1 (January 1922): 24–40.

43. Ibid., 39–40.

44. Ibid., 34.

45. Walter Lippmann, "The Mental Age of Americans," *New Republic*, October 25, 1922, 213–214.

46. Walter Lippmann, "The Mystery of the 'A' Men," *New Republic*, November 1, 1922, 246–247.

47. Walter Lippmann, "The Reliability of Intelligence Tests," *New Republic*, November 8, 1922, 276.

48. Walter Lippmann, "A Future for the Tests," *New Republic*, November 29, 1922, 10.

49. Walter Lippmann, "The Abuse of the Tests," *New Republic*, November 15, 1922, 297.

50. Lewis M. Terman, "The Great Conspiracy, or the Impulse Imperiouis [*sic*]

of Intelligence Testers, Psychoanalyzed and Exposed by Mr. Lippmann," *New Republic*, December 27, 1922, 116.

51. After the war, Strong taught at the Carnegie Institute of Technology from 1919 to 1923, until going to Stanford. John G. Darley, "Edward Kellogg Strong, Jr." *Journal of Applied Psychology* 48, no. 2 (April 1964): 73.

52. "Looking for Right Job? Strong Test Reveals All," *SD*, March 30, 1948.

53. "Test '1000' for Vocation," *SD*, October 23, 1934. The then-current version of the Strong test was described as consisting of eight pages of "pertinent and varied questions calculated to rate occupational interests. Such data as likes and dislikes in occupations, amusements, activities, peculiarities of people, and a self-rating of present abilities and characteristics."

54. Terman and Cowdery, "Stanford's Program," 266.

55. Questionnaires were filled out by 287 men, which was two-thirds of the class. Edward K. Strong, Jr., "Predictive Value of the Vocational Interest Test," *Journal of Educational Psychology* 26, no. 5 (May 1935): 331, 332.

56. "Check Your Preference," *SD*, April 19, 1927.

57. Edward K. Strong, Jr., "Differentiation of Certified Public Accountants from Other Occupational Groups," *Journal of Educational Psychology* 18, no. 4 (April 1927): 235.

58. Strong, "Predictive Value," 331-333, 343.

59. "Strong Vocational Results Prove Valid After 19 Years," *SD*, September 26, 1952.

60. The Stanford University Press sold the rights in 2004. "CPP, Inc., Purchases Strong Interest Inventory Assessment from Stanford University Press," PR Newswire, September 8, 2004.

61. Lemann, *The Big Test*, 30-31.

CHAPTER 13. THE STRENGTH OF WEAK TIES

1. "European-American Relations to Be Studied in New Course," *SD*, March 4, 1943.

2. Stanford University, *Study of Undergraduate Education, The Study of Undergraduate Education at Stanford University (SUES)* (Stanford: The Office of the Vice Provost for Undergraduate Education, Stanford University, 2012), 17.

3. Grangaard's father had gone on to earn an MBA at the University of Chicago.

4. The Band's scatter formations, field-show themes that mock and torment the school's athletic opponents, and adoption of Free's "All Right Now" as the school's unofficial fight song are among its signatures. The Band describes itself as equipped with "the weapons of student autonomy, rock-and-roll music and bad fashion sense." History page, LSJUMB website, http://lsjumb.stanford.edu/history.html, accessed January 3, 2017.

5. For an introduction to Meraki's technology, see Randall Stross, "Wireless Internet for All, Without the Towers," *NYT*, February 4, 2007. The size of the company when Grangaard's friend had joined in January 2011 can be guessed by Meraki CEO Sanjit Biswas's mention in November 2012 that the company had grown the previous year from 120 to 330 employees. If the 120 employees refers to November 2011, it would be reasonable to assume that the number in January 2011 would have been

fewer than one hundred, perhaps many fewer. "Letter to Employees from Meraki CEO, Sanjit Biswas," [November 12, 2012], Cisco Meraki blog, https://www.meraki.com/company/cisco-acquisition-faq#ceo-letter.

6. The number of actual employees at that moment would have been smaller than 286, as the employee number reflects the number of employees who have ever worked at a company, not the current headcount.

7. "Cisco Announces Intent to Acquire Meraki," Cisco press release, November 18, 2012; "Cisco Completes Acquisition of Meraki," Cisco press release, December 20, 2012.

8. For his doctoral dissertation at Harvard, Mark Granovetter interviewed one hundred men in 1969, residents of Newton, Massachusetts, who had changed jobs in the previous year. In addition to the one hundred interviews, he also collected completed questionnaires from 187 other men. The resulting dissertation was titled "Changing Jobs: Channels of Mobility Information in a Suburban Population" and was submitted in 1970. The theoretical formulation was presented in "The Strength of Weak Ties," *American Journal of Sociology* 78 (May 1973): 1360–1380. The revision of the dissertation was published as *Getting a Job: A Study of Contacts and Careers* (Chicago: University of Chicago Press: 1974); a second edition was published in 1995.

9. Granovetter found that 56.1 percent of his subjects in the professional category got their jobs by personal contacts; technical, 43.5 percent; and managerial, 65.4 percent. *Getting a Job*, 2nd ed., 19.

10. *Getting a Job*, 2nd ed., 148.

11. Granovetter's article "The Strength of Weak Ties" would become one of the most cited articles in social science. Google Books tallied more than forty-one thousand citations as of January 7, 2017.

CHAPTER 14. THE SHINY NEW THING

1. Graduate totals are based on searches by major of the database maintained by the Stanford Alumni Association.

2. In 2015, Eric Roberts, a professor of computer science, complained to the *Stanford Daily* about the lack of resources: "We're all teaching three times as many students as we were six years ago, and we don't have any more of us and any more money." "A Look at Stanford Computer Science, Part II: Challenges of a Growing Field," *SD*, April 16, 2015.

3. "John Herriot—Stanford Math Pioneer," *SFC*, April 14, 2003. In an oral history recorded twenty-six years after establishing the Center, Herriot described the process of programming the CPC as easy: "It's not like getting out your solder gun or anything like that." John George Herriot, oral history, May 22, 1979, Charles Babbage Institute, University of Minnesota, Minneapolis.

4. Alexandra I. Forsythe, oral history, May 16, 1976, Charles Babbage Institute, University of Minnesota, Minneapolis.

5. George E. Forsythe, "Educational Implications of the Computer Revolution," talk given at the American Association for the Advancement of Science meeting, Denver, Colorado, December 1961, transcript, 1–2, in H&SR, Box 8, Computer Science Division 1962–69, SCUA. Forsythe pointed out that in 1945 a desk calculator operated

by a human could complete one multiplication operation about every ten seconds. But in 1962 it would be possible to have the computer do the same operation in 0.000025 seconds, an improvement by a factor of about half a million. He reasoned that such an improvement could not help but produce epochal changes. He drew an analogy to changes that followed the advent of jet-powered aircraft, which brought a speed improvement over walking of only about one-hundred-fold. "Jets have caused a totally new approach to commerce, vacations, management of industries, and international government. They have brought new industries, new kinds of jobs, new problems, new ways of thinking and certainly new fears," he said. "All this from an acceleration of merely 100. . . . Now what may we expect of the almost million-fold increase in man's speed of computation?"

6. Ibid., 14.

7. In 1959, George Forsythe noted that the United States had three thousand "automatic digital computers" installed around the country, and he estimated that each machine needed ten college-trained mathematicians to tend to its needs as programmers, analysts, and supervisors. George E. Forsythe, "The Role of Numerical Analysis in an Undergraduate Program," *American Mathematical Monthly* 66, no. 8 (October 1959): 651.

8. As more applied mathematicians with an interest in computing joined the department, a gap appeared between them and some of their colleagues. David Gilbarg, then head of the mathematics department, was uneasy about the "technological character" of computer science and the propriety of keeping the field in H&S. David Gilbarg to Philip H. Rhinelander [dean, H&S], memo, January 9, 1960, H&SR, Box 8, Computer Science Division 1962–69, SCUA.

9. Forsythe, "Educational Implications," 16. Forsythe could see the case to be made for locating CS in engineering, too, but he was inclined to keep it in H&S. He was less concerned about location than about the "personnel shortage" that afflicted the field. The pool of computer scientists who had not been lured by industry to work outside of academe was small. Forsythe wrote, "The demands of these commercial installations have sucked into industry very many of the persons whose presence on campus is necessary for the development of knowledge in computing. As a result, it is astonishingly hard to find well-qualified persons to assume professorships in computing. Those who come command salaries much higher than their more traditional academic brethren."

10. G. E. Forsythe to R. R. Sears, January 15, 1962, H&SR, Box 8, Computer Science Division 1962–69, SCUA.

11. George Forsythe to Dean Sears, "Preliminary Budget Planning for 1963–64," memo, October 10, 1962, H&SR, Box 8, Computer Science Division 1963–64, SCUA.

12. George Forsythe to Robert R. Sears, August 21, 1963, H&SR, Box 8, Computer Science Division 1963–64, SCUA.

13. An example of Forsythe's reports on the diffusion of computer science is the cover letter he sent out in May 1963 with a detailed report of a new computer science program at the University of Colorado, Boulder. He noted that Carnegie Tech, the University of Pennsylvania, and MIT still kept computer science within existing departments, but Wisconsin and Purdue had established new programs. George E. Forsythe to Profes-

sors Bowker, Gilbarg, Herriot, Lederberg, McCarthy, Parter, Royden, and Sears, "University of Colorado Institute for Computing Science," n.d. [stamped "Received May 17 1963, Dean of H&S"], H&SR, Box 8, Computer Science Division 1962–69, SCUA.

14. The same year that Stanford established its computer science department, so too did many others. By June 1965, George Forsythe was worried that other institutions were in a rush to staff new departments and would try to lure members of Stanford's computer science faculty. "Of the top 15 universities, ten either have such departments now or have phoned me personally (Yale, Cornell) in the past few months, requesting advice about organization and personnel! Yet only two or three years ago there were none." Forsythe predicted, "In the face of this panic, Stanford's Computer Science faculty are going to be raided very hard. We are going to have to raise our salary levels very substantially to hold people." G. E. Forsythe to H. L. Royden, June 7, 1965, H&SR, Box 8, Computer Science 1965–66, SCUA.

15. Robert R. Sears to Donald W. Taylor, February 1, 1965, H&SR, Box 8, Computer Science 1964–65, SCUA.

16. The potential usefulness of computing to humanities research was remarked upon in 1965 by Forsythe. Yale University, using a grant from IBM, held a two-day conference that year titled "Computers for the Humanities?" A copy of the program was sent to Stanford by Don Taylor, a former Stanford faculty member, and circulated from dean to faculty member to faculty member. Forsythe passed it on with a note that said, "A year ago the director of the Computation Center at Princeton told me that within five years he expected to get a vastly increased demand for computing from the humanities people. He called humanities a 'sleeping giant'[for computing]. I haven't checked lately on how it has been going." Robert R. Sears to Professor George Forsythe, January 28, 1965, and George E. Forsythe to Virgil K. Whitaker, February 4, 1965, George E. Forsythe Papers (SC98), Box 6, Folder 6, SCUA.

17. In 1967, Ying Y. Lew, a sophomore, asked the university to permit him to create his own customized major that would be labeled "computer science," proposing to draw upon courses in mathematics, electrical engineering, philosophy, and physics. "Interdepartment Majors Proposed By H-S Deans," SD, December 1, 1967. The next year Lew received approval for a revised version of his proposed interdisciplinary major, "computer methods and designs." "15 Students Receive Approval for Interdepartmental Study," SD, May 8, 1968. When Lew graduated in 1970, however, his major was not this but English.

18. George E. Forsythe to Julian W. Hill, February 3, 1965, H&SR, Box 8, Computer Science, 1964–65, SCUA. When computer science was still merely a division of the Department of Mathematics, the faculty boasted of their service to undergraduates, teaching 2,475 student-equivalents of introductory-level courses in the 1963–64 academic year. Halsey Royden to Frederick E. Terman, October 26, 1964, H&SR, Box 8, Computer Science Division 1964–65, SCUA. The Computation Center, for which Forsythe served as director, had grown apace. In 1962, it was used by nearly 1,600 Stanford students in forty-three courses. See "Eichler Awarded Building Contract," SD, August 2, 1962.

19. George E. Forsythe to Provost's Computer Committee, "Meeting of 7 July 1969," memo, July 8, 1969, George E. Forsythe Papers (SC98), Box 11, Folder 20, SCUA. Forsythe said that around 675 undergraduates were enrolled in one of four el-

ementary courses in 1968–69. He then estimated that about 2,000 current undergraduates had taken one of them, or 40 percent. He estimated that another 10 percent were students who had arrived with some computing experience. Consequently, "we feel that 50% of the undergraduates are now being reached with computing." The expansion of courses was accomplished without full financial support from the administration. In his oral history of this period, John Herriot said that the administration provided support for less than half of the faculty's salaries; the remainder came from grants, contracts, and funds allocated to the Computation Center. He said, "I think we had 15 people, we had [only] about 6 full-time equivalent positions, or something like that. So, convincing the Dean at all times that we needed more money was one of Forsythe's big things. It was a hard job." Herriot, oral history, 23–24.

20. Disclosure: Lyman Van Slyke was one of my two principal graduate advisors at Stanford.

21. L. P. Van Slyke to All Colleagues, "Interest in Computer Applications in the History Department," memo, January 20, 1969, Richard W. Lyman, provost of SU, Papers (SC0099), Box 14, History Department, SCUA.

22. Ibid.

23. Fred Hargadon to Norman Wessells, "Undergraduate Major in Computer Science," memo, March 10, 1983, H&SR, Box 9, Computer Science 1982–83, SCUA.

24. Ibid.

25. Russell Berman and Brian Cook, representing the Policy & Planning Board, "Changes in the Academic Interests of Stanford Undergraduates," SU, Forty-Ninth Senate Report No. 1, October 13, 2016, 11. The qualifying modifier "about" that precedes the two percentage figures for 1986 indicates that when I pulled them from a line graph, I had to guess the starting points for the corresponding lines in the absence of actual figures.

26. Ibid., 13.

27. Ibid., 17.

28. Ibid., 12.

29. These numbers rely on the online alumni directory.

30. "Tech Culture Yields Opportunities and Challenges for Stanford," *SD*, January 29, 2016.

31. "CS'[s] Rise in Popularity Poses Pressing Questions," *SD*, June 5, 2013. [The online version of the story uses a slightly different headline, "CS's Rising Popularity Poses Pressing Questions," and uses June 4, 2013 as the publication date.]

32. "For Stanford Programming Class, the Bigger the Better," SU, School of Engineering, press release, December 13, 2012.

33. Students who had taken AP computer science in high school or had prior programming experience skipped Programming Methodology, and instead of taking Programming Abstractions CS 106B, they took an accelerated version, CS 106X, which covered the same topics as CS 106B but moved at a faster pace and tackled more challenging projects. This course may have only seventy-five to one hundred students each quarter, and the students who did well in this course formed a pool of prospective undergraduate teaching assistants for the department.

34. Mehran Sahami had a BS, MS, and PhD, all in computer science and all earned at Stanford.

35. "CS'[s] Rise in Popularity."

36. Marisa Messina, "Content to Code? Straddling Silicon Valley's Techie-Fuzzie Divide," *Stanford Magazine*, September/October 2015, 40.

37. Messina, "Content to Code?"

38. Dylan Sweetwood, interview, May 8, 2015. After graduating in June 2015, Sweetwood directly went to Oxford University, where he earned a master's in English.

39. "Equity and Excellence: Mayor de Blasio Announces Reforms to Raise Achievement Across All Public Schools," Office of the Mayor, NYC, press release, September 16, 2015.

40. Jeff Atwood, "Learning to Code Is Overrated," *New York Daily News*, September 27, 2015.

41. "New Joint Program to Be Offered in Fall," *SD*, April 3, 2014. The survey was distributed to about 2,000 students who were either CS majors or who took CS106A during the 2012–13 academic year; 603 responses were received. Sixty-three percent of respondents expressed greater inclination to double major if the number of classes were reduced for each by two courses, for a total of four fewer courses. The slices in the pie chart that accompanies the story are labeled incorrectly. Author email correspondence with Mehran Sahami, December 16, 2015. Sahami also said that many of the students who indicate in a survey like this that they would be more inclined to double major do not follow through. The number of participants in the inaugural CS+X initiative was lower than had been expected. Even in February 2016, the university declined to disclose the number of students who had chosen a CS+X major. The one Stanford student who was interviewed for a *Chronicle of Higher Education* story about the program was a sophomore who had chosen Stanford over other schools because of its welcome of students like her, with twin interests in music and technology. She was not certain she would stick with her CS+Music major, however, as she said "it feels like you have three majors, and it's hard to focus." "Computer Science, Meet Humanities: In New Majors, Opposites Attract," *Chronicle of Higher Education*, February 5, 2016.

42. Liam Kinney, "CS+X-traordinary," *SD*, May 15, 2014. (Kinney will be the primary subject of Chapter Seventeen.)

43. Jess Peterson, interview, October 23, 2014.

44. "Not So Different," Inside Higher Ed blog, March 7, 2014.

45. Tallies of double majors for the Class of 2014 are based on searches by major of the database maintained by the Stanford Alumni Association.

46. Department of English, SU, CS+English web page, https://english.stanford.edu/csenglish, accessed January 2, 2017.

CHAPTER 15. FIRST GEN

1. This was the second "Out for Undergraduate Technology Conference," which was hosted at Facebook's headquarters and drew 400 student applications for 170 slots. See "Silicon Valley Meets at Facebook Campus to Recruit LGBT Students," Xconomy.com, February 1, 2013.

2. "Early Android Veterans Raise $18M from Accel, Google Ventures for Stealth Company, NextBit," TechCrunch, January 14, 2014.

CHAPTER 16. THE ART OF LIVING

1. "Saving the 'Fuzzy,'" *SD*, October 20, 2011.

2. SU, *Study of Undergraduate Education, The Study of Undergraduate Education at Stanford University* (SUES) (Stanford: The Office of the Vice Provost for Undergraduate Education, SU, 2012), 17–18. The university presently does not release a top-ten list of majors, only a top-five list. Tallying the majors in the undergraduate degrees conferred in 2014–15, the rank order was (1) computer science, (2) human biology, (3) engineering, (4) science, technology and society, and (5) economics. http://facts.stanford.edu/academics/undergraduate-facts, accessed January 7, 2017.

3. The language departments are French and Italian; German Studies; Iberian and Latin American Cultures; and Slavic Languages and Literature.

4. "Saving the 'Fuzzy.'"

5. Philippe Buc, "Op-Ed: The Humanities at Stanford," *SD*, April 26, 2011.

6. "Faculty Senate Addresses Humanities, Hears from Trustees," *SD*, March 4, 2011.

7. SU, *Study of Undergraduate Education*, 17.

8. "Computerizing the Farm: Dorm, Class Use Foreseen," *SD*, May 20, 1983. The facility that Gorin directed was LOTS (the Low Overhead Time-Sharing System), which provided students with terminals connected to a DEC minicomputer. The highest priority was given to students enrolled in computer science classes, but other students, such as graduate students in history, including me, were permitted unlimited access to terminals in the wee hours of the night. At 3 a.m. on a random weeknight a visitor would have seen most of the terminals occupied by students typing their dissertations. (Our large text files had to be loaded on reels of magnetic tape and walked across campus to another facility for printing). In 1982, as computer science enrollments grew and CS students were complaining that they could not get access to terminals, Gorin announced that the machines were not to be used for word processing. At a public meeting between Gorin and unhappy students, I recall standing up to vigorously argue that all students who were doing school-related work on the machines, whatever the application, should be welcomed and accommodated. Gorin responded with a counterargument put in the form of a rhetorical question, to which I had no answer: The university doesn't provide every student with his or her own typewriter, does it?

9. SU, *Study of Undergraduate Education*, 17.

10. "CS'[s] Rise in Popularity Poses Pressing Questions," *SD*, June 5, 2013.

11. "Tech Culture Yields Opportunities and Challenges for Stanford," *SD*, January 29, 2016.

12. "CS'[s] Rise in Popularity."

13. Even though Eric Roberts authored textbooks on Java and C++, his teaching repertoire extended to the outer boundaries of computer science and ventured into the humanities. It included such courses as The Two Cultures, Technological Visions of Utopia, and Computers, Ethics, and Public Policy.

14. "A Look at Stanford Computer Science, Part II: Challenges of a Growing Field," *SD*, April 16, 2015.

15. "Saving the 'Fuzzy.'"

16. Ibid.

17. Ibid.

18. The university placed the video, "In Defense of the Humanities," which runs a little more than six minutes, on YouTube: https://www.youtube.com/watch?v=L8VssKBCQ4A. The university news service also built an article around the segment and an interview that a staff member did with Landy: "Lit Classes Under Attack? Stanford's Joshua Landy to the Rescue," *Stanford Report*, December 7, 2010.

19. Emphasis in original. Persis Drell, "Stanford Engineering: The Path Forward," SU, Forty-Eighth Senate Report No. 3, November 5, 2015, https://stanford.app.box.com/s/d563ao3dqs322i3z2c587rwjve91yym1. If the amusement produced in the faculty meeting by the "she doesn't think [engineering is] that interesting" remark was from the listeners' appreciation of the sense of humor of the speaker—why of course the dean of engineering would think that engineering is the most interesting field of all, wouldn't she?—Drell's curriculum vitae tells us that she may not have been joking that day, that she really didn't think that engineering is that interesting. None of her degrees were in engineering. She received an AB from Wellesley College, where she majored in mathematics and physics, and a PhD in atomic physics from the University of California, Berkeley. She had directed the SLAC National Accelerator Center for five years. At the time of her appointment in 2014 to the deanship in the School of Engineering, she held no position in that school: she had a joint appointment as a professor of physics in H&S and of particle physics and astrophysics at SLAC. "Former SLAC Director Persis Drell Named Dean of Stanford Engineering," *Stanford Report*, June 4, 2014.

20. Drell, "Stanford Engineering."

21. "Pediatrics and Immunology Expert to Speak on Emerging Trends in Medicine," *Fordham News*, October 4, 2011.

22. The phrase was used by Russell Berman, a professor of German studies and comparative literature.

23. "Stanford Distinguished Careers Institute to Offer Transformative Experience," *Stanford Report*, April 2, 2014.

24. SU's Academic Council, Forty-Eighth Senate, Report No. 3, November 5, 2015, 29–30.

25. Ibid., 30.

26. SU, *Study of Undergraduate Education*, 18.

27. Ray Lyman Wilbur had been among the earliest graduates of the newly founded Stanford University, graduating in 1896. He remained in school, earning a master's degree at Stanford the next year and his MD two years later at Cooper Medical College, in San Francisco. He became president of Stanford in 1916.

28. Ray Lyman Wilbur, "The Junior College in California," *Bulletin of the American Association of University Professors* 14, no. 5 (May 1928): 363–364.

29. Ibid., 365.

30. "University Must Welcome Change Says Dr. Wilbur," *SD*, July 9, 1926.

31. Ray Lyman Wilbur, "Introduction," *Junior College Journal* 1, no. 1 (October 1930), 3.

32. "Faculty Considers Instruction Change," *DPA*, April 23, 1920.

33. "New System at Stanford Will Offer Change," *SFC*, July 18, 1920.

34. The passage from the 1920 report by the Commission on the Reorganization of Undergraduate Education is quoted in SU, *Study of Undergraduate Education*, 18.

35. The Problems of Citizenship course was dropped in 1934 and replaced by a three-quarter history course sequence, Western Civilization, a requirement that ran until the 1960s. When Western Civ was dropped, nothing immediately replaced it. Twelve years later, Western Culture became a new requirement for all students. It was succeeded in 1988 by the nominally broader Culture, Ideas, and Values requirement, a three-quarter thematic sequence in the freshman year that students selected before arriving to campus. Its replacement, Introduction to the Humanities, was broken into two parts: a team-taught introductory course for the fall, which was selected in advance of arrival, and then a two-quarter thematic sequence that students would pick later. It was also supposed to do better in representing non-European, non-male voices—and, addressing another student complaint, reducing the amount of assigned reading to a quantity that was more realistic. One of the introductory courses was The Word and the World, which assigned only five books instead of the ten that were used in the pre-IHUM version of the course. "A New Era: CIV Sweeps in Fac Sen," *SD*, April 1, 1988; "CIV Replacement Pilot Begins," *SD*, September 24, 1997; "Course Changes," *SD*, September 18, 1998.

36. Registrar's Office, SU, *Stanford Bulletin*, Archive 2008–09, https://web.stanford.edu/dept/registrar/bulletin0809/65097.htm.

37. Students had to take two courses: one centered on analysis and research-based arguments, the other on writing, research, and oral presentation. A third requirement, Writing in the Major, was fulfilled by a writing-intensive course in the major. "Understanding the Writing and Rhetoric Requirements," Program in Writing and Rhetoric website, https://undergrad.stanford.edu/programs/pwr/courses/understanding-writing-and-rhetoric-requirements, accessed January 7, 2017.

38. The 150 figure is from Stanford, *Study of Undergraduate Education*, 2012, 46; the 250 figure is the number given by Harry Elam in "Departments Assess Impact of Thi-Mat," *SD*, September 18, 2012.

39. Stanford, *Study of Undergraduate Education*, 46.

40. Ken Auletta, "Get Rich U.," *New Yorker*, April 30, 2012.

41. SU, Forty-Fourth Senate of the Academic Council, March 8, 2012, Minutes, 18, https://stanford.app.box.com/s/el0ewruz6n8t1nuuxnbn.

42. Ibid.

43. "Faculty Back IHUM Successor," *SD*, February 28, 2012.

44. "Despite Warm Reception, Some Faculty Find Fault with Thinking Matters," *SD*, January 11, 2013.

45. "Faculty Back IHUM Successor."

CHAPTER 17. BILINGUAL

1. In a column that he wrote regularly for the *Stanford Daily*, Liam Kinney described to readers his yet-unsuccessful search for a summer internship as a symbolic systems major: "I'm cornered into giving this feeble excuse about how the Computer Science major is too many units to double with, and how I would never dream of leaving the classics major, and how Symbolic Systems is the next best thing to Computer Science." Liam Kinney, "CS+X-traordinary," *SD*, May 15, 2014. At the *Daily*'s website, an anonymous commentator took aim at Kinney's description of SymSys as "the next best thing to Computer Science." The critic wrote, "I know a score of people who could have majored in either CS or SymSys but chose the latter because its interdisciplinary focus offered distinct advantages. The fact that you underrate it as a major, and sell it short in conversation, is your fault. Most major Silicon Valley tech companies probably know what a Stanford SymSys degree is—Marissa Mayer, after all, front-lines a group of prominent tech leaders who possess that degree." Mayer, an early employee at Google who would rise to senior leadership before moving to Yahoo to become its chief executive, does not illustrate the commentator's point, however. Mayer was a SymSys major but stayed to earn her master's degree in computer science in 1999 before seeking her first professional job, which would be Google.

2. Kinney, "CS+X-traordinary."

3. Thomas L. Friedman, "How to Get a Job at Google, Part 2," *NYT*, April 19, 2014.

4. Kinney's mother settled on Airbnb as the ideal workplace before Glassdoor.com anointed Airbnb as the top choice in its annual rankings, announced in December 2015. Airbnb displaced Google from the top spot and had not been on Glassdoor's previous year's list. "Airbnb Tops List of 'Best Places to Work' for 2016," *USA Today*, December 9, 2015.

5. When the *Harvard Crimson* in 2005 ran a sidebar about the cofounders of "TheFacebook," which had been founded the year before, it listed computer science and psychology as Mark Zuckerberg's concentrations at Harvard. "Key Players," *Harvard Crimson*, February 24, 2005.

6. Mark Zuckerberg's own recollections in 2012 of his student days bring out the primacy of his interest in programming, not the humanities. The occasion for the event was Startup School, a one-day program of speakers addressing startup life, sponsored by seed-stage fund Y Combinator, which rented the auditorium at Stanford for the day. In a question-and-answer session, Zuckerberg told a story of how he had prepared for an art history final exam by quickly coding a website that displayed two hundred images of artworks and sending the link to this "study tool" to his classmates, inviting them to add their thoughts about the significance of each image. The annotations came in quickly—and he aced the exam. (The interlocutor, Y Combinator cofounder Paul Graham, quipped, "So you crowdsourced studying.") "Zuckerberg Admits: If I Wasn't the CEO of Facebook, I'd Be at Microsoft," VentureBeat blog, October 20, 2012.

7. Grace Chao, a senior who was an English major, defended students like Kinney in an opinion piece published in 2014 in the *Stanford Daily*. She addressed fellow students in the humanities: "Denigrating CS as boring, unoriginal or 'selling-out' in order to make humanities majors feel better about their futures should be discouraged."

Grace Chao, "In Defense of the Humanities, Computer Science, and the Not-So-Book-Drunk English Major," *SD*, April 8, 2014.

8. The link pointed to Richard Saller, "Enlightenment in Unexpected Places," *SD*, April 7, 2014.

9. Lloyd Minor, "The Humanities and Medicine," *SD*, April 6, 2014; Dan-el Padilla Peralta, "Why 'Why Classics?'" n.d., SU, Department of Classics website, https://classics.stanford.edu/dan-el-padilla-peralta-why-why-classics; Mary Beard, "Do the Classics Have a Future?" *New York Review of Books*, January 12, 2012.

10. Liam Kinney, "12 Reasons to Study Classics in the 21st Century," n.d., SU, Department of Classics website, https://classics.stanford.edu/sites/default/files/final_project_0.pdf, linked on the department's Why? Classics web page, https://classics.stanford.edu/academics/why-classics, accessed January 7, 2017.

CHAPTER 18. A HISTORY OF THE FUTURE

1. "Stanford 2001," *SD*, January 29, 1969.

2. Raj Reddy earned his PhD in computer science at Stanford, finishing in 1966, and had accepted a position on the faculty. He would move to Carnegie Mellon in 1969.

3. In the 1960s, Patrick Suppes, a professor of philosophy at Stanford, was a national pioneer of computer-aided instruction, first addressing mathematics education at the elementary level (his first course offering was in set logic). He predicted in 1966, "In a few more years, millions of schoolchildren will have access to what Philip of Macedon's son Alexander enjoyed as a royal prerogative: the personal services of a tutor as well informed and as responsive as Aristotle." In 1967, he founded the Computer Curriculum Corporation to commercialize the technology he developed; it enjoyed great success, and Suppes made generous donations to Stanford. "Patrick Suppes, Pioneer in Computerized Learning, Dies at 92," *NYT*, December 3, 2014.

4. What would be called "distance learning" did not need the arrival of the Internet. At the moment that Reddy was speaking, Stanford had secured permission from the FCC to launch a four-channel television broadcast system, the Stanford Instructional Television Network, to deliver lectures of graduate courses, mostly in engineering, to the employees of partner companies and organizations who were part-time graduate students. The network utilized a segment of the microwave band that required special television sets to receive. FM-based audio links between the lecture hall at Stanford and the receiving room at the companies provided a rudimentary form of interactivity. The broadcasts began in the early 1970s, and SU later boasted that its network was the largest university provider of live, graduate-level engineering courses. "TV Circuit to Link Colleges," *SD*, May 22, 1968; "Area Businesses Ally with Stanford," *SD*, January 15, 1969; "Stanford TV Transmits Education," *SD*, February 19, 1974; "Top Prize for SITN," *SD*, December 2, 1993; "Distance Learning Successful," *SD*, December 1, 2011.

5. "Stanford 2001."

6. "D.School Presents the Future of Higher Education," *SD*, May 2, 2014.

7. Sebastian Thrun was a co-instructor; the other co-instructor was Peter Norvig, director of research at Google.

8. "Virtual Classroom," *SD*, February 21, 2012. In this trio, Koller was the first

to move one of her courses online, in winter quarter 2010, then just for her Stanford students.

9. Sebastian Thrun, "University 2.0," presentation at DLD12, Munich, Germany, January 23, 2012, https://www.youtube.com/watch?v=SkneoNrfadk.

10. Thrun implied that he had just resigned in order to pursue work on his startup but, in fact, he had been forced by the university to give up the position the year before because he had been on a leave of absence the previous two years working at Google as a Google Fellow and Stanford imposed on faculty members a strict limit of two years of leave in any seven-year period. "Thrun Starts Web-Based University," *SD*, February 9, 2012.

11. "Online Education Venture Lures Cash Infusion and Deals with 5 Top Universities," *NYT*, April 18, 2012.

12. Ken Auletta, "Get Rich U.," *New Yorker*, April 30, 2012.

13. David Black, "Udacity's Sebastian Thrun, Godfather of Free Online Education, Changes Course," *Fast Company*, November 13, 2014.

14. "Penn GSE Study Shows MOOCs Have Relatively Few Active Users, with Only a Few Persisting to Course End," University of Pennsylvania press release, December 5, 2013; Slides for presentation, Laura Perna et al., "The Life Cycle of a Million MOOC Users," given at the MOOC Research Initiative Conference, University of Texas at Arlington, December 5, 2013, http://www.gse.upenn.edu/pdf/ahead/perna_ruby_boruch_moocs_dec2013.pdf.

15. Thrun said that the adaptation of Udacity's technology for San Jose State was prompted by a phone call, out of the blue, from California Governor Jerry Brown, who, according to Thrun, had said, "Hey, Sebastian, we have a crisis in the state." "California to Give Web Courses a Big Trial," *NYT*, January 15, 2013.

16. "Udacity's Partnership with SJSU Furthered [*sic*] Explained to Campus Community," *Spartan Daily*, February 3, 2013; "After Setbacks, Online Courses Are Rethought," *NYT*, December 10, 2013.

17. "SJSU and Udacity Offer Summer Courses," *Spartan Daily*, April 30, 2013.

18. "San Jose State U. Puts MOOC Project with Udacity on Hold," *Chronicle of Higher Education*, July 19, 2013. The university's partnership with Udacity had been championed most enthusiastically by the university's provost, Ellen Junn. The unhappy ending to the trial was followed by her departure from the university on short notice in January 2014. Junn described the online experiment this way in her farewell message that was emailed to the faculty: "Perhaps our boldest adventure was the partnering with edX and Udacity. These opportunities were exciting and challenging, and helped put San Jose State into the national news arena. President Qayoumi and I were able to meet with Bill and Melinda Gates, Sebastian Thrun, the governor and lieutenant governor and other noted leaders. We also experienced the highs and lows of press coverage. All and all it was an invigorating experience and we learned a great deal. We were able to secure NSF funding to research the possibility of these new delivery methods and their applicability for under-prepared students still in high school and/or who already failed remedial math. The initial results were mixed, but it was one of the first empirical studies to determine student learning in actual university courses." Ellen Junn, "Dear

Friends and Colleagues," email sent out by the Office of the Provost, San Jose State University [January 10, 2014], http://us7.campaign-archive2.com/?u=bee290757ecb 4d88376ed920d&id=3c09b0d55d.

19. "Demystifying the MOOC," *NYT*, October 29, 2014.

20. Udacity website, https://www.udacity.com/nanodegree, accessed January 4, 2017.

21. Susan Matt and Luke Fernandez, "Before MOOCs, 'Colleges of the Air,'" *Chronicle of Higher Education*, April 23, 2013. New York University had established its radio station by 1922, through which "virtually all the subjects of the university [would] be sent out." Columbia, Harvard, Kansas State, Ohio State, Purdue, Tufts, and the Universities of Akron, Arkansas, California, Florida, Hawaii, Iowa, Minnesota, Nebraska, Ohio, Wisconsin, and Utah offered courses broadcast by radio.

22. Stanford 2025: Open Loop University web page, http://www.stanford2025 .com/open-loop-university.

23. Ibid.

24. Ibid.

25. Stanford 2025: Axis Flip web page, http://www.stanford2025.com/axis-flip.

26. Stanford 2025: Purpose Learning web page, http://www.stanford2025.com/ purpose-learning.

27. Stanford 2025: Paced Education web page, http://www.stanford2025.com/ paced-education.

28. Ibid.

29. Ibid.

30. Stanford 2025: Axis Flip.

31. Peter N. Miller, "Is 'Design Thinking' the New Liberal Arts?" *Chronicle of Higher Education*, March 26, 2015.

32. Ibid.

33. Stanford 2025, www.stanford2025.com.

34. Jeanne Meister, "Job Hopping Is the 'New Normal' for Millennials: Three Ways to Prevent a Human Resource Nightmare," *Forbes*, August 14, 2012.

35. The quotation from Swearer was used in SU, *The Study of Undergraduate Education at Stanford University* (SUES) (Stanford: The Office of the Vice Provost for Undergraduate Education, SU, 2012), 12. In turn, Stanford 2025 used the SUES report as its source for the quotation.

36. Harry Elam, "Our Shifting Educational Environment: Why Stanford's Leadership in Higher Education Is Critical Now," SU, Forty-Eighth Senate Report No. 5, January 21, 2016.

CHAPTER 19. DO-OVER

1. Blumeyer is listed in the Stanford alumni directory as a member of the Class of 2007, but he took a year of leave while a student and actually graduated in 2008.

2. "Generating Brain Power for 1950," General Electric Company advertisement, *Stanford Illustrated Review*, April 1929, 367.

3. "Alumni Placement Service," *Stanford Illustrated Review*, June 1934, 258.

4. In 2017, SU's Department of Computer Science advised applicants, "The MSCS program is 45 units, and most full-time students take two years to complete it. That works out to roughly 8–10 units per quarter, which is the most common course load for MSCS students (and the maximum allowed if you are doing a 50% TAship or RAship). This typically translates to two or three classes." "Program Planning," Department of Computer Science, SU, http://mscs.stanford.edu/classes/planning/, accessed January 4, 2017.

5. Nick Toscano, "The Complete List of Coding Camps in San Francisco," January 6, 2015, http://www.skilledup.com/articles/bootcamps-san-francisco. The guide subsequently was revised. But when the revised page was revisited on April 4, 2017, it had disappeared.

6. The App Academy advertisement ran at the top of an emailed digest of *Stanford Daily* stories that was sent out daily to subscribers.

7. App Academy also collected a $5,000 deposit from each applicant upon acceptance, which was refunded at the completion of the course; this ensured that the applicant would follow through and attend.

8. Kyle Wiens, "I Won't Hire People Who Use Poor Grammar. Here's Why," *Harvard Business Review*, July 20, 2012. Also see Kristian Glass, "Cover Letters: Always Send One," Kristian Glass—Do I Smell Burning? blog, January 15, 2016, http://blog.do ismellburning.co.uk/cover-letters-always-send-one/. Glass, who was the London-based chief technology officer for LaterPay, attempted to dissuade software engineers who applied for jobs from treating cover letters as a waste of time, especially candidates whose experience does not match up exactly with what is requested. "We're a bunch of people from different nationalities with different backgrounds and that diversity strengthens us," Glass wrote. "Even if your CV feels like a perfect fit, give me a short cover letter that makes it painfully clear. Humans are imperfect. Data transmission is unreliable. Redundant methods of indicating your suitability are unlikely to hurt."

9. At Lyft, Stephen Hayes received a number of résumés from graduates of Hack Reactor, some of whom were humanities majors, that a Stanford friend who had also gone to Hack Reactor sent him. Hack Reactor is highly regarded but expensive: tuition for its twelve-week program in early 2016 was $17,700. Its participants, who, as at App Academy, had to have some programming knowledge, liked to say that instead of undergoing training that took their skills from "0 to 60," it was "20 to 120." Hayes forwarded the résumés to software engineering groups at Lyft, but none that he passed on were hired.

10. Matt Weinberger, "Why Ford's CEO Invested $182 Million in the $2.8 Billion Startup That Teaches How to Be More Like Google," Business Insider blog, July 14, 2016.

11. Ibid.

CHAPTER 20. LIBERAL EDUCATION IS VOCATIONAL

1. Office of the President, SU, Biography.

2. "Prepared Text of Inauguration Address, 'The Purposeful University,' by Stanford President Marc Tessier-Lavigne," Stanford News, October 21, 2016.

3. Marc Tessier-Lavigne, "The Purposeful University: Dialogue with the University Senate," SU, Forty-Ninth Senate Report No. 2, October 27, 2016. Tessier-Lavigne

was familiar with computer science's preeminent position at Stanford because he had been present at the meeting of the faculty senate two weeks before, when a report on trends in undergraduate majors had been presented: Russell Berman and Brian Cook, representing the Policy & Planning Board, "Changes in the Academic Interests of Stanford Undergraduates," SU, Forty-Ninth Senate Report No. 1, October 13, 2016.

4. Tessier-Lavigne, "Purposeful University."

5. Ibid.

6. William A. Cooper et al. to J. C. Branner, June 14, 1915, Wilbur Presidential Papers (SC 064A), Box 2, Folder 11, SCUA.

7. "His Diploma," *Stanford Chaparral* 6, no. 6 (November 23, 1904), 1.

8. "To the Man at the End of the Plank," *Stanford Chaparral* 3, no. 15 (May 22, 1902), 1.

9. "A Defect in the Major-Subject System," *Stanford Alumnus* 12, no. 2 (October 1910), 43; "Professor R. M. Alden to Leave Stanford," *SD*, April 4, 1911.

10. "Defect," 43–44. Voices on campus that defended the practicality of a liberal education, even within the English department, were rare then. Walter Miller, the professor of classical philology who in the commencement ceremonies in 1898 had eloquently defended the humanities and the undergraduate education that was "not for learning things, but for learning how to learn things," had departed from the campus shortly after delivering the speech. "Stanford Now Loses One More from Its Staff of Professors," *San Francisco Call*, May 26, 1902.

11. Stanford's first president, David Starr Jordan, was succeeded in 1913 by John C. Branner, the professor of geology who had been Herbert Hoover's professor and advisor. Branner was in the president's office only three years and was succeeded by Ray Lyman Wilbur, a medical doctor who had served as dean of Stanford's new School of Medicine in San Francisco, created when the university acquired the freestanding Cooper Medical College. A year after assuming the president's position, Wilbur at an assembly mentioned "the danger of too much specialization in preparing for a vocation." But making the public case for a liberal education did not emerge as a top priority in what would turn out to be a very long tenure, twenty-seven years, as Stanford's president. "Dr. Wilbur Tells of Stanford's Problems," DPA, January 11, 1917.

12. Ibid.

13. "'Choosing a Life Work' Is Subject of Freshman Talk," *DPA*, December 1, 1919.

14. Stanford University Committee on Vocational Guidance, *Vocational Information* (Stanford: Stanford University, 1919), 2, 13.

15. Ibid., 34.

16. Ibid., 6–7.

17. Ibid., 147.

18. Ibid., 63–64.

19. Among the careers that were offered up for the consideration of male graduates, the one that was promoted by an anonymous writer with great gusto as offering "an exciting life" was a most unlikely choice: "railroading," that is, working as a manager for a railroad. "No two days are ever alike," the brochure gushed, and "the lack of

monotony and the demand for aggressiveness make this a very attractive field for young men of energy." SU, *Vocational Information*, 53–54.

20. "A Job! My Kingdom for a Job!" *SD*, January 29, 1930.

21. "Share the Wealth," *SD*, May 10, 1940. The same point was made in 1951: "The series of Vocom programs will be aimed toward those graduating seniors who have majored in such fields as social science, English, or history; who have thus had no intensified training for a given job; and who may or may not have decided on the field of activity they wish to enter." "Senior Vocom Outlines Jobs," *SD*, April 5, 1951.

22. The 1929 start date is inferred by Wrenn's being in place in early January 1930 and by a reference to his seven years of service when he resigned in 1936 to take a position at the University of Minnesota. "Dr. C. G. Wrenn Resigns Office," *SD*, July 2, 1936.

23. "Committee Offers Information on Careers Open to Graduate," *SD*, January 9, 1930. For a description of Wrenn's dissertation research on personality traits and careers and on his subsequent career, see Clyde Parker, "Charles Gilbert Wrenn (1902–2001)," *American Psychologist* 57, no. 9 (September 2002): 721–722.

24. "Committee Offers Information," *SD*, January 9, 1930.

25. "Vocom Aids in Evaluating Professions," *SD*, May 11, 1939, and "Advice on That Career Hunt," *SD*, February 28, 1951. Interest flagged most visibly in the Depression years: see "Lectures Cancelled," *SD*, May 12, 1937 and "Vocom Asks Farm Ideas on Projects," *SD*, February 16, 1940, which suggests the committee had disappeared by its reference to "the newly formed Men's Vocational Guidance Committee." The women's committee was officially discontinued in 1951 and so too was the remaining Vocational Guidance Committee two years later: "Interest Lag Is Reason for Ending Vocom," *SD*, October 5, 1951, and Eugene Dils, Director of the Placement Service, "From Another Viewpoint," *SD*, January 13, 1953.

26. The women students developed the superior communications system at the system's peak: every women's dorm and sorority house on campus had its own Vocational Guidance Committee representative to spread notices of upcoming speakers and to gather program suggestions.

27. "Forum Plans Merchandise Talk Tonight," *SD*, January 29, 1940.

28. "A Job!"

29. "Vocom to Discuss Fashion Designing," *SD*, January 30, 1940.

30. The importance of personality surfaced in 1945, when the National Association of Manufacturers organized a panel of five representatives from large San Francisco Bay Area businesses, including Standard Oil, General Electric, and a department store in Oakland. The representatives were asked to talk about careers at their firms. All agreed that what was most appreciated was "a well-rounded education" that came from the liberal arts. The same group of representatives went a bit further, however, and said something, in unison, that today's corporate communications minders would never permit their company's official ambassadors to say, anywhere, which was that the degree that the applicant earned was secondary to the applicant's personality, which the group agreed was the most important factor in getting and holding a job. "'Rounded Education' Favored," *SD*, November 28, 1945.

31. "Wrenn Advises Job-seeking '500,'" *SD*, February 17, 1932.

32. "Vocom Aids."

33. "Vocom Gives Students Aid Through Files," *SD*, May 12, 1939. The location of Doyle's office was described as an "obscure" one in the Administration Building.

34. "Majors Will Be Subject," *SD*, May 22, 1951.

35. "Farouk Dey Is New CDC Head," *SD*, January 16, 2013.

36. "'Vision 2020' Re-Envisions Career Services Model," *SD*, November 1, 2013.

37. "Career Development Center Renamed BEAM," *SD*, September 17, 2015.

38. Farouk Dey, "Our Name Story," n.d., Stanford Career Education, https://beam.stanford.edu/about-us/our-name-story, accessed January 7, 2017.

39. "Q & A: Farouk Dey," *SD*, May 21, 2013; "Stanford BEAM Celebrates Name Change with BEAM Connection Event," *SD*, January 15, 2016.

40. "Stanford's Most Popular Class Isn't Computer Science—It's Something Much More Important," *Fast Company*, March 26, 2015.

41. "Designing Your Life, ME104B," course syllabus, identified as "v5," n.d., http://web.stanford.edu/class/me104b/cgi-bin/uploads/Syllabus-Designing-Your-Life-ME104B-v5.pdf, first retrieved November 10, 2015.

42. "Forum Plans."

43. "Stanford's Most Popular Class." In 2016, Burnett and Evans shared their ideas with the general public, publishing a book, *Designing Your Life: How to Build a Well-Lived, Joyful Life* (New York: Knopf, 2016), that swiftly ascended bestseller lists. It is a self-advice book, addressing the reader in the second-person voice, provisioned with practical "actionable" advice on every page. Here's an example (p. 11): "To change the median income of poets, you'd somehow have to alter the market for poetry and get people to buy more poetry or pay more for it. Well, you could try for that. You could write letters to the editor in praise of poetry. You could knock on doors to get people out to the poetry night at your local coffeehouse. This one is a long shot. Even though you can work on this 'problem' . . . we'd recommend that you accept it as an inactionable situation. If you do that, then your attention is freed to start designing other solutions to other problems."

44. Jaison R. Abel and Richard Deitz, "Agglomeration and Job Matching Among College Graduates," *Regional Science and Urban Economics* 51 (2015), 16. In passing, the authors happened to mention that 44 percent of studio arts majors hold jobs related to their major. This astonishing figure—it is almost as high as the 53 percent of accounting majors who are well-matched to their jobs—suggests that the 1 percent figure for matches for all of the liberal arts would be even lower were it not for studio arts.

45. Steven Pearlstein, "Meet the Parents Who Won't Let Their Children Study Literature," *Washington Post*, September 2, 2016.

46. "As Interest Fades in the Humanities, Colleges Worry," *NYT*, October 31, 2013.

47. Amanda Rizkalla, "From Lower Class to Literature Class," *SD*, October 24, 2016.

48. The first study was Stacy Berg Dale and Alan B. Krueger, "Estimating the Payoff to Attending a More Selective College: An Application of Selection on Observables and Unobservables," *Quarterly Journal of Economics* 117, no. 4 (November 2002): 1491–1527. It followed more than fourteen thousand individuals who were entering freshmen

in 1976 at the thirty colleges and universities that were participating in Andrew W. Mellon Foundation's College and Beyond data-gathering project and gathered self-reported earnings in 1995. The second study was Dale and Krueger, "Estimating the Return to College Selectivity Over the Career Using Administrative Earnings Data," NBER Working Paper Series, Working Paper 17159, June 2011. It followed a cohort that were entering freshmen in 1989 at twenty-seven of the colleges and universities that were willing to participate in the follow-up study, and it used earnings data obtained from the Social Security Administration. The authors listed the names of the twenty-seven schools that participated in the follow-up study: Barnard College, Bryn Mawr College, Columbia University, Duke University, Emory University, Georgetown University, Kenyon College, Miami University of Ohio, Morehouse College, Northwestern University, Oberlin College, Penn State University, Princeton University, Smith College, Stanford University, Swarthmore College, Tufts University, Tulane University, University of Michigan, University of Pennsylvania, Vanderbilt University, Washington University, Wellesley College, Wesleyan University, Williams College, Xavier University, and Yale University. Thirty-five percent of the students in each of the two cohorts the authors studied did not attend the most selective school to which they were admitted. Dale and Krueger, "Estimating the Return," 26.

49. Dale and Krueger, "Estimating the Payoff," 1499.

50. "Revisiting the Value of Elite Colleges," *NYT*, February 21, 2011.

51. Debra Humphreys and Patrick Kelly, *How Liberal Arts and Sciences Majors Fare in Employment* (Washington, DC: Association of American Colleges and Universities, 2014), 6.

52. SU Committee, *Vocational Information*, 34.

INDEX

Abel, Jaison R., 236
account associate, 35, 36
account coordinator, 85
account management, 34
account manager, 84
"Adventures in Stupidity" (L. Terman), 140–41
Agassiz, Louis, 245n15
Airbnb, 174–80, 199–200, 223, 272n4
Ajax (Sophocles), 123
Alden, Richard, 228–29
Amazon, 12–13, 202
American Association for the Advancement of Science, 159
American Colleges and Universities, 240
American Nickel Company, 25
American Psychological Association, 114, 135
American Tobacco Company, 134
American Trust Company, 232
Anderson, Lanier, 192
Anderson, Melville, 71
Andrew Carnegie (Nasaw), 237
Anyone Can Learn To Code, 216
App Academy, 216–19, 221–23, 276n7
Apple, 217
Arizona State University, 129
Arkansas Geological Survey, 70
Army Alpha test, 137, 139, 146
Army Beta test, 137

Arrington, Michael, 259n1
Arthur Andersen, 77–78
assembly language, 10–11
AT&T, 128
Atlantic Monthly, 23
Atwood, Jeff, 167
Auletta, Ken, 207
Authentic Happiness (Seligman), 235–36
The Autobiography of Malcolm X, 147
Autonomic Technologies, 151
Ayres Handwriting Scale, 134

bachelor's degree, 15, 45, 50
Bain & Company, 55
Bard Graduate Center, 212
BASIC, 219
Benchmark Capital, 17
Bergstrom, John A., 113, 114, 116
Berman, Russell, 163
Bethlehem Steel Company, 25
Bewick, Moreing and Company, 74
Binet, Alfred, 120, 121, 142–43, 144
Binet-Simon Intelligence Scale, 120
Bizo, 131
Blumeyer, Doug, 215–24
Bock, Laszlo, 106, 197
Boeing, 159
Bok, Derek, 233
Bolles, Richard, 236
Bow, Clara, 85

Branner, John C., 51, 68–69, 73–74, 87, 277n11
British education, 28
Brown, Barbara, 7
Brown, Jerry, 274n15
Brown University, 213
Bryan, William Lowe, 113, 114, 257n7
Buc, Philippe, 181–82
Burnett, Bill, 235, 236, 279n43
Bush, Arthur Dermont, 258n31
business education, 22, 25, 91–98

C programming language, 11, 197
C++, 180
California Institute of Technology, 109, 163, 181
California State University, Long Beach, 239
Camplife Chickamauga, 138
Capital Business College, 66
Card Programmed Electronic Calculator, 158
Carlson School of Management, 148
Carnegie, Andrew, 86, 237
Carnegie Foundation for the Advancement of Teaching, 117
Carnegie Institute of Technology, 144
Carnegie Mellon University, 233
Carter, Jimmy, 251n1 (chap. 6)
Center for Democratic Institutions, 9
Center Magazine, 9
Central Normal College, 112–13, 114
Central Pacific Railroad, 19, 20, 47
Chang, Michael, 197–98
Chao, Grace, 272n7
Charles, John, 42
Chico State University, 129
Choosing Employees by Mental and Physical Tests (Kemble), 134–35
Chronicle of Higher Education, 212
Chuard, Alain, 259n8
Cisco, 156
Citi, 102
Civil Service Commission, 92

Clark, George A., 91
Clark University, 113, 114–15, 116, 257nn7–8
classics and classical languages, 21, 23–24, 86, 113, 116, 194, 201, 202–4
Clothier, Robert C., 132
Coder Camps, 216
coding boot camps, 216
Coding Dojo, 216
College Entrance Examination Board, 139
Collison, John, 38
Collison, Patrick, 38
Colorado School of Mines, 17
Columbia University, 117, 119, 135, 136, 139, 257n21
Committee on Classification of Personnel, 135
CompuCorp, 10–11
Computer Curriculum Corporation, 273n3
computer science, universal proficiency 8, 167
computer science major, 11
computing education, 165–67, 170
Confucianism, 14
"Content to Code? Straddling Silicon Valley's Techie–Fuzzie Divide" (Messina), 165
Cool Careers for Dummies (Nemko), 236
Cooper Medical College, 277n11
Cooper, Peter, 24
Cooper Union, 24, 26
Cornell, Ezra, 24–25, 246n22, 246n25
Cornell University, 20, 24–25, 28, 42–43
Coursera, 207, 208
Cowdery, Karl M., 145
CPP, 146
Crandell, Michael, 7–13, 16
Crown-Zellerbach Corporation, 232
Csikszentmihalyi, Mihalyi, 236
Cubberley, E. P., 116
Curtis Publishing Company, 132–33
customer success manager, 13

Cypress String Quartet, 152–53, 155

Dale, Stacy Berg, 238–39
Damon, William, 18
Dartmouth University, 22, 95
Davis, Daniel, 128–29, 130, 131, 260n9 (chap. 11)
Davis, Horace, 86–87
de Blasio, Bill, 166–67
Dead Space, 127–28
Deitz, Richard, 236
Deloitte, 102
Dev Bootcamp, 216
Dey, Farouk, 233–34
DirectTV, 198
discriminatory admissions, 139
Doyle, Anastasia, 233
Doyle, Edmund, 68
Drell, Persis, 186–87, 188–89, 270n19
Dropbox, 179
Drummond, David, 107
DuBois, W. E. B., 186

Earlham College, 66
East Asian languages and cultures major, 16
eBay, 204
Edelstein, Dan, 183
edX, 274n18
eFax, 12
Elam, Harry, 213–14
The Electric Kool-Aid Acid Test, 147
Electronic Arts, 127–28
Eliot, Charles W., 19, 23, 26, 246
Elliott, Orrin Leslie, 43
Emergency Economic Stabilization Act of 2008, 149
employers: appearance of applicants, 132, 134; liberal arts, 3, 226, 239–40; majors, applicants' choice of, 227; personality attributes preferred, 84, 278n30; political opinions of applicants, 135; power, 228; soft skills, 14–15; at Stanford, 4; technical inter-

views, 200, 223; work ethic sought, 128–29, 131
engineering education, 88–89, 188–89
engineers viewed by non-engineers, 9, 107–8, 156, 168
English major, 16
environmental studies major, 13
eugenics, 115
Evans, Dave, 235, 279n43

Facebook, 128, 148, 173, 177, 179, 201–2
Fazzino, Gary, 13–14, 244n13
Federal Reserve Bank of New York, 236
Feinstein, Dianne, 54
film theory, 220
Fisher Investments, 260n9 (chap. 11)
Fisher, M. F. K., 35
flappers, 77, 85
Flow (Csikszentmihalyi), 236
Forbes, 109, 213
Fordham University, 188
Forsythe, George E., 158–60, 161, 162, 264n4, 265n7, 265n9, 266n14
France, education in, 23, 28
Freedman, Estelle, 101–2
French major, 165
Friedman, Thomas, 197
Friends Pacific Academy, 65

Galvanize, 216
Gates, Bill, 274n18
Gates, Melinda, 274n18
Genentech, 225
General Assembly, 216
General Electric, 105, 106, 215, 278n30
General Motors, 62
"Genius and Stupidity" (L. Terman), 115
George Mason University, 237
George Peabody College for Teachers, 135
Georgetown Preparatory School, 124
Germany, education in, 23, 28–29, 116
"Get Rich U" (Auletta), 207

Gill, Dan, 83
Gladwell, Malcolm, 244n12
Glass, Kristian, 276n8
Google: brain teasers, 57; Build
    Opportunities for Leadership &
    Development, 103, 104; campus
    recruiting, 148; commutes, 179;
    contractors, 56–57, 105, 178; for-
    mer employees, 36, 175, 179, 180,
    216; Google Fellows, 274n10; hiring
    process, 177–78; imprimatur, 104;
    internships, 102, 104; interviews, 56;
    job–seeking graduates' interest in,
    173, 256n9; liberal arts majors, recep-
    tiveness to, 105, 110; Management
    Leadership for Tomorrow, 102;
    People Operations, 56–58, 104–5,
    109; scale of organization, 178, 180;
    selection criteria, 106, 108–9; TGIF,
    108; training, 105–7, 256n8; Wildfire
    Interactive acquisition, 129–30
Gordon Biersch, 150
Gorin, Ralph, 182–83, 269n8
government-relations manager, 13
The Graduate, 147, 244n11
Grangaard, Elise, 147–57
Granovetter, Mark, 157, 264nn8–9
GRE General Test, 204
Great American Universities (Slosson), 117
Great Recession, 147, 149, 182

Hack Reactor, 216, 276n9
Hackbright Academy, 216
Hall, Stanley, 113–15, 116
handshake interepretation, 132
handwriting analysis, 134
Hargadon, Fred, 162
Harvard Business Review, 223
Harvard University: academic repu-
    tation, 257n21; Agassiz, Louis,
    245n15; alumni, 86; Bok, Derek,
    233; Business School, 78, 95; classi-
    cal curriculum, 21; Crimson, 18, 20;
    Divinity School, 9; Eliot, Charles W.,

    19, 23–24, 26, 246n20; founding,
    18; General Education, Program in,
    19; Lawrence Scientific School, 22,
    245n15; Lepore, Jill, 237; MBAs,
    259n8; Royce, Josiah, 249n16; sala-
    ries, 119; Stanford, Leland, and, 25,
    26; Stanford University and, 18–19,
    21, 181; University of Virginia and,
    21–22; Yerkes, Robert, 135
Hastorf, Albert, 262n41
Hayes, Stephen, 53–63, 105, 276n9
Hazy, Meredith, 31–40
Head-Fi.org, 82
Heald Business College, 91–92
Heisman Trophy, 124
Hennessy, John, 207
Herodotus, 54, 77, 101
Herriot, John George, 264n3
Hertz, 62
Hewlett-Packard, 13–14
Hilton, Paris, 186
Hobbs, Alyson, 100
Homer, 123
Hoover, Herbert, 64–76, 87, 251n2
    (chap. 6)
Hoover, Theodore, 65, 66, 75
Huberich, Charles Henry, 90
Huddler, 82–84
Huey, Katharine, 132
humanities majors: employment,
    184–85; English majors favored by
    employers, 78; female students, 45;
    future learning, accelerates, 95, 149;
    as general preparation, 7, 74, 184;
    GRE scores, high, 204; human po-
    tential, fulfilling, 50; language skills, 9,
    156, 167, 185; as MBA students, 96;
    peer pressure on, 183; skills, suppos-
    edly fail to confer, 85
Huntington, Collis, 249n29

IBM, 158
IBM PC, 11
iFixit, 223

Indeed.com, 173, 79, 80, 173
The Independent, 117
Indiana University, 42, 113–14, 116, 257nn7–8
Inkling, 58–61, 105
intelligence tests, 111, 115, 119, 120–22, 132–44, 141–42, 146
internships: Airbnb, 174, 199–200; anxiety about, 200–201; Bain, 55; DirectTV, 198; geological survey, 70; juniors, for rising, 78–79; law firm, 124; public service, 33; seniors, for rising, 30, 54; SoundHound, 202; Target Corporation, 148, 149, 155; in Washington, DC, 31
interviews: Airbnb, 199–200; App Academy, 218; consulting firm, 126; Google, 56; Lyft, 62; questions, 57–58, 84, 132–33; Rocket Lawyer, 81; Twitter, 35
IQ, 111, 121, 141, 143
Irwin, Will, 65, 71
"Is 'Design Thinking' the New Liberal Arts?" (P. Miller), 212–13
Ivy League, 128, 163, 181, 219

J2 Global, 12
Jackson, J. Hugh, 96
James, William, 119
Janin, Louis, 72–74
Java, 166, 180, 218
JavaScript, 217
Jefferson, Thomas, 21–22, 123
JetFax, 12
Johns Hopkins University, 26
Johnson, Samuel, 120
Jordan, David Starr: faculty, clashes with, 118, 258n26; faculty recruitment, 249n16, 249n21, 257n7; general education, opposition to, 189; graduate programs, favoring of, 250n41; Hoover, Herbert, and, 73, 74; Huntington, Collis, on, 249n29; lower division, proposal to excise, 47,

249n33; Stanford, Leland, advice from, 71; Stanford University president, early tenure as, 42–45, 68; stenography, students trained in, 92–93
Journal of Educational Psychology, 146
Junn, Ellen, 274n18

Kaiser Family Foundation, 31
Kellogg, Vernon Lyman, 250n43
Kemble, William Fretz, 134–35
Kenen, Stephanie H., 19
Kennedy, David, 191–92
Kennedy, Donald, 4–6
Kimball, E. B., 252n29
Kinney, Liam, 194–204, 223
Koller, Daphne, 206–7
Krebs, Christopher, 195, 197
Krueger, Alan B., 238–39

Ladies' Home Journal, 132
Landy, Joshua, 185–87, 187, 202
LaserFAX, 12
LaterPay, 276n8
legal education, 88
Lehman Brothers, 149
Lepore, Jill, 237
Lew, Ying Y., 266n17
LGBT recruiting, 175
liberal arts: business leaders' attitudes toward, 84–85, 94–95, 106, 197; computing and, 161–62, 165, 167; engineers defense of, 167, 187, 190; Hoover, Herbert, 75, 76; multiplicity of perspectives, 168, 193; virtues, 213, 225–26, 230, 239
liberal arts majors: earnings, 3–4, 243n2; employment, 243n1; occupational matching, 236; practicality, 2, 3, 7, 13–14, 84–85; underemployment lore, 5, 95; versatility, 5, 7
Lindgren, Waldemar, 72
Lindley, Ernest H., 113, 114
LinkedIn, 131, 177
Lipman, Edward C., 232

Lippmann, Walter, 142–44
Los Angeles State Normal School, 115
Luck, Andrew, 124
Lyft, 61–63, 276n9

Macalester College, 16
Macarthur Foundation, 211
Make School, 216
Management Leadership for Tomorrow,
    101, 103
Marcus, Roger, 10
Martin, Richard, 123, 184–85
Marx, Guido H., 88–89
Massachusetts Agricultural College, 25
Massachusetts Institute of Technology,
    23, 24, 26, 38, 87, 109, 163, 185
Master of Commerce, 131
Mathematica Policy Research, 238
Matson Navigation Company, 7
Mayer, Marissa, 105, 256n8, 272n1
McIntire School of Commerce, 125–26,
    129, 131
Measurement of Intelligence (L Terman),
    120, 121
medical education, 88
"Meet the Parents Who Won't Let
    Their Children Study Literature"
    (Pearlstein), 237
Mellon Foundation, 101
Mellon Mays fellowship, 101, 103, 256n4
Meraki, 154, 155–57, 263n5
Messina, Marisa, 165, 166
Microsoft Office, 11–12
Miller, Derek, 19
Miller, Peter N., 212
Miller, Walter, 49–50, 277n10
Minor, Lloyd, 202
Monitor, 54–55
MOOCs (Massive Open Online
    Courses), 206, 208–9
Moore, Jessica, 99–110
Moore, Maryellie, 7
Morrill Act of 1862, 23
music major, 16

Myers-Briggs Type Indicator test, 146

Nasaw, David, 237
National Association of Corporation
    Schools, 133
National Association of Manufacturers,
    278n30
National Bureau of Standards, 159
National Football League, 124
National Science Foundation, 274n18
Natives Land Act of 1913, 53
Negroponte, Nicholas, 185
Nemko, Marty, 236
"The New Education" (Eliot), 23–24
New Republic, 142, 143
New York Times, 197
New York Tribune, 20
New York University, 135, 220, 221,
    275n21
New Yorker, 207
Nextbit, 177, 179
Ng, Andrew, 206–7
Northwestern University, 95, 133,
    245n16
Norton, Peter, 11, 13
Nostalghia, 220

Obama, Barack, 54
Oberlin College, 28
Ockelmann, Jennifer, 77–85
Odyssey (Homer), 123
Olmsted, Frederick Law, 42
Omeros (Walcott), 123
Oracle, 196
Orange Bowl, 124
Otis, Arthur S., 136

Pacific Foundation Services, 33
Pacific Gas and Electric Company, 54
Page, Larry, 108
pair programming, 218, 222, 224
Patel, Kush, 216
Pearlstein, Steven, 236–37
Peirce School, 93, 254n19

Pennsylvania State University, 238
Pepsi, 128
Perl, 218
Peterson, Jess, 168
Philips Exeter Academy, 194, 195, 201
Phillips, Andrew, 123–31, 184, 224
Philoctetes (Sophocles), 123
PHP programming language, 218
phrenology, 132
physiognomy, 132
Pinterest, 179
"Pity the Fuzzy Study Major" (Young), 5
Pivotal Labs, 223–24
Pixar, 153
Pizzo, Philip, 188–89
Pomona College, 106
Princeton University, 117, 163, 181, 238
Proctor, W. M., 229
program manager, 156
Pulitzer Prize, 183, 192
Python, 218

Qayoumi, Mo, 274n18
Quora, 173

Rakove, Jack, 183, 192
Randau, Clem J., 95
Ransom, Victoria, 259n8
recruiter, 177
recruiter coordinator, 173
Reddy, Raj, 205–6, 273n2
Rensselaer Polytechnic Institute, 24, 88
Reynolds, Jackson, 69–70, 74
RightScale, 8, 12, 13
risk analyst, 37–38
Rizkalla, Amanda, 237
Roberts, Eric, 184, 264n2, 269n13
Rockefeller University, 225
Rocket Lawyer, 81–82
Rocket U, 216
Royce, Josiah, 249n16, 249
Ruby on Rails, 217, 218
Ruggeri, Ned, 216
Rutgers University, 246n21

Saavedra, Rafael, 12
Sahami, Mehran, 165, 268n34
SAIL programming, 8, 12
Saint Anselme, 12
sales associate, 130
Saller, Richard, 202–3
San Francisco Chronicle, 27, 28–29, 41, 44, 190
San Francisco Municipal Railway, 7
San Francisco Performances, 152
San Jose State University, 17, 208, 274n15, 274n18
Sanchez, Mike, 171–80
Saturday Evening Post, 132
Satz, Debra, 184
Scholastic Aptitude Test, 122, 136, 139, 146, 238–39
The School Review, 116
Scott, Walter Dill, 133–34
Scribner's Magazine, 115
Sears, Robert S., 160, 262n41
Seligman, Martin, 235–36
Shakespeare, William, 123
Shanks, Michael, 212
Shazam, 201
Sheffield Scientific School, 22
Shepley, Rutan and Coolidge, 42
Silicon Valley: acquisitions of smaller firms, 131; LGBT recruiting, 175; new graduates, turning away, 63; software engineers, recruiting of, 176; Stanford University and, 1, 2–3, 19, 191–92, 258n26
Simon, Theodore, 120
Slosson, Edwin E., 117–19, 250n44
soft skills, 14–15, 40
Sophocles, 123
SoundHound, 201–2
sourcing, 174, 175–80
South Africa, 53, 56
Southern Pacific Railroad, 46–47
Spiegel, David, 18
Spielberg, Steven, 239
SQL, 40, 107

Stack Overflow, 167

Standard Oil Company, 232, 278n30

Stanford, Jane, 25–28, 41, 42, 47, 51–52, 86, 87–88, 250n47

Stanford, Leland: business–skills education, advocacy of, 91; campus design, 41–42; David Starr Jordan and, 44–45, 71; death, 46–47; equal treatment of students, 68; faculty hiring, cap on, 249n17; initial plans for a university, 19–21, 25–28, 46; preparatory schools, plans for, 246n26

Stanford, Leland, Jr., 19, 41

Stanford University: 2025 project, 206, 209–13; Academic Council, 140, 186, 188; academic ranking, 89, 109, 117; academic reputation, 162, 39, 89, 90, 162, 171, 173, 258n24; Academic Secretary, 187; admissions, dean of, 162; admissions standards, 49, 66–67, 111, 117–18, 140, 182; African–American students, 99, 256n1; agriculture, 28, 46; Alumni Association, 151; alumni network, 3, 39, 56, 58, 61–62, 83, 126, 151–52, 154–55, 156–57, 179, 238; alumni, occupations of, 90; Alumnus, 94; American Studies major, 147, 149; App Academy and, 216, 219; Applied Sciences, 43; Art and Ideas, 191; art history major, 78, 80; The Art of Living, 185–86, 202; Artificial Intelligence (AI), 220; Artificial Intelligence: Principles and Techniques CS 221, 199; Band, Leland Stanford Junior University Marching, 147–48, 150, 154, 156–57, 263n4; baseball team, 69; BEAM (Career Development Center), 234; biological sciences major, 83; bionomics major, 51, 250n43; business courses, earliest, 91–94; Business, Graduate School of, 95–98, 202; Camp Stanford, 55;

Career Development Center, 78, 102, 233–34; career fairs, 31–32, 54, 78, 102, 124, 196, 201; Career Planning and Placement Center, 4; Center for Computer Research in Music and Acoustics (CCRMA), 199, 201; chemistry major, 33; Chinese history, 16–17; classics department, 202–3; classics major, 124, 125–26, 129, 194, 195, 198, 200, 202–4; climate as attraction, 67; commencement addresses, 47–48, 48–49, 94–95; Computation Center, 158, 161, 266n18; computer labs, 8–9, 182; Computer Organization and Systems CS 107, 197; computer science course enrollments, 161, 163, 182–83, 225, 266n19; computer science courses for nonmajors, 7, 160; computer science department, 166, 168–69, 196, 206–7; computer science division, 159, 265n8, 266n18; computer science major, 158, 161, 162–64, 168, 183, 196; computer science master's degree, 198, 199, 202, 216, 276n4; coterm, 168, 169, 198, 202; CS+X, 168–70, 184, 268n41; Culture, Ideas, and Values, 271n35; Daily, 5, 182, 184, 205, 235; Designing Your Life, 235–36; Designing Your Stanford, 30; disciplinary breadth requirements, 195; Distinguished Careers Institute, 188; double major, 165, 168, 185, 187, 197; d.school (Hasso Plattner Institute of Design), 206, 212–13; dual major, 169; earnings of graduates, 239; East Asian Studies major, 171, 172, 171, 172, 177, 180; East Coast, students from, 67, 182; economics major, 50, 77, 95, 96, 147, 185; education department, 92, 94, 116–17, 144; education major, 50; Education Program for Gifted Youth, 79; Education, School of, 18; educational department, 227; engineering major, 4, 9, 34–35, 51, 88–89, 95, 99, 154, 163, 186–89, 227, 258n26; Engineering, School of, 162, 188, 258n26; English department, 71, 169–70; English major, 31, 33, 36, 39, 40, 50, 51, 78, 147, 164, 228; Epic Journeys, Modern Quests, 191; faculty recruitment, 44, 45; faculty, reputation of, 111, 119; faculty senate, 213; The Fate of Reason, 191; female students, 45, 49, 51–52, 97, 229, 230–31, 232–33, 251n48; film and media studies major, 215, 221, 223; Film Society, 220; finances, 26, 43–47; first–generation college students, 171, 237; football, 124, 126, 127; foreign language majors, 50; founding, 19–21, 25–29, 41–45; French major/minor, 149, 165; freshman seminars, 53, 123, 184; future, imagined, 205–6, 209–13; "fuzzies"/"techies," 5, 102–3, 165, 169–70, 214; general education requirements, 189–93; geology major, 64; German major, 51, 228; Global Affairs and World History track, 181, 184; Government and Community Relations, Office of, 173; Greek, 124, 194; Haas Center for Public Service, 32–33; Harvard University and, 18–19, 21, 181; history department, 54, 161, 181, 184; history major, 5, 7, 50, 53, 77, 78, 84–85, 99, 100, 106, 110, 164, 168, 228; Hospital, 129; human biology major, 158; Humanities and Sciences, School of, 1, 6, 98, 160, 162, 202; humanities, decline of, 98, 181–82, 183, 192, 202; humanities departments, 168, 182; Humanities House, 183; humanities majors, 5, 15, 45, 169, 170, 185–86; inexpensiveness, 67, 252n11; instructional television, 273n4; intelligence tests in admissions, 140;

Introduction to Artificial Intelligence, 206; Introduction to Computers CS 105, 166, 173; Introduction to Databases, 206; Introduction to the Humanities (IHUM), 189, 190–92, 271n35; Italian, 129; job board, 79, 173; Job Faire, 32; joint degrees, 168–69; Latin, 51, 91, 194, 195; Latin major, 51; law department, 90; law major, 47, 50–51, 69, 89, 90, 254n9; Law School, 59, 60; leaves of absence, 274n10; Liberal Arts and Sciences, 43; liberal arts education, advocates for, 49–50, 225–26; liberal arts majors, 4; A Life of Contemplation or Action? Debates in Western Literature and Philosophy, 191; liquor-sales ban in vicinity, 247n36; Literature, Cultures, and Languages division, 181; Low Overhead Time-Sharing System (LOTS), 269n8; lower division, proposal to excise, 47, 190; Machine Learning, 206; The Major Decision, 6, 7, 13, 14; major requirements, 87–88, 168, 192, 195, 196; majors, distribution of, 48, 50–51, 183–84, 187–88, 213–14, 225–26, 252n28, 269n2; Management Leadership for Tomorrow, 101, 102, 103; Mandarin, 172, 172, 174, 180; Mass Violence from Crusades to Genocides, 191; mathematics department, 159, 160, 265n8; MBAs, 97, 259n8; mechanical engineering major, 195; Medicine, School of, 18, 188, 202; mining and metallurgy department, 75; mining engineering, 64, 93, 227; multidisciplinary majors, 147, 163, 266n17; nonprofessional majors, 228–29, 230; on-campus job interviews, 4; online instruction, 205, 206–7, 208; parental pressure when major chosen, 100, 145, 168, 172, 185, 186, 194, 226,

236–37; parents who are alumni, 77, 99, 147; philosophy major, 7; Pioneer Class, 47–49, 64, 72–73, 74, 252n28; political science major, 187; Problems of Citizenship, 190, 191, 271n35; product design major, 195; professions and undergraduates, 88–91, 95; Programming Abstractions (Accelerated) CS 106X, 220, 267n33; Programming Abstractions CS 106B, 164, 166, 196, 220; Programming Methodology CS 106A, 19, 55, 79–80, 164, 166, 173, 183, 187, 195, 196, 199, 220; psychology department, 111, 144; psychology minor, 77, 79; public policy major, 100; Ram's Head Theatrical Society, 147; Rebellious Daughters and Filial Sons of the Chinese Family, 191; religious studies major, 7, 8, 9, 11, 13–14; residential education, 209; salaries, 119; sciences, majors in the, 50; seniors seeking work upon graduation, 5, 32, 227–28, 229–30, 231; Silicon Valley and, 1, 2–3, 19, 191–92, 258n26; social science majors, 96, 163; socioeconomic background of students, 67–68; Stanford-Binet, 120, 122, 132, 133, 136, 141; student body, characteristics of, 2; Summer Institute for General Management, 97, 98, 202, 255n36, 255n40; Summer Institute for Undergraduates, 97; symbolic systems major (SymSys), 164, 165, 168, 196–97, 198, 272n1; teaching credential, earning, 227; technical education, advocates for, 20–21, 26–27, 28–29, 41, 46, 47–48, 74–75; Thinking Matters, 192–93; tour guides, 54; tuition, 26, 43, 55, 66, 67; University Press, 146; Visions of the 1960s, 147; vocational guidance committees, 229–32, 232, 233; Washington, DC, internship, 31; Western Civilization, 190, 271n35;

Western Culture, 271n35; women, careers designated for, 230–31, 232–33; women's dorm, 248n5; work–study, 28, 67, 69–70, 103; World History of Science, 191; Writing and Rhetoric, Program in, 54, 191; writing requirement, 66, 70–71

Startup School, 272n6
STEM, 5, 187, 192–93, 222, 225
Stillman, John Maxson, 47–48
Stripe, 37–40
Strong, Edward K., 135, 144–46
Strong Vocational Interest Blank, 144–46
Suppes, Patrick, 273n3
Swain, Joseph, 66
Swearer, Howard, 213
Sweetwood, Dylan, 166
Synack, 202

Target Corporation, 148, 155
Tarkovsky, Andrei, 220
Taylor, Donald W., 266n16
Teach for America, 33, 55–56
team coordinator, 155
TechCrunch, 259n1
technical education, advocates for, 86–87
technical skills, 13, 15
Terkel, Studs, 236
Terman, Frederick E., 113, 258n26
Terman, Lewis M., 111–22, 132, 135–36, 140–45, 141, 257n1, 262n41
Tessier–Lavigne, Marc, 225–26
Thorndike, Edward L., 135, 139
Thorndike Intelligence Examination, 139–40, 144
Thrun, Sebastian, 206–7, 209, 274n10, 274n15
Ticknor, George, 21–22
training, employer-provided, 36, 40, 63, 104–7, 130, 180, 215, 240
Troilus and Cressida (Shakespeare), 123
Twitter, 33–39, 247n5

Uber, 179

UCLA, 115, 239
Udacity, 207–8, 208, 211, 274n15, 274n18
Unilever, 128
United Airlines, 61
University of California, 94, 139–40
University of Chicago, 89, 92, 117, 216, 257n21
University of Illinois, 133, 258n28
University of Minnesota, 91, 148
University of Missouri, 25
University of Notre Dame, 245n16
University of Pennsylvania, 25, 91, 95, 208
University of Southern California, 239
University of Virginia, 21–22, 125, 129, 131
Ursinus College, 106
U.S. Army, 135–38, 146
U.S. Geological Survey, 69, 70, 71, 72, 73
U.S. Military Academy, 21, 88, 118
U.S. News & World Report, 89, 219

Van Rensselaer, Stephen, 21
Van Slyke, Lyman, 161–62
Visa, 99
vocational majors, 14
vocational tests, 144–46
von Eicken, Thorsten, 12

Walcott, Derek, 123
Walker, Francis A., 26
Washington Post, 237

Weiler, Hans, 187
Weinstock, Harris, 94–95
Weinstock-Lubin Company, 94
West Point, 21, 88, 118
Wharton, Joseph, 25
Wharton School of Finance and Economy, 25, 91, 95
What Color Is Your Parachute? (Bolles), 236
Whipple, Guy Montrose, 133
White, Andrew Dickson, 24–25, 42
Widom, Jennifer, 169, 183
Wiens, Kyle, 223
Wigen, Karen, 184
Wikia, 83
Wilbur, Ray Lyman, 189–90, 270n27, 277n11
Wildfire Interactive, 127–31
William Penn College, 66, 75
Williams College, 238
Working (Terkel), 236
Wrenn, C. Gilbert, 231, 232
writing skills, 7, 9, 56, 71, 78, 107, 184, 223

Xavier University, 238, 239

Y Combinator, 17, 38, 272n6
Yale University, 22, 26, 106, 181, 238, 266n16
Yerkes, Robert, 135
Young, Stan, 5–6

Zuckerberg, Mark, 201, 272nn5–6